THE BEST RECIPES FROM NEW ENGLAND INNS

Compiled and edited by Sandra J. Taylor
Designed by Jill Shaffer
Illustrated by Alison Scott, and Erick Ingraham

First Edition
Sixth printing, 1990

Library of Congress Catalogue Card Number: 83-62864
ISBN: 0-89909-321-3

The Best Recipes From NEW ENGLAND INNS

More than 100 country inns share their traditional favorites and specialties of the house.

Camden, Maine

CONTENTS

INTRODUCTION

Known for their delicious meals, warm hospitality, and comfortable guest rooms, country inns are an inherent part of New England. But it is their cooking that attracts the most people because locals, as well as travelers, will frequent an inn that serves good food.

Just as New England inns vary one from the other, so do the chefs, each giving a distinctive touch to his or her cooking. Therefore, when we contacted the inns about this cookbook, we asked that they send us recipes that were most often requested, house specialties, or the chefs' favorites. We received a bountiful assortment — for outstanding appetizers; excellent soups and salads; aromatic breads and rolls; elegant entrées of poultry, beef, fish, pork, or lamb; plus devastatingly delicious desserts of every kind.

Given the individuality of the creative minds at work, some of the chefs' recipes, we discovered, were as personal as a signature, zealously protected against even the slightest "forgery." I am reminded of a call I made to one chef, asking if a more familiar ingredient could be included as an alternate to the hard-to-find one he used. "No!" he said, with alarm. "It won't taste the same." Another time, I checked with a chef about a specific step in making his cream sauce. "Describe it however you feel would be best understood," he blithely told me. Two extremes, with two entirely different approaches to cooking. And that is exactly what this book is meant to be — a collection of excellent recipes that offers you an abundance of culinary experiences. From elegant simplicity to gourmet extravaganza, each one comes highly recommended by the inn that supplied it.

Don't be deterred if you occasionally encounter an unusual ingredient like chanterelles, morels, Tamari sauce, or walnut oil (there aren't many). If you can find it in a nearby market or gourmet foods shop, by all means, use it as instructed in the recipe; but if it isn't available or is obtainable only at great effort, substitute something else — domestic mushrooms, soy sauce, or a favorite salad oil, for example. You won't recreate the exact dish that the inn serves, but you will come close and should be pleased with the results. And who knows, maybe you will devise a masterpiece of your own while you're at it. That's part of the fun of cooking — and a big part of the appeal of this book.

At the same time, I don't wish to imply that you should ignore the importance of the ingredients either. Go ahead and make that dish using all four cloves of garlic, even though you think it might be too much for your palate. Do include that dash of allspice or extra spoonful of molasses, in spite of how insignificant it might seem. So often it is the addition — liberal or minuscule — of a special ingredient that makes all the difference in the world. And having made these recipes innumerable times, the chefs have honed them to perfection and know the ideal blends or exact proportions that create memorable meals.

Incidentally, not all the foods in this book are complicated or time-consuming by any means. Many New England inns are famous for their traditional dishes, so you will also find choices for New England Clam Chowder, Yankee Pot Roast, Codfish Balls, Old-Fashioned Chicken Pie, Anadama Bread, Apple Crisp, and Indian Pudding, to name just a few. Every recipe here is well worth making at least once, and more than likely, once won't ever be enough!

A sure sign of a successful cookbook is when one returns frequently to its pages — perhaps leaving behind a smudge from a drop of chocolate, an ink-like drip from blueberries, a dab of flour that gets compressed between two pages. Whether your books evidence such marks or not, my hope is that you will refer to this book often, use it, and enjoy it — my hunch is that you will.

Sandra J. Taylor
October 1983

Breakfast, Brunch, & Luncheon Dishes

The Four Chimneys Inn, Nantucket, Massachusetts

BREEZEMERE FARM
South Brooksville, Maine

BREEZEMERE GRANOLA

"Breezemere Granola is kept in a large glass jar in the dining room at breakfast time. It is so popular we have had to put a small sign on the jar asking the guests to 'please control yourself to three scoops.'"

5 cups uncooked oats
1 cup sliced almonds
1 cup broken walnut meats
1 cup chopped pecans
1 cup sesame seeds
1 cup unsalted sunflower seeds
1 cup wheat germ
1 cup shredded coconut
1 cup safflower oil
1 cup honey
1 cup golden raisins
1 cup currants

Preheat oven to 325°. Combine oats, nuts, seeds, wheat germ, and coconut in a very large mixing bowl and mix well. Heat oil and honey together in small pan just enough to meld them. Pour over dry ingredients and mix well. Spread mixture onto two 17x11-inch cookie sheets. Bake for 45 minutes or until lightly browned, watching carefully toward the end. Stir and turn with spatula every 10 or 15 minutes so granola will brown evenly. Remove from oven and when cool stir in the raisins and currants.

Makes 14 cups.

THE FOUR CHIMNEYS INN
Nantucket, Massachusetts

APPLE CRISP

"We cut this into 9 squares and serve it hot for our complimentary breakfast." Takes less than 10 minutes to prepare for the oven.

4 cups cored and sliced unpared apples
¼ cup water
1 teaspoon cinnamon
½ teaspoon salt
⅓ cup soft butter
1 cup sugar
¾ cup flour

Place apples in a 10-inch-square pan that has been lightly greased with butter. Sprinkle water, cinnamon, and salt over top. With a pastry blender, cut butter into sugar and flour and spread over apples. Bake at 350° for 40 minutes. *Serves 9.*

BLUEBERRY STREUSEL COFFEE CAKE

"This recipe is a special favorite with our guests and is requested over and over." Alternate layers of moist sour-cream cake and chewy fruit streusel.

2¾ cups flour
1½ teaspoons baking powder
1½ teaspoons baking soda
1 teaspoon salt
¾ cup softened margarine
1 cup granulated sugar
3 eggs
1 pint sour cream
2 teaspoons vanilla
¾ cup light brown sugar
¾ cup chopped nuts
1 teaspoon cinnamon
2 cups blueberries

Combine flour, baking powder, soda, and salt. Set aside. Cream margarine and granulated sugar with electric mixer. Add eggs one at a time, beating well. Add flour mixture alternately with sour cream and vanilla to batter. Combine brown sugar, nuts, and cinnamon for streusel and set aside ½ cup. Toss the remainder in with the blueberries. Spread one third of batter in a 10-inch greased and floured tube pan. Sprinkle with half of the berry mixture, then spread another third of batter and sprinkle with remaining berry mixture. Top with remaining batter. Sprinkle on ½ cup reserved streusel. Bake at 350°-375° for 60-65 minutes. Cool 10 minutes. *Serves 16.*

SOUR CREAM-APPLE COFFEE CAKE

Excellent with morning coffee or afternoon tea or served for dessert with a dollop of whipped cream.

1 cup butter, softened
2 1/4 cups granulated sugar
4 eggs
2 1/2 cups flour
1/2 teaspoon salt
1/2 teaspoon baking powder
1/2 teaspoon baking soda
1 cup sour cream
1 teaspoon vanilla
3 cups peeled, cored, and coarsely chopped apples
1/4 cup brown sugar, packed
1/2 teaspoon cinnamon
1 cup chopped nuts

Heavily grease and flour Bundt pan. In a large bowl, cream butter with 2 cups granulated sugar until light and fluffy. Beat in eggs. Add flour, salt, baking powder, soda, and sour cream. Add vanilla.

In medium-sized bowl, stir together apples and remaining 1/4 cup granulated sugar. Fold into batter. Spoon half of batter into prepared pan. Smooth with spatula. Combine brown sugar and cinnamon and stir in nuts. Sprinkle this mixture over batter in pan and top with remaining batter. Bake at 350° for about 70 minutes or until toothpick inserted in the middle comes out clean. Turn immediately onto plate to cool. *Makes 1 cake.*

CINNAMON COFFEE CAKE

"We like to serve this warm for that freshly baked taste. Pineapple chunks and raisins also taste great in this cake."

1 1/4 cups sugar
1/4 cup chopped pecans
1 tablespoon cinnamon
1/2 cup butter
2 eggs (large)
1 teaspoon vanilla
1 tablespoon lemon juice
2 cups sifted all-purpose flour
1/4 teaspoon baking powder
1 teaspoon salt
1 teaspoon baking soda
1 cup sour cream

Preheat oven to 350°. Mix 1/2 cup sugar with nuts and cinnamon and set aside. Cream butter and beat in remaining sugar and the eggs. Add vanilla and lemon juice. Combine the dry ingredients and add alternately with sour cream to the butter, sugar, and egg mixture. Spread half the batter in a greased 9-inch-square cake pan. Sprinkle with half the cinnamon mixture. Spread the remaining batter and sprinkle with remaining cinnamon. Bake for 35-45 minutes. *Makes 12 squares.*

MORNING CAKE WITH BREAKFAST TOPPING

A nice touch for that special Sunday brunch. For an eye-pleaser, spoon chopped strawberries or bananas on top of each piece, then add a generous amount of Breakfast Topping.

½ cup butter
¾ cup honey
1 teaspoon vanilla
1 teaspoon almond extract
½ cup milk
2 cups flour
1 teaspoon baking soda
3 medium apples or pears, peeled, cored, and finely chopped
¾ cup walnuts
1 teaspoon cinnamon
½ teaspoon ginger
Breakfast Topping (recipe follows)

Beat together butter, honey, vanilla, almond extract, and milk. Combine flour and soda and add to wet mixture. Stir in fruit, walnuts, cinnamon, and ginger. Bake at 350° for 40 minutes in a greased 8½-inch-square baking dish. Serve with Breakfast Topping. *Serves 8-9.*

BREAKFAST TOPPING

½ cup whipping cream
1 teaspoon vanilla
½ teaspoon almond extract
¼ cup sour cream
¼ cup plain yogurt
3 teaspoons orange marmalade

Whip the cream with extracts and then gently fold in remaining ingredients. *Makes 1¼ cups.*

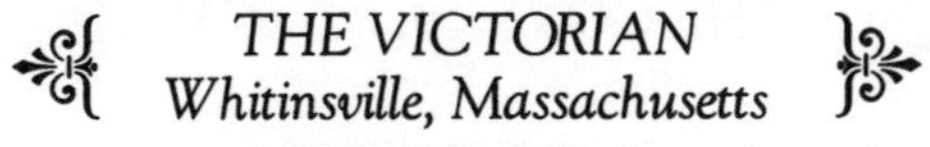

MARZAPYNE

"A big favorite with the local residents of Dutch descent, Marzapyne can be served for brunch or tea. It is especially appropriate for holidays. The almond and lemon combination is delicious."

DOUGH

½ pound cold butter
2 cups flour
1 tablespoon sugar
1 teaspoon salt
½ cup water
1 tablespoon white vinegar

Work like a pie dough, cutting cold butter into the flour. Add sugar, salt, and liquid ingredients gradually. Place in refrigerator.

FILLING

2 medium eggs plus 1 yolk (save white)
½ cup sugar
8 ounces almond paste
½ teaspoon lemon extract
½ teaspoon vanilla extract

Beat eggs and yolk. Beat in sugar. Beat in paste. Add lemon and vanilla extracts. Beat one minute. Place in refrigerator till firm.

Roll out dough into an 8x12-inch rectangle on a cookie sheet. Place filling in tube shape down long side, leaving space at either end to seal dough. Roll up. Seal edges, brush outside with reserved egg white, and score every half inch with a sharp knife. Bake at 425° for 15 minutes, then at 350° for about 10 minutes or until browned and firm. *Serves 10.*

THE GOVERNOR'S INN
Ludlow, Vermont

RUM RAISIN FRENCH TOAST

"Imagine sunshine in the breakfast room, a cozy fire in the Crawford wood stove, hot cereal, freshly ground coffee, and Charlie's famous French toast."

¾ cup rum raisin ice cream, melted
3 large eggs, beaten
1 tablespoon vanilla (or dark rum)
¼ teaspoon cinnamon
5 tablespoons finely ground walnuts
6 slices raisin bread
6 tablespoons sweet butter
Vermont maple syrup
Rum raisin ice cream

Combine melted ice cream, eggs, vanilla (or rum), cinnamon, and nuts in a bowl. Beat well with wire whisk. Dip raisin bread into egg mixture, coating well on both sides. Sauté in butter over medium-low heat until "toasted." Serve on heated plate with a small scoop of rum raisin ice cream capped with Vermont maple syrup. *Makes 6 slices.*

THE CAPTAIN JEFFERDS INN
Kennebunkport, Maine

CAPTAIN JEFFERDS FANCY FRENCH TOAST

"This is a favorite dish served at breakfast or brunch. I like to accompany it with a good-sized country sausage and a slice of fresh orange twisted as a garnish. It is a variation of French toast, only I use French bread. It makes all the difference!"

9 eggs
1 cup milk
3 tablespoons Grand Marnier liqueur
18 slices French bread (about ¾ inch thick)
Confectioners sugar
Maple syrup

In a large bowl mix eggs, milk, and Grand Marnier. Beat until fluffy. Soak several slices French bread in the mixture. Grease skillet or grill and cook toast on both sides until golden brown. Arrange 3 slices (overlapping slightly) on a plate and sprinkle with confectioners sugar. Serve with maple syrup. *Serves 6.*

THE VICTORIAN
Edgartown (Martha's Vineyard), Massachusetts

STRAWBERRY CRÊPES

Tender French pancakes with strawberries-and-cream filling.

6 cups fresh strawberries
1/3 cup granulated sugar
1 cup cottage cheese
1 cup dairy sour cream
1/2 cup confectioners sugar
10 to 12 cooked crêpes

Hull and slice strawberries, add granulated sugar, and set aside. Whip cottage cheese until smooth; stir in sour cream and confectioners sugar. Fill crêpes with about two thirds of creamy mixture and berries; fold over. Top with remaining strawberries and cream. *Makes 10-12 crêpes.*

THE VICTORIAN
Edgartown (Martha's Vineyard), Massachusetts

BREAKFAST PANCAKES

Delicate pancakes with a nice nutty flavor.

1 1/2 cups unbleached white flour
1 tablespoon sugar
1/4 teaspoon salt
1 1/2 tablespoons baking powder
3 eggs, separated
2 cups milk
1/4 cup melted sweet butter (unsalted)
1 cup chopped walnuts or pecans

Sift dry ingredients into bowl. Beat the egg yolks with milk and cooled melted butter and stir into the flour. Add nuts and blend. Beat egg whites until fluffy, then fold into batter.

Heat large skillet or griddle and oil lightly. Drop batter by small ladleful and brown on both sides. Serve with hot buttered syrup or honey. *Serves 10.*

THE CHURCHILL HOUSE INN
Brandon, Vermont

COTTAGE CHEESE PANCAKES

"These light, tender pancakes are always a hit and are our number one recipe request."

1 cup cottage cheese
½ cup flour
4 eggs
6 tablespoons melted butter

Combine cottage cheese, flour, and eggs in the bowl of a food processor and process briefly. Add melted butter and process until it is blended. Batter should be slightly lumpy. Drop on preheated griddle using ¼-cup measure. Cook for 1½-2 minutes, lift to see if golden brown, and if so, flip over and cook other side until golden. Do not overcook. Pancakes will be moist because of the cheese. *Makes 10 four-inch pancakes.*

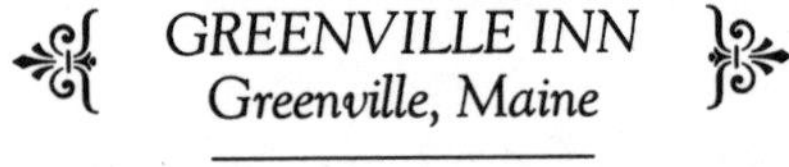

GREENVILLE INN
Greenville, Maine

GERMAN PANCAKE

Delightful for breakfast, lunch, or a light supper.

3 eggs
¼ teaspoon salt
½ cup sifted flour
½ cup milk
2 tablespoons melted butter

Lightly beat eggs with a wire whisk. Add salt to flour. Add flour mixture and milk to eggs in 3 or 4 portions alternately, beating well after each addition. Add melted butter and beat well. Pour into 2 well-buttered pie pans. Bake at 400° for 30-35 minutes or until puffed and light brown. Serve immediately, with lemon wedges, melted butter, and confectioners sugar. *Serves 2.*

BIRCH HILL INN
Manchester, Vermont

EGG IN THE HOLE

Also known as "egg in a nest," "eye of Egypt," and "one-eyed pirate," this is easy to make, fun to serve, and good to eat.

2 tablespoons margarine
1 slice firm wheat bread
1 egg
Salt and pepper

On griddle, melt margarine. Cut a circle in the center of the bread with a 3-inch-round cookie cutter (leave center piece in bread slice at this time). Brown bread, turn, and brown second side. Remove center of bread and keep warm on side of griddle. Drop egg into hole, add salt and pepper to taste, and cook until set. Turn and cook briefly on second side. Serve with toast round atop. *Serves 1.*

THE VICTORIAN
Edgartown (Martha's Vineyard), Massachusetts

EGGS VICTORIAN

Hearty and filling breakfast-in-one-dish to be made ahead and baked the next day.

1 pound breakfast sausage
1 loaf French bread
4 tablespoons flour
2 tablespoons dry mustard
Black pepper
Basil
5 cups milk
10 eggs
4 tablespoons melted butter
1 cup grated cheddar cheese

Boil sausage in water to cover for 3-5 minutes in a skillet. Drain into colander and set aside to cool. Break bread into small pieces and spread in a large greased baking pan. Cut up sausage and add. Combine flour, mustard, pepper, and basil and sprinkle over sausage and bread. Mix milk, eggs, and melted butter together and pour over top, making sure all is covered. Sprinkle grated cheese over top. Cover with aluminum foil and refrigerate. Bake, covered, next day at 350° for 1 hour. *Serves 10-12.*

EGGS PORTUGUESE

Prepare these for brunch or lunch, top with your favorite hollandaise sauce, and serve immediately.

- **4 patty shells, prepared according to package directions**
- **2 ounces chopped onion**
- **1 clove garlic, crushed and mashed**
- **Cooking oil**
- **1 can (1 pound) stewed tomatoes**
- **1/8 teaspoon basil**
- **1/8 teaspoon oregano**
- **1 bay leaf**
- **Salt and pepper to taste**
- **4 poached eggs**
- **Hollandaise sauce**

Remove caps from patty shells and reserve for another use. Place shells on individual plates. Sauté onion and garlic in small quantity of oil until translucent. Add crushed or chopped stewed tomatoes, herbs, and salt and pepper and simmer. Remove bay leaf, then spoon some of tomato mixture into each shell, top with a poached egg, drape hollandaise sauce over egg and shell, and garnish as desired. *Serves 2-4.*

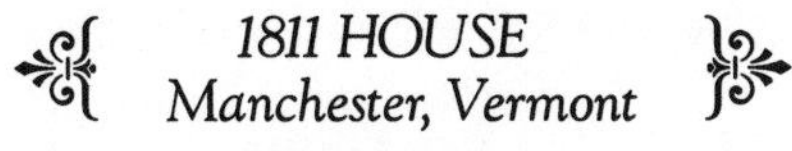

1811 HOUSE
Manchester, Vermont

SCOTCH EGGS

Halve eggs and serve with salad for luncheon or a light supper, or quarter them, sprinkle yolks with paprika, and present as canapés.

4 hard-boiled eggs
1 pound fine sausage meat
1 egg, beaten
Finely ground bread crumbs
Salt and pepper to taste
Vegetable oil

Peel eggs and wrap in sausage meat. Roll in beaten egg and then in seasoned bread crumbs. Heat oil in skillet and roll around eggs until sausage meat is thoroughly cooked. Drain and cool well.
Serves 2.

OAKLAND HOUSE
Herricks (Sargentville P.O.), Maine

NEW ENGLAND CODFISH BALLS

"A favorite treat for Sunday-morning breakfast at Oakland House. We serve 3 golden fishballs with chunks of corn bread and crisp bacon."

1/4 pound dried salt codfish
6 potatoes, cooked, drained, and mashed
3 eggs
1 cup bread crumbs

Cook cod in water until it flakes well; rinse with fresh water several times and drain well. In mixer blend potatoes and fish. Add eggs and bread crumbs to form a proper consistency for making into balls. Chill overnight.

Form into balls (a #40 ice cream scoop works well) and cook until golden in 350° fat. Drain on paper towels. *Makes about 24.*

GRANES HAM AND CHEESE SOUFFLÉ

"The smell from this soufflé, as it is baking, permeates the whole 20-room inn. By the time it's ready to serve, everyone is at their table — fork in hand. It makes such a pretty dish we have had guests run back upstairs to get their cameras to take pictures of it!"

8 slices homemade white bread, cubed
1 1/2 cups chopped ham
1 1/2 cups grated cheddar cheese
1 small onion, minced
Salt and pepper to taste
10 eggs
2 1/2 cups milk
1/2 stick margarine or butter, melted
2 teaspoons dry mustard
1/2 cup grated Parmesan cheese
Paprika

In a buttered 2-quart soufflé dish layer a third of the bread cubes and half of the ham, cheddar cheese, onion, and salt and pepper. Repeat layers, topping with last third of bread. Beat eggs in a bowl; add milk, cooled melted margarine, and dry mustard and mix well. Pour over bread in dish. Sprinkle with grated Parmesan and paprika. Refrigerate overnight. Bake uncovered at 350° for 1 hour and serve immediately. *Serves 6-8.*

ZUCCHINI SOUFFLÉ

"This is a very 'forgiving' recipe and ideal for the busy innkeeper or harried housekeeper. First, almost any vegetable can be used. Although zucchini is our family favorite, we have also used broccoli, corn, and French green beans. Leftover vegetables can be used, too, as long as they were not overcooked the first time around. If leftovers are to be used, boil onions alone for 3 minutes.

"Second, you need not be entirely accurate in your measurements of the vegetables or cheese. We often use ¼ cup more of cheese than is called for in the recipe.

"Third, this recipe can be prepared up to 4 hours in advance. If you choose to do this, do not mix the vegetables into the cheese mixture until you are ready to place in the casserole dish and bake.

"Fourth, and finally, if your guests linger over their first course, turn the oven down as low as it will go. The soufflé may get a little browner and may not be quite as high but will taste just as good."

2 cups sliced or diced fresh vegetable
½ cup diced onion
3 eggs
½ cup milk
1 teaspoon salt
¼ teaspoon pepper
1 tablespoon sugar
1 tablespoon flour
½ cup diced cheddar or Jack cheese
4 tablespoons melted butter

Parboil vegetable and onion together in a large saucepan until done but not soft. Drain very well and return to saucepan.

Place remaining ingredients, except butter, in blender and blend at high speed until cheese chunks cannot be seen.

Drain vegetables again, then add cheese mixture to the vegetables. Place in greased 1½- to 2-quart casserole. Pour melted butter over top. Bake at 350° for 45 minutes. *Serves 6.*

CHEESE PIE

The mixture of Swiss and cheddar cheeses gives tang to this versatile quiche, which holds its shape but is creamy-soft like a custard. Mushrooms, vegetables, or seafood may be added for variety.

9-inch pie crust, unbaked and refrigerated
6 slices bacon
Melted butter
1 cup grated cheese (half Swiss, half cheddar)
4 eggs
2 cups thin cream
3/4 teaspoon salt
Pinch of nutmeg
Pinch of cayenne pepper
Pinch of sugar
1/2 teaspoon black pepper

Fry bacon until crisp, then crumble into bits. Take pastry-lined pie plate out of refrigerator and brush with melted butter. Sprinkle bacon bits over crust. Sprinkle grated cheese over bacon. Combine eggs, cream, and remaining ingredients and pour over this. Bake at 425° for 15 minutes. Lower temperature to 300° and bake approximately 30 minutes longer or until silver knife inserted comes out clean.

Serves 6.

OAKLAND HOUSE
Herricks (Sargentville P.O.), Maine

SPINACH PIE

"This recipe was given to us by a friend. We usually serve it at our Wednesday noon buffet luncheon. It can be served hot or cold and looks so pretty cut in eighths, with a tomato slice garnishing each piece."

1 package (10 ounces) frozen chopped spinach
1 carton (12 ounces) cottage cheese
1 cup grated cheddar or mozzarella cheese
3 eggs
2 tablespoons oil
1 teaspoon onion or garlic salt
Freshly ground pepper

Cook spinach about 5 minutes, drain, and press out all water. Combine cottage cheese, cheddar or mozzarella, spinach, eggs, oil, and seasonings. Pour mixture into lightly oiled 9-inch pie plate. Bake at 350° for 40 minutes or until knife comes out clean. Dot with butter or oil for a golden top. *Serves 8.*

THE BLACKBERRY RIVER INN
Norfolk, Connecticut

APPLE AND WALNUT QUICHE

Good for early-day tastebuds — at breakfast, brunch, or lunch. Use only those apples that hold up well and don't turn mushy when cooked.

4 eggs
$1\frac{1}{3}$ cups light cream
Pinch of nutmeg
Salt (to taste)
White pepper (to taste)
2 apples, peeled and chopped (Granny Smith, McIntosh, or a combination)
2 ounces walnuts, chopped
6 ounces Swiss cheese, shredded
Cinnamon (sprinkled on top)
9-inch pie crust, prebaked for 10 minutes at 400°

Beat eggs and cream together; add nutmeg, salt, and white pepper to taste. Spread apples, walnuts, and Swiss cheese evenly in the pie shell and pour liquid over all. Sprinkle cinnamon on top of quiche. Bake at 375° for approximately 45 minutes.

Serves 6-8.

CRAB MEAT QUICHE

If you have extra filling, pour it into buttered ramekins and bake along with the quiche.

1½ cups crab meat, fresh or canned
1 tablespoon chopped celery
1 tablespoon chopped onion
2 tablespoons finely chopped parsley
2 tablespoons sherry
Pastry for 9-inch pie shell
4 eggs, lightly beaten
2 cups cream, or 1 cup each milk and cream
¼ teaspoon nutmeg
½ teaspoon salt
¼ teaspoon white pepper

Pick over the crab meat to remove bits of shell and cartilage. Combine crab meat, celery, onion, parsley, and sherry and refrigerate 1 hour.

Preheat oven to hot (450°). Line pie plate with pastry and bake 5 minutes. Sprinkle the inside of the partly baked pastry shell with the crab-meat mixture. Combine eggs, cream, nutmeg, salt, and pepper and strain over the mixture in the pie shell. Bake 15 minutes, reduce the oven temperature to moderate (350°), and bake about 10 minutes longer or until a knife inserted 1 inch from the pastry edge comes out clean. Serve immediately. *Serves 6-10.*

THE WHITE HOUSE
Wilmington, Vermont

SEAFOOD QUICHE

Sautéed scallops, shrimp, and crab meat combined with 2 flavorful cheeses. Superb! (Be sure to simmer the cream; otherwise the custard won't hold together.)

1 quart heavy cream
5 whole eggs
1 clove garlic, crushed and minced
1 teaspoon celery seed
3/4 cup grated Vermont cheddar cheese
Unbaked pie crust in 10-inch quiche pan
1/4 pound shrimp
1/4 pound shredded crab meat
1/4 pound scallops
Butter for sautéing seafood
1/4 cup freshly grated Parmesan cheese
1 teaspoon Spanish paprika

Pour heavy cream in saucepan and heat to a simmer (tiny bubbles will form around inside of pan). Remove from heat. In a large bowl, whisk together eggs, garlic, and celery seed, then add heavy cream. Place cheddar cheese in bottom of pie crust. Sauté all of the seafood in a large saucepan in butter. When seafood is cooked place over cheddar cheese. Then pour cream liquid over all ingredients in the pie crust. Sprinkle Parmesan cheese and paprika over top. Bake in 350° oven for approximately 30 minutes. Insert knife in center of quiche. If knife comes out clean, quiche is done. *Serves 6-8.*

THE BIRCHWOOD INN
Temple, New Hampshire

LOBSTER QUICHE

A festive blend of cubed lobster meat, chopped green pepper, chunks of fresh tomato, and grated Jarlsberg cheese.

1 green pepper, chopped fine
1/2 small onion, chopped fine
1 tablespoon basil
1 clove garlic, minced
1/4 cup parsley flakes
1 tablespoon chives
1/4 pound butter
1 whole egg
2 egg yolks
1/2 cup mayonnaise
3/4 pound Jarlsberg cheese, grated
2 fresh tomatoes, seeded and cut in chunks
3/4 pound fresh lobster meat, cut in cubes
10-inch pie shell, unbaked
Bread crumbs
Paprika

Sauté green pepper, onion, basil, garlic, parsley, and chives in butter. Mix egg and yolks with mayonnaise in bowl. Add cheese and tomatoes. Add lobster and sautéed herbs and vegetables, and mix well. Place in pie shell. Sprinkle with bread crumbs and paprika. Bake at 350° for 45 minutes.

Serves 8 as main course or 12 as appetizer.

PEG LEG INN
Rockport, Massachusetts

LOBSTER STEW

Rich, creamy, and reminiscent of Lobster Newburg. Be sure to use heavy cream, as specified, as it will not break when boiled.

12 ounces lobster meat
4 ounces melted butter
1 cup sherry wine
Dash Tabasco sauce
3 cups heavy cream
Salt and white pepper to taste

In a small saucepan sauté lobster meat in melted butter along with sherry and Tabasco. Add heavy cream and simmer for 5 minutes. Adjust salt and pepper to taste. Bring to a boil to allow stew to thicken slightly. Serve in heated bowls, each topped with a piece of whole butter.

Serves 4.

LOBSTER OMELETTE

Keep the accompaniments to this extraordinary omelette simple. Cooked spinach or grilled tomatoes and French bread would go well with it.

1 tablespoon butter
2 shallots or scallions
2 mushrooms, thinly sliced
1 tablespoon flour
1 teaspoon tomato paste
½ cup dry white wine
2 tablespoons whipping cream
1 cup canned or fresh lobster
4 eggs
Pinch salt
2 tablespoons butter
1 teaspoon melted butter
1 teaspoon grated Parmesan cheese

Melt 1 tablespoon butter and sauté shallots until softened, then add mushrooms. Stir in flour and tomato paste, gradually add wine and cream, and fold in cleaned lobster.

Prepare omelettes, using 2 eggs beaten with pinch of salt for each. Melt 1 tablespoon butter in omelette pan, pour in beaten eggs, and cook until surface sets. Place half of the lobster mixture on omelette, fold over, brush surface with ½ teaspoon melted butter, and sprinkle with ½ teaspoon Parmesan cheese. Make second omelette in the same way. Brown both under a preheated broiler and serve immediately. *Serves 2.*

LOVETT'S BY LAFAYETTE BROOK 
Franconia, New Hampshire

SALMON MOUSSE

"This is one of the specialties of the house. The requests for the recipe are constant."

2 cups cooked, flaked salmon, bones removed
1 envelope gelatin
3 tablespoons cold water
½ cup béchamel sauce (or ½ can condensed cream of chicken soup)
½ tablespoon dry mustard
Salt to taste
Cayenne pepper
1 cup lightly salted whipped cream
Mayonnaise
Fresh lemon juice
Fresh chopped dill

Force salmon through a fine sieve or use a food processor. Soften gelatin in cold water and dissolve over hot water. Combine béchamel sauce, mustard, salt, and pinch of cayenne and work into the salmon. Add gelatin, mix well, and cool over a bowl of cracked ice. When mixture begins to set, fold in whipped cream. Divide among individual molds, then chill. Unmold on lettuce and serve with mayonnaise to which lemon juice and dill have been added.

Serves 4-6.

LAKHANIKA

"Based on a classic Greek soup, this is aromatic and fulfilling, yet light enough to be served in hot weather. I have made an equally delicious vegetarian version without the chicken and broth by adding mushrooms and more tomato juice."

3 whole chicken breasts
4 to 5 peppercorns
4 to 5 whole cloves
1 bay leaf
Cooking oil
2 cloves garlic, minced
2 quarts eggplant, cut in 1-inch pieces
1 onion, coarsely chopped
1 quart zucchini, cut in 1-inch pieces
1 quart whole tomatoes in juices, coarsely chopped
1/4 cup dry red wine
1 tablespoon oregano
1 tablespoon garam marsala*
1 tablespoon chopped parsley
2 teaspoons basil
Salt and pepper to taste
1 cup coarsely chopped cabbage
1/2 cup macaroni

Place chicken in pot with peppercorns, cloves, and bay leaf. Cover with water and bring to a boil. Skim, cover, and simmer for 45 minutes. Remove chicken to cool and set aside stock. Bone chicken, degrease and strain stock, and save for later.

Heat oil in heavy-bottomed soup pot. Sauté garlic, add eggplant and onion, and continue to sauté, adding more oil as needed. When eggplant has softened and glistens, add zucchini. Toss lightly and sauté 3-4 more minutes. Add tomatoes along with their juice, the wine, and the spices and herbs. Add enough chicken stock to create a good stew-like appearance — not too soupy. Bring just to a boil, then turn off heat and let stand 1-2 hours to increase the flavor. Thirty minutes before serving, reheat and add cabbage and macaroni. Add boned cooked chicken, torn in large pieces, 5 minutes before serving and stir gently. Adjust seasonings and serve. *Serves 6-8.*

*This is an Indian spice mixture which can be found in most gourmet food shops, but I prefer to make my own. Combine 1/3 cup cardamom pods, 2 tablespoons peppercorns, 2 sticks cinnamon, 1 tablespoon whole cloves, 2 tablespoons ground cumin, 1 teaspoon ground mace, 3 tablespoons ground coriander, and 2 bay leaves. Spread the spices on a baking sheet and roast at 200° for 20 minutes, stirring frequently. Let cool; shell the cardamom and discard the pods. Crush the spices and grind into fine powder. Store in a jar with a tight-fitting lid.

SPANAKOPITA

"Rich with cheese — a meal in itself. Making your own filo dough is an ambitious undertaking but you can buy excellent frozen pastry. You must work with it very quickly and carefully as it is fragile and dries out rapidly. If you've never used it before, be sure to read the instructions on the package."

3 pounds cottage cheese
8 ounces feta cheese, crumbled
2 cups grated cheddar cheese
3 eggs
3 tablespoons dill weed
1 teaspoon pepper
2 teaspoons oregano
1/2 teaspoon garlic powder
2 pounds frozen spinach, cooked and drained well
1/2 cup melted butter
1 pound filo pastry
1 cup dry bread crumbs
Caraway seeds

Combine the cheeses, eggs, and herbs. Squeeze excess liquid out of drained spinach, add to cheese mixture, and mix well. Brush a 13x9-inch pan with butter. Lay a sheet of pastry in pan, allowing edges to extend beyond sides of pan. Brush with butter and sprinkle with bread crumbs. Lay another sheet of dough on top and again brush with butter and sprinkle with bread crumbs. Continue to layer the pastry dough in this fashion until there are 6 layers. Fill shell with cheese and spinach mixture. Fold edges of dough over top and again start to layer sheets of pastry dough for a total of 8 layers on top of mixture. End with brushed butter on the top sheet. Tuck the extra dough that extends beyond the edges down inside the pan around the cheese and spinach mixture. Slash the top and sprinkle with caraway seeds. Bake for 30 minutes at 425°.

Serves 8.

PHILBROOK FARM INN
Shelburne, New Hampshire

BEEF MIRATONI

A great way to use up leftover pot roast or roast beef.

3 large onions, finely chopped
3 tablespoons butter
1 tablespoon flour
2 tablespoons wine vinegar
1 cup beef stock or consommé
2 tablespoons tomato paste or catsup
Salt, pepper, and garlic to taste
Sliced leftover pot roast or roast beef
Bread crumbs
Parmesan cheese

Simmer onions in butter, stirring often. Cook until golden. Sprinkle in flour and blend thoroughly. Add wine vinegar, beef stock, and tomato paste. Season with salt and pepper and touch of garlic and simmer 20 minutes.

Pour half sauce in bottom of baking dish. Add meat and cover with rest of sauce. Sprinkle with bread crumbs and Parmesan cheese. Bake at 350° until heated through. *Serves 4.*

THE VILLAGE INN OF WOODSTOCK 
Woodstock, Vermont

RED PLAID HASH

Prepare on a chilly day for a substantial breakfast or brunch dish. By adding a cup of cooked beets you have Red Flannel Hash.

4 medium red potatoes
1 pound leftover cooked meat (corned beef or roast beef)
1 small onion
1 can red kidney beans
1 tablespoon Worcestershire sauce
1 tablespoon steak sauce
2 tablespoons catsup
4 shots Tabasco sauce
Salt and pepper to taste
1 poached egg per serving

Boil potatoes with skins on until tender (approximately 20 minutes) and cool. Then cut them into bite-size pieces. Grind meat and onion in food processor or meat grinder. Mix with potatoes and remaining ingredients except salt and pepper and eggs and place in greased 11x7-inch pan. Cover and bake at 350° for 1 hour, stirring occasionally. Salt and pepper to taste. Serve hot directly from oven and top each serving with a poached egg. Hash can be cooled and reheated in a frying pan. *Serves 6.*

BREADS

Mountain View Inn, Waitsfield, Vermont

YEAST BREADS

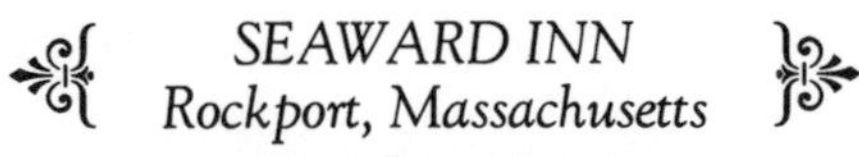

SEAWARD INN
Rockport, Massachusetts

MUFFIE'S SHREDDED WHEAT BREAD

Shape the dough into rolls, if you prefer, and bake for 20-25 minutes.

2 cups boiling water
3 large shredded wheat biscuits
8 tablespoons shortening
⅓ cup sugar
⅓ cup molasses
1½ packages dry yeast
1 tablespoon sugar
¼ cup lukewarm water
2 teaspoons salt
5 to 6 cups flour

Put boiling water, shredded wheat, and shortening in large bowl. Cool and add ⅓ cup sugar and molasses. Dissolve yeast and 1 tablespoon sugar in warm water. Add to shredded wheat mixture and blend. Stir in salt and gradually beat in flour. Turn out on floured board and knead. Put in greased bowl, turning dough until it is coated. Cover with damp towel and let stand until doubled in bulk. Punch down and shape into 2 loaves (or pan rolls). Place in greased pans, cover, and let stand again until doubled in bulk. Preheat oven and bake at 375° for 45-50 minutes.

Makes 2 loaves.

ANADAMA BREAD

"It took me 2 years of trial and error to get the perfect Anadama recipe and this is it. The culmination of many variations, it makes the best toast, which we serve with our own strawberry jam. Originally the bread was perfected in Maine and eaten by fishermen. The wives would make cornmeal mush for their tired and cold husbands coming off the fishing boats. One day a fisherman tired of just cornmeal mush said to his wife, 'Anna, damn it, I'm tired of mush — make bread,' and she did and he called it Anadama bread. How true, I don't know, but it makes all us Mainers laugh!"

1 cup molasses
1/4 pound margarine
3 1/2 cups water
1 cup cornmeal
3 1/2 cups flour
1 tablespoon salt
2 packages dry yeast
3 1/2 cups flour

Bring just to boiling point molasses, margarine, and water. Lower heat to simmer and add cornmeal, whisking as you add slowly. Simmer 15 minutes, stirring occasionally. Cool. In large bowl mix all dry ingredients except last 3½ cups flour. Add cooled wet ingredients to dry and beat for 2 minutes. Add last 3½ cups flour and blend with hands. Turn out on floured board and knead for 5 minutes, adding more flour if needed for right bread consistency. Let rise in greased bowl until double; punch down and let rest 5 minutes. Make into 2 loaves and put in two 9x5-inch greased bread pans. Let rise until double again. Bake at 400° for 45-50 minutes. Cool on rack. *Makes 2 loaves.*

"HEALTHY" WHOLE-WHEAT BREAD

In every way an excellent bread — plain or toasted. Moist, fine-textured, and nutritious.

2 packages dry yeast (or 4 teaspoons if you buy it in bulk)
2½ cups warm water
3 eggs
½ cup sugar
¼ cup vegetable oil
1½ teaspoons salt
½ cup soy flour
4 cups unbleached white flour
½ cup dry milk solids
3 tablespoons wheat germ
4 cups whole-wheat flour

Dissolve yeast in warm water. Add eggs, sugar, oil, and salt and beat together. Add soy flour and 2 cups white flour, beating thoroughly. Add dry milk and remaining 2 cups white flour, beating thoroughly. Mix in wheat germ and whole-wheat flour. Knead 10 minutes by hand or 5 minutes with electric mixer and dough hook. Put in well-oiled bowl, turning to coat dough. Cover with plastic wrap and let rise in warm place until double. Punch down and form into 3 loaves. Put in greased 8½x4½x2⅝-inch loaf pans. Grease tops of loaves, cover, and let rise until double. Place in cold oven and turn heat to 400°. After 15 minutes, reduce heat to 375° and bake 20 minutes more. Remove from oven and immediately remove loaves from pans. Brush crusts with butter and place loaves on racks to cool. *Makes 3 loaves.*

WHOLE-WHEAT COFFEE CAN BREAD

An easy and economical recipe that produces a firm-textured and slightly sweet bread that children as well as adults will love.

1 package dry yeast
½ cup warm water
1 egg, beaten
2½ cups warm water
½ cup melted butter or margarine
½ cup maple syrup or honey
1 teaspoon salt
5 cups whole-wheat flour
3 cups King Arthur unbleached flour
⅔ cup chopped walnuts
Sesame seeds

In bowl dissolve yeast in ½ cup warm water. Beat together egg, 2½ cups warm water, butter, maple syrup, and salt. Stir in yeast and whole-wheat flour. Then add unbleached flour and walnuts. Cover with cloth. Let rise for 1 hour on stove top or warm place.

Remove dough and divide into 5 equal parts. Sprinkle sesame seeds on counter and knead into dough. Place in 5 greased and floured 1-pound coffee cans. Bake at 350° for 45 minutes. Remove from oven and take bread out of cans as soon as it shrinks (about 15 minutes). *Makes 5 loaves.*

THE GOSNOLD ARMS
New Harbor, Maine

MY OATMEAL BREAD

"Our guests enjoy this bread with dinner as well as toasted for breakfast. Try it fresh from the oven, dripping with butter!"

2 teaspoons dry yeast
1/2 cup warm water (110°)
1/8 teaspoon sugar
1 cup oats
2 tablespoons bacon drippings
1 1/2 teaspoons salt
1/4 cup molasses
3/4 cup boiling water
1/2 cup cool water
3 3/4 to 4 1/4 cups bread flour

Sprinkle yeast over warm water. Add sugar. Set aside in a warm draft-free place. In a large mixing bowl place oats, bacon drippings, salt, and molasses. Add boiling water, stir, and set aside for 5 minutes. Add cool water to oats mixture and blend. Add yeast mixture and 1 1/2 cups flour and mix well. Work in remaining flour and knead until dough is smooth and elastic (the dough will still be a little sticky). Place dough in lightly buttered bowl, turning to coat dough. Cover with a tea towel. Set aside in warm, draft-free place until double in size (about 1 hour). Punch down dough and knead 1 minute. Shape into desired form and let rise until double in bulk.

Loaf Bread — 1 1/2 pounds dough per 9x5x3-inch bread pan. Bake at 375° for 30-35 minutes.

Dinner Rolls — 1 1/2 ounces each. Bake at 375° for 12-18 minutes.

Makes 1 loaf plus 10-12 rolls.

LINCOLN HOUSE COUNTRY INN
Dennysville, Maine 

FENNEL SEED BREAD

"A recipe that has been handed down for four generations. This wholesome whole-wheat bread is sold by the loaf at our inn."

2 tablespoons dry yeast
⅓ cup warm water
2 tablespoons brown sugar
1 tablespoon salt
¼ cup oats
¼ cup cornmeal
1 tablespoon wheat germ
¼ cup molasses
2 tablespoons Crisco
¼ cup dry milk powder
1 tablespoon fennel seed
3 cups hot water
5½ cups whole-wheat flour
3 to 4 cups white flour

Combine yeast, ⅓ cup water, and sugar in small bowl and set aside. In large bowl combine next 8 ingredients, add 3 cups hot water, and stir well. Add yeast mixture to large bowl. Add to this the whole-wheat flour and mix well. Cover and set in warm place and allow to rise to double its bulk — about 45 minutes. Pour onto floured board and knead in white flour for 10 minutes. Divide into 2 loaves and place in greased bread pans. Cover and allow to rise until double in bulk. Bake at 350° for 40-50 minutes. Remove from pans immediately and brush tops with butter.

Makes 2 loaves.

GREENVILLE INN
Greenville, Maine

MOOSEHEAD BREAD

The aroma of this bread baking will knock your socks off! And the flavor is just as appealing. Serve with soup or stew.

1 can (12 ounces) beer, preferably Moosehead
1/2 cup water
1/4 cup bacon drippings
2 cups whole-wheat flour
1/3 cup sugar
2 packages dry yeast
2 teaspoons salt
3 to 3 1/2 cups all-purpose flour
2 eggs
1 1/2 cups oats
1 cup grated Parmesan cheese
1 tablespoon caraway seeds

Combine beer, water, and bacon drippings in saucepan and heat to 120°-130°. Combine with whole-wheat flour, sugar, yeast, and salt and beat at medium speed about 2 minutes. Blend in 2 cups all-purpose flour and the eggs. Beat at high speed for about 2 minutes. Stir in oats and Parmesan cheese and mix well. Stir in enough remaining flour to make a stiff batter. Place in greased bowl, cover, and let rise in warm place until double in size (about 1 hour). Punch down and divide between 2 well-greased 9x5-inch loaf pans. Sprinkle with caraway seeds and press lightly into dough. Let rise uncovered in warm place for about 45 minutes or until double in size. Bake at 375° for 20-25 minutes. Cool 10 minutes, remove from pans, and cool completely on wire racks.

Makes 2 loaves.

POPCORN BREAD

A "mystery" bread to serve at a party and see if the guests can guess the secret ingredient. Makes 3 big and beautiful loaves of a good-tasting, slightly sweet all-purpose bread. Be sure the water-and-milk mixture is not too warm before adding the yeast.

1 cup boiling water
1 cup cold milk
1½ tablespoons dry yeast
¾ cup sugar
4 cups popped popcorn (no old maids)
1 teaspoon salt
3 eggs
⅓ cup butter, melted
7 cups all-purpose flour

Combine water and milk in a large bowl. Stir in yeast and sugar and let them "work" about 10 minutes. Run popcorn through a blender or food processor until it is the consistency of cornmeal. Add popcorn and salt to the mixture in the bowl. Then add eggs and cooled melted butter and gradually work in all 7 cups of flour.

If you don't have a machine, knead the mixture well by hand. Let dough rise (usually 25-30 minutes). Punch it down then let rise once more. Put dough out onto a rolling board. Separate into 3 equal pieces. Roll into shape and place in greased bread pans. Let rise until doubled in size.

Bake at 350° for 35-40 minutes or until loaves are golden brown. Remove from oven and butter the crusts. *Makes 3 loaves.*

BRAIDED PEPPER BREAD

Large, thick-crusted, golden-brown loaves with a mouth-tingling aftertaste. Best warm or toasted. Serve with a ripened wedge of Brie.

1 cup milk
½ cup butter
¼ cup sugar
2 teaspoons salt
½ cup warm water
2 tablespoons dry yeast
4 eggs
2 tablespoons coarsely ground pepper
7 cups flour
1 egg, beaten
Caraway seeds

Scald the milk. Add butter, sugar, and salt and let the mixture cool. Combine water and yeast and proof for 10 minutes. When milk mixture is cool, add to yeast. Beat in 4 eggs and pepper. Beat in flour a few cups at a time. Then knead in enough of remaining flour to make dough smooth and elastic.

Divide dough into 6 pieces and roll each out on a floured surface, using your hands to form each into a long rope about 1-2 inches in diameter. Braid each loaf using 3 ropes apiece. Tuck ends under and place each loaf on a greased 15x10-inch sheet pan. Brush tops liberally with a beaten egg and sprinkle with caraway seeds. Bake 25-30 minutes at 375° or until golden brown.

Makes 2 loaves.

ITALIAN BREAD RING

A no-knead yeast bread that makes a huge round loaf. For variety, use part whole-wheat flour or throw in some wheat germ.

1 package dry yeast
1/4 cup warm water
1/2 teaspoon sugar
8 cups flour
5 tablespoons butter, cut into bits and softened
1 tablespoon salt
2 eggs, lightly beaten
2 to 3 cups warm water
Cornmeal

In small bowl proof yeast in 1/4 cup warm water and sugar. In large bowl combine flour, butter, and salt. Blend in yeast mixture and eggs and gradually add 2 to 3 cups warm water — enough to make a soft dough. Transfer to a greased bowl, cover, and let rise in warm place for 2 hours, or until double in bulk. Punch down dough. Sprinkle a greased or Teflon-coated baking sheet with cornmeal. Form dough into a ring on baking sheet, let rise for 10 minutes, and bake in preheated 400° oven for 10 minutes. Reduce heat to 300° and bake 1 1/2 hours more or until lightly browned. Cool on rack.

Makes 1 ring.

PUMPERNICKEL RYE BREAD

A chewy, moist rye bread that makes good sandwiches. It has a dark crust but is not as dark on the inside as are most pumpernickels.

3 packages dry yeast
1½ cups warm water
½ cup molasses
1 tablespoon salt
2 tablespoons vegetable oil
4 cups medium rye flour
2 to 3 cups all-purpose or bread flour

Dissolve yeast in warm water in large bowl. Add molasses, salt, and oil; then add flours alternately. Knead about 12 minutes, turn into a greased bowl, and cover. Allow to rise till almost double in size. (On a cold day it will take a few hours unless you have a warm, humid kitchen.) Divide in half and let rest for about 10 minutes. Form into round loaves, place on greased baking sheet, and let rise until double in size. Stick with a skewer several times (this helps prevent the crust from lifting off while baking) and bake at 375° for 45-60 minutes. *Makes 2 round loaves.*

CUBAN BREAD

Crusty, chewy loaves that are an easy substitute for French bread.

1½ packages dry yeast
1 tablespoon sugar
2 cups warm water
1 tablespoon salt
5 to 7 cups all-purpose or hard wheat flour
3 tablespoons cornmeal
1 tablespoon egg white mixed with 1 tablespoon cold water

Combine yeast with sugar and water in bowl and allow to proof. Mix salt with flour and add to yeast mixture, a cup at a time, until you have a stiff dough. Remove to lightly floured board and knead until no longer sticky, about 10 minutes. Place in buttered bowl. Cover and let rise until doubled, about 1½-2 hours. Punch down. Turn out on floured board and shape into 2 long, French-bread-style loaves. Place on baking sheet that has been sprinkled with cornmeal. Brush with egg wash. Place in cold oven, set temperature at 400°, and bake about 35 minutes or until well browned. *Makes 2 loaves.*

PARMESAN CHEESE ROLLS

In addition to their light texture and crunchy crust, the beauty of these rolls is that they can be readied for baking in less than an hour! Marvelous accompaniment to soups, stews, or spaghetti.

3½ to 4 cups flour
2 packages dry yeast
2 tablespoons sugar
2 teaspoons garlic salt
2 teaspoons Italian seasoning
1 cup milk
½ cup water
2 tablespoons butter
1 egg
½ cup grated Parmesan cheese
2 tablespoons butter, melted
¼ cup grated Parmesan cheese

In a large bowl combine 1½ cups flour, yeast, sugar, salt, and seasoning. Mix well. In a saucepan heat milk, water, and butter until warm. Add to flour mixture. Add egg and blend at low speed for 1 minute, then medium speed for 3 minutes. By hand blend in ½ cup cheese and enough flour to make a firm dough. Knead on a well-floured surface 5 minutes. Place in greased bowl, cover, and let rise 15 minutes. Punch down dough and divide into 16 pieces. Form into balls and dip tops into melted butter and ¼ cup cheese. Place in a well-greased 13x9-inch pan or two 8-inch-square pans. Cover and let rise for 10 minutes. Bake at 375° for 20-25 minutes or until golden brown. Remove from pan.

Makes 16.

COLBY HILL INN
Henniker, New Hampshire

CINNAMON BUNS

Sure to lure even the sleepiest heads out of bed in the morning.

1/4 cup warm water
1 scant tablespoon dry yeast
1 tablespoon granulated sugar
1 teaspoon salt
1 1/4 cups milk
5 cups flour
1/2 cup shortening or butter
3/4 cup granulated sugar
2 eggs
Melted butter
Brown sugar
Cinnamon
Raisins (optional)
Sticky Mixture (recipe follows)

Measure warm water into a cup and sprinkle on yeast and 1 tablespoon granulated sugar. Set aside. Add salt to milk and scald. Cool to lukewarm. Stir yeast mixture and add it to milk, then gradually beat in 2 cups flour, blending well. Cover and set aside in warm place to get bubbly. Meanwhile beat shortening, 3/4 cup granulated sugar, and eggs until very creamy and smooth. When yeast is bubbly, add sugar and egg mixture — a small amount at a time — until well blended. Then add remaining flour, 3/4 cup at a time, beating lightly after each addition until all flour is added. Dough will be sticky and soft but don't be alarmed — don't add too much flour. Cover and let rise until double in bulk. Turn out on floured board and knead to get air bubbles out and then roll out quite thin to rectangle shape. Spread with melted butter and sprinkle with brown sugar and cinnamon; add raisins if desired. Roll up jelly-roll style and cut into slices 1/2 inch thick. Place in two 8- or 9-inch-square pans that have been greased and have Sticky Mixture on bottom; let rise until doubled and bake at 350° for 35-40 minutes. Turn out from pans as soon as removed from oven. *Makes 2 dozen.*

STICKY MIXTURE

1/2 cup butter, melted
1 1/2 cups dark Karo syrup
1/2 cup brown sugar

Combine ingredients and heat until well blended. Pour into 2 greased 8- or 9-inch-square pans.

QUICK BREADS

 *THE KENNEBUNK INN*
Kennebunk, Maine 

MARBLE SOUR CREAM AND ALMOND BREAD

Rich with sour cream, crunchy with almonds, and marbled with semi-sweet chocolate. The extra loaf would make an attractive gift — if you can bear to part with it!

3 cups granulated sugar
6 eggs
3 cups sour cream
3 teaspoons baking soda
1½ teaspoons salt
6 cups flour
½ teaspoon each ginger, nutmeg, cinnamon, and allspice
1 cup finely grated almonds
1 cup grated semi-sweet chocolate
Confectioners sugar
Cinnamon or unsweetened cocoa

Cream together granulated sugar and eggs. Add all but last 3 ingredients and blend well. Mixture will be thick. Butter and flour two 9x5-inch loaf pans and spread batter in evenly. Put chocolate on top of batter in each pan and run a fork halfway through and once around in a circular motion. Bake at 325° for about 1 hour and 20 minutes or until inserted silver knife comes out clean. Sprinkle with confectioners sugar and cinnamon or confectioners sugar and cocoa while warm. *Makes 2 loaves.*

BLACK LANTERN INN
Montgomery Village, Vermont

WHOLE-WHEAT QUICK BREAD

Subtly sweet and attractive. Keeps well if refrigerated, wrapped in aluminum foil or plastic wrap. The recipe can easily be doubled or tripled.

- **1½ cups sifted all-purpose flour**
- **3 teaspoons baking powder**
- **½ teaspoon salt**
- **1 cup unsifted whole-wheat flour**
- **1 egg, beaten**
- **1 teaspoon vanilla**
- **¾ cup sugar**
- **¼ cup melted butter**
- **1¼ cups milk**
- **1 cup finely chopped walnuts (optional)**

Preheat oven to 350°. Sift all-purpose flour with baking powder and salt. Stir in whole-wheat flour. In a large bowl, combine egg, vanilla, sugar, and butter. Beat until well mixed. Stir in milk. Add flour mixture and combine until blended. Do not overbeat. Add nuts if desired. Pour into greased 9x5-inch loaf pan and bake 1 hour. Cool in pan 10 minutes before removing.

Makes 1 loaf.

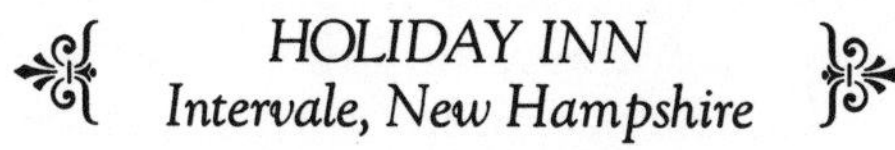

HOLIDAY INN
Intervale, New Hampshire

POPPY SEED BREAD

"One of the most requested recipes at Holiday Inn, this bread is easy to make, freezes well, and can be used as a tea bread as well as with a meal."

- **4 eggs**
- **2 cups sugar**
- **1 can (14 ounces) evaporated milk**
- **1½ cups salad oil**
- **3 cups flour**
- **4 teaspoons baking powder**
- **1 teaspoon salt**
- **½ cup poppy seeds**

Mix in order given with electric mixer, beating constantly at medium speed. Pour into 3 greased and floured 9x5-inch loaf pans. Bake at 350° for 45-60 minutes. *Makes 3 loaves.*

VERMONT MAPLE POPPY SEED BREAD

"This sweet bread goes well with afternoon tea or a chef salad with Lime-Sesame Seed Salad Dressing (see page 146). For the best flavor use Vermont grade "B" syrup and for a variation substitute almond extract for the vanilla. Be careful not to overmix the batter."

2½ cups sugar
2 cups salad oil
½ cup Vermont maple syrup
2 cups evaporated milk
5 large eggs
½ cup milk
5 cups all-purpose flour
4½ teaspoons baking powder
¼ teaspoon salt
½ cup poppy seeds
2½ teaspoons vanilla

Combine first 6 ingredients in a mixer and blend on low speed for 3 minutes. Sift flour, baking powder, and salt together and gradually add to the batter, stopping to scrape the bowl after each addition. Add poppy seeds and vanilla and mix till blended. Divide the batter among 4 greased and floured 8½x4½-inch loaf pans, filling no more than half full. Bake in preheated 350° oven for 60-65 minutes and cool 5 minutes before removing from pans.

Makes 4 loaves.

THE WILDWOOD INN
Ware, Massachusetts

STURBRIDGE SORCERY BREAD

"The early American furnishings of Wildwood attract many who've been touring nearby Old Sturbridge Village or Historic Deerfield, and we treat them to this pioneer favorite — a spicy, sweet, and moist applesauce nut bread."

2 cups sifted flour
1/2 cup granulated sugar
1/4 cup brown sugar
1 teaspoon baking powder
1/2 teaspoon baking soda
1/2 teaspoon nutmeg
1 teaspoon cinnamon
1/2 cup walnuts
1 egg, beaten
1 cup applesauce

Preheat oven to 350°. Mix all ingredients together, stirring just enough to moisten. Pour into greased and floured 9x5-inch baking pan. Bake for 50-60 minutes or until toothpick comes out clean when inserted in center. Allow to cool for 10-15 minutes before removing from pan. *Makes 1 loaf.*

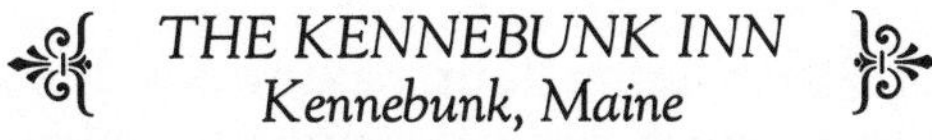
THE KENNEBUNK INN
Kennebunk, Maine

CRANBERRY APPLE BREAD

Worthy of slicing thick and serving as dessert, topped with a sauce.

1/2 cup butter
2 cups sugar
2 eggs
2 cups chopped cranberries
1 cup applesauce
1 cup chopped walnuts
1/4 teaspoon nutmeg
1/4 teaspoon cinnamon
1/4 teaspoon allspice
3 1/2 cups flour
1 teaspoon baking powder
3 1/2 teaspoons baking soda

Cream butter, sugar, and eggs. Add cranberries, applesauce, nuts, and spices, and blend well. Sift together flour, baking powder, and soda, and stir into mixture. Pour into 2 greased and floured medium-sized loaf pans and bake 1 hour at 325° or until loaves test done. *Makes 2 medium loaves.*

APPLE CRANBERRY BREAD

"Excellent with cream cheese and good hot coffee! Our guests from abroad especially like the tart flavor of the cranberries."

¼ cup butter or margarine, softened
1 cup sugar
2 eggs
1 cup sour cream
2 teaspoons grated lemon peel
3 cups all-purpose flour
4 teaspoons baking powder
1 teaspoon baking soda
½ teaspoon salt
1½ cups peeled and chopped apples
1½ cups chopped cranberries
½ cup walnuts

Cream butter and sugar until light. Beat in eggs, sour cream, and lemon peel. Sift together flour, baking powder, soda, and salt. Add to creamed mixture. Fold in apples, cranberries, and walnuts. Turn batter into a greased 9x5x3-inch loaf pan. Bake at 350° for 60-65 minutes. Cool in pan 15 minutes. Let mellow 24 hours before slicing. *Makes 1 loaf.*

CRANBERRY NUT BREAD

A slightly cinnamony cranberry bread made even more special by a tart and creamy topping.

2 cups sifted flour
3/4 cup sugar
3 teaspoons baking powder
1/2 teaspoon baking soda
1 teaspoon salt
1 teaspoon cinnamon
1 cup chopped walnuts
1 egg
1 cup whole cranberry sauce
2 tablespoons vegetable oil
1/2 cup cranberry sauce
3 ounces cream cheese
1 teaspoon grated lemon rind

Sift onto waxed paper all the dry ingredients. Add the walnuts. In mixing bowl beat egg and add 1 cup cranberry sauce and oil. Add the dry ingredients. Stir till blended. Pour into greased loaf pan and bake at 350° for 55 minutes. Cool. Blend 1/2 cup cranberry sauce with cream cheese; mix in grated lemon rind. Spoon over each slice when ready to serve. *Makes 1 loaf.*

CRANBERRY CHEESE BREAD

The cheese and cranberry combination creates an unusually delicious flavor that is difficult to identify. Serve with lunch or dinner.

2 cups flour
1 cup sugar
1½ teaspoons baking soda
½ teaspoon salt
2 teaspoons grated orange rind
2 tablespoons shortening
1½ cups shredded cheddar cheese
1 egg, beaten
1 cup cranberries, halved
½ cup chopped walnuts
Juice of 1 orange, plus water to make ¾ cup

Combine first 5 ingredients, then cut in shortening. Mix remaining ingredients together and combine with dry mixture. Turn into greased 9x5-inch loaf pan and bake at 350° for 1 hour. Let cool before slicing. *Makes 1 large loaf.*

BLUEBERRY QUICK BREAD

A versatile recipe that can be doubled or halved with ease and made with different nuts, liquids, or fruits. Try Strawberry-Orange Bread, for example, using fresh strawberries and 1 cup orange juice in place of 1 cup milk. If you use bananas for the fruit, reduce the liquid by a half cup.

5 cups white flour
2 tablespoons baking powder
1 teaspoon salt
1½ cups sugar
¾ cup butter (6 ounces)
4 eggs
2 cups milk
2 teaspoons vanilla
3 cups blueberries
1½ cups chopped walnuts (optional)

Sift flour, baking powder, salt, and sugar together. Cut butter into flour mixture as you would when making pie dough. In a separate bowl, thoroughly blend eggs, milk, and vanilla. Add blueberries and nuts if desired. (If you use frozen blueberries, it's better not to defrost them before adding to liquid ingredients.) Grease bread pans: five 6½x3-inch or two 9x5-inch. Add wet ingredients to dry ingredients and blend together thoroughly but quickly. Pour batter into pans and put immediately into a preheated 350° oven. Bake for 40-50 minutes.

Makes 2 large or 5 small loaves.

PEAR BREAD

A lovely tea bread that is special enough to be dessert for a picnic. It freezes well so keep an extra loaf on hand for unexpected guests.

1/2 cup sweet butter (1 stick), room temperature
1 cup sugar
2 large eggs
2 cups all-purpose flour
1/2 teaspoon salt
1/2 teaspoon baking soda
1 teaspoon baking powder
Pinch nutmeg
1/4 cup buttermilk
1 cup coarsely chopped cored pears (or puréed in food processor or blender)
1 teaspoon vanilla
1/2 cup chopped walnuts

Cream butter, gradually beat in sugar, and add eggs one at a time, beating after each addition. Combine dry ingredients and add to egg mixture alternately with buttermilk. Stir in pears, vanilla, and nuts. Pour into a greased loaf pan and bake at 350° for 1 hour. Cool. Slice and serve plain, with Quick Apple Butter (recipe follows), or with cream cheese. *Makes 1 loaf.*

QUICK APPLE BUTTER

2 cups unsweetened applesauce
1/2 cup sugar
1/4 teaspoon ground allspice
Pinch each of ginger and cloves

Combine all ingredients in a saucepan, bring to a boil, and simmer 30 minutes. Cool and spread on Pear Bread (or toast).
Makes 1 1/2 cups.

RHUBARB BREAD

A very moist quick bread best suited for breakfast or tea time. After baking, let loaf sit for 10 to 15 minutes before turning it out of the pan. Cool completely — preferably overnight — before slicing.

1½ cups brown sugar, packed
⅔ cup oil
1 egg
1 cup buttermilk or sour milk
1 teaspoon baking soda
2½ cups flour
1 teaspoon salt
1 to 1½ cups chopped raw rhubarb, depending on the juiciness of the variety
½ cup chopped nuts
½ cup granulated sugar
1 tablespoon butter or margarine
½ teaspoon cinnamon
¼ cup chopped nuts

Combine brown sugar, oil, egg, milk, and soda. Sift together flour and salt and add to liquid mixture. Fold in rhubarb and ½ cup nuts. Pour into greased and floured 9x5-inch loaf pan. Combine granulated sugar, butter, and cinnamon until crumbly. Add ¼ cup nuts and sprinkle topping over batter in pan. Bake at 350° for about 1 hour or until done. *Makes 1 loaf.*

THE RED LION INN
Stockbridge, Massachusetts

PINEAPPLE BREAD

Tastes like pound cake and adds a fancy touch to any meal.

1/4 pound butter
1 cup sugar
2 eggs
2 cups flour
1 teaspoon baking powder
Pinch salt
1 cup crushed and drained pineapple
1/2 to 3/4 cup chopped nuts

Cream butter and sugar. Beat eggs in one at a time. Sift flour, baking powder, and salt. Alternate adding flour mixture and pineapple to egg mixture. Add nuts. Pour into greased and floured pans. Bake at 350° for 45-60 minutes.

Makes 2 small or 1 large loaf.

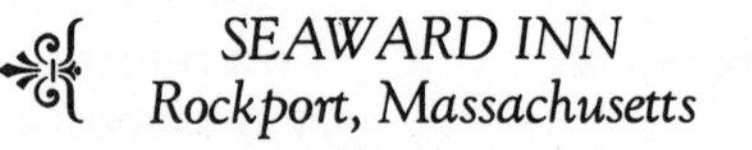

SEAWARD INN
Rockport, Massachusetts

SQUASH BREAD

This goes well with dinner as it isn't overly sweet. For variety, add 2/3 cup chopped nuts, raisins, or dates, and bake in muffin tins at 400° for about 25 minutes.

2/3 cup margarine
2 2/3 cups sugar
4 eggs
1 can (15 ounces) winter squash or pumpkin purée
2/3 cup water
3 1/3 cups sifted flour
1/2 teaspoon baking powder
2 teaspoons baking soda
1 1/2 teaspoons salt
1 teaspoon cinnamon
1 teaspoon cloves
1/4 teaspoon each ginger and nutmeg

Cream margarine and sugar. Add eggs, one at a time, beating well after each addition. Add squash and water. Sift together remaining ingredients and stir into squash mixture. Pour into 2 greased and floured 9x5-inch loaf pans and bake in preheated 350° oven for 50-60 minutes or until done. *Makes 2 loaves.*

THE JOHN HANCOCK INN
Hancock, New Hampshire

DANIEL'S PUMPKIN BREAD

"The aroma of pumpkin and spices never fails to whet the appetite as it fills the inn. We serve this bread every day and present it as a special gift on holidays."

1½ cups granulated sugar
1½ cups brown sugar, firmly packed
1 cup oil
3 eggs
2 cups pumpkin purée
3 cups flour
1½ teaspoons ground cloves
1½ teaspoons cinnamon
½ teaspoon allspice
1½ teaspoons nutmeg
½ teaspoon baking powder
1 teaspoon baking soda
½ teaspoon salt

Mix together sugars and oil. Beat in eggs and pumpkin. Sift together remaining ingredients and add to creamed mixture, blending well. Pour into lightly greased loaf pans. Bake at 350° for 1-1¼ hours. Other goodies such as raisins, nuts, or chopped dates may be added. *Makes 5 small or 2 medium loaves.*

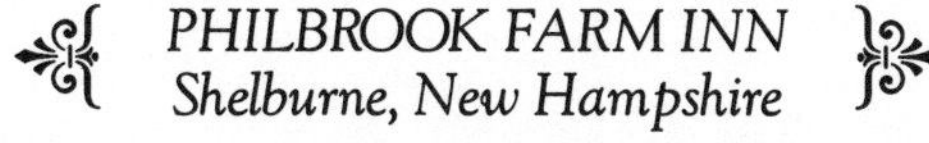
PHILBROOK FARM INN
Shelburne, New Hampshire

GRAHAM DARK BREAD

The ingredients are simple, the directions are easy, and the bread tastes as good as it looks. Has the slightly sweet molasses flavor and chewy consistency of brown bread.

1½ cups graham flour
2 cups white flour
½ cup dark brown sugar
½ cup dark molasses
2 cups sour milk or buttermilk
2 teaspoons baking soda
1 teaspoon salt

In a bowl combine all ingredients, mixing well. Pour into greased 9x5-inch loaf pan and bake 1 hour (or until tests done) at 350°. *Makes 1 loaf.*

THE PASQUANEY INN
Bridgewater, New Hampshire

ZUCCHINI BREAD

A great recipe for zucchini season, when the fresh vegetable abounds. Makes a large loaf, loaded with nuts and raisins.

3 eggs
1 cup oil
1/2 cup sugar
2 cups grated and drained zucchini
2 teaspoons vanilla
2 cups flour
1/4 teaspoon baking powder
2 teaspoons baking soda
3 teaspoons cinnamon
1 teaspoon salt
1 cup raisins
1 cup chopped walnuts

Beat eggs slightly in a large bowl; stir in oil, sugar, zucchini, and vanilla. Sift together flour, baking powder, soda, cinnamon, and salt. Stir into egg mixture until well blended, then add raisins and nuts and stir. Bake in large greased loaf pan at 375° for 1 hour.

Makes 1 large loaf.

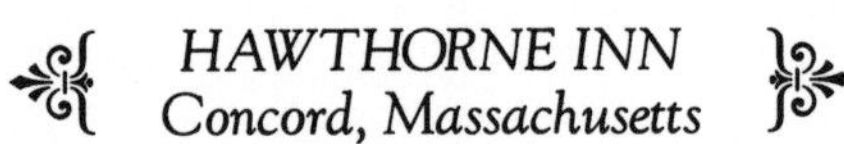
HAWTHORNE INN
Concord, Massachusetts

BROWN BREAKFAST BREAD

Dark brown, dense, sweet, and spicy. Be sure the baking dish is well greased so the bread can be easily removed. Serve warm from the oven with butter or cream cheese.

3/4 cup honey
3/4 cup molasses
3 1/2 cups flour
2 teaspoons baking soda
2 teaspoons ginger
2 teaspoons cinnamon
2 teaspoons allspice
Dash of salt
2 cups milk
1 cup raisins
1 to 2 tablespoons marmalade

Beat together honey and molasses. Add all but last ingredient and blend well, then stir in marmalade. Bake in a large well-greased baking dish at 350° for 1 1/4 hours. *Serves 10-12.*

THE WILDWOOD INN
Ware, Massachusetts

BUNDT BEAUTY BREAD

"This wholesome bread is so beautiful to look at and so satisfying to eat that our guests are doubly delighted when they find out it is such a healthy bread as well! We invert it onto an early American round pine serving platter and let it make a mouth-watering centerpiece for any breakfast spread."

2 cups whole-wheat flour
1 cup unbleached flour
2 teaspoons baking soda
2 cups buttermilk
½ cup honey
½ cup dark molasses
1¼ cups raisins

Preheat oven to 400°. Grease and flour a Bundt pan (even if it's nonstick). Mix all the ingredients together, blending well, and then pour into pan. Turn the oven down to 350° and bake for about 45-60 minutes, testing to see if toothpick comes out clean and bread leaves pan sides easily. *Makes 1 Bundt ring.*

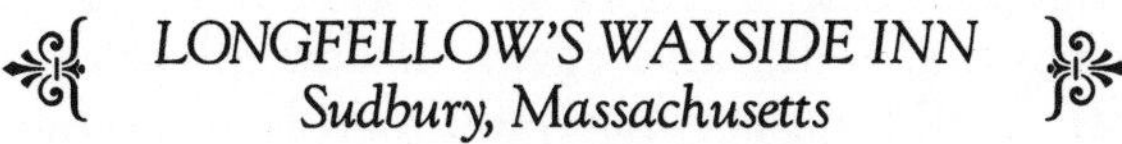

LONGFELLOW'S WAYSIDE INN
Sudbury, Massachusetts

CORN MUFFINS

There's just the hint of corn flavor in these sweet muffins, which are not at all like corn bread in taste or texture.

1½ cups sugar
Pinch of salt
2 tablespoons baking powder
3½ cups bread flour
1 cup cornmeal
4 large eggs
1½ cups milk
⅓ cup salad oil

Combine sugar, salt, baking powder, flour, cornmeal, eggs, and 1 cup milk until well blended. Add remaining ½ cup milk and the salad oil and mix for 3 minutes. Place in well-greased muffin tins and bake at 400° for about 20 minutes or until golden. *Makes 2-3 dozen.*

MANDARIN MUFFINS

Not at all mundane muffins — these are sweet and spicy with plump morsels of mandarin orange and a buttery sugar topping.

1½ cups sifted flour
½ cup sugar
2 teaspoons baking powder
½ teaspoon salt
½ teaspoon nutmeg
¼ teaspoon allspice
¼ cup melted margarine or butter
½ cup milk
1 egg, slightly beaten
1 can (11 ounces) mandarin oranges, well drained
Melted butter or margarine
½ cup sugar combined with 1 teaspoon cinnamon

Sift together first 6 ingredients. Combine ¼ cup cooled melted margarine, milk, and egg, and add all at once to flour mixture. Stir until flour is moist. Add mandarin oranges and mix lightly. Pour batter into well-greased muffin tins and bake in preheated 400° oven for 15-20 minutes. Remove from tins and while hot dip tops of muffins in melted butter and roll in cinnamon-sugar mixture. *Makes 1 dozen.*

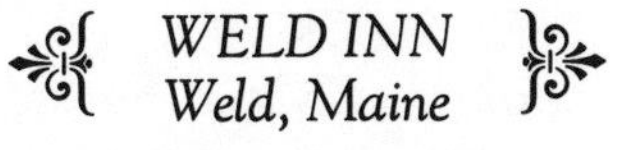

WELD INN ORANGE-RAISIN MUFFINS

Light and delicate bran muffins with an appealing orange flavor. They freeze well, too, if you ever have any left over.

2 eggs, slightly beaten
1 1/2 cups orange juice
1/4 cup vegetable oil
2 cups raisin bran cereal
2 1/2 cups flour
1/2 cup sugar
2 1/2 teaspoons baking powder
1/2 teaspoon salt

Combine eggs, orange juice, oil, and cereal. Sift together flour, sugar, baking powder, and salt. Add all at once to liquid ingredients and stir just until moistened. Pour into greased muffin tins and bake at 375° for 20-25 minutes. *Makes 1 dozen.*

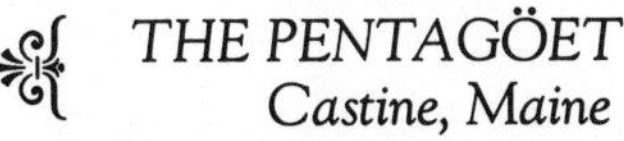

PENTAGÖET INN BRAN MUFFINS

You can make fresh muffins daily or as often as you wish with this batter, which will keep in the refrigerator for about 6 weeks.

2 cups boiling water
2 cups All-Bran cereal
3 cups sugar
1 cup melted butter
4 eggs, beaten
1 quart sour milk
5 cups flour
4 cups raisin bran cereal
5 teaspoons baking soda
1 teaspoon salt
2 cups chopped dates

Pour boiling water over All-Bran and set aside. Mix sugar and melted butter, beat in eggs, and stir in sour milk. Add All-Bran mixture. Combine flour, raisin bran, soda, salt, and dates. Stir into wet mixture. Store in refrigerator at least overnight. Bake in greased muffin tins at 400° for 20-25 minutes.

Makes 3-4 dozen.

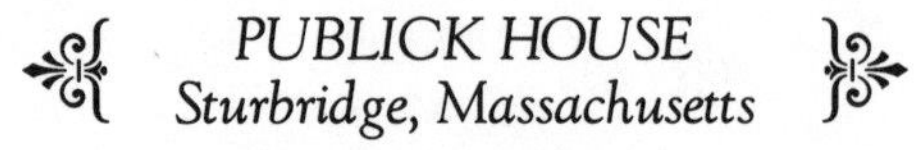

PUMPKIN MUFFINS

"Sweet, golden, and jam packed with raisins and nuts. Fresh or frozen pumpkin can also be used."

2 cups sugar
1/2 cup vegetable oil
3 eggs
1 1/2 cups canned pumpkin
1/2 cup water
3 cups bread flour
1 1/2 teaspoons baking powder
1 teaspoon baking soda
1 teaspoon salt
1/2 teaspoon cloves
3/4 teaspoon cinnamon
1/2 teaspoon nutmeg
1 1/2 cups raisins
1 cup chopped walnuts

Place sugar, vegetable oil, eggs, pumpkin, and water in bowl and mix. Sift flour, baking powder, soda, salt, and spices. Stir into first mixture. Add raisins and walnuts. Let stand 1 hour at room temperature. Place in greased muffin pans. Bake in preheated 400° oven approximately 15 minutes. *Makes 2 dozen.*

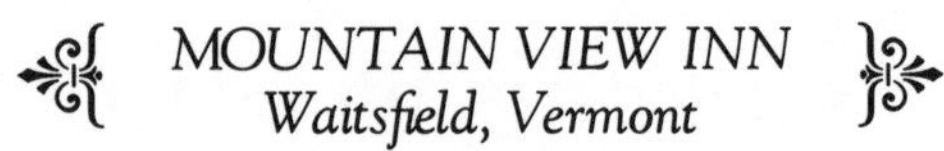

BLUEBERRY MUFFINS

"I got this recipe from my mother-in-law who lives in Maine and says that blueberry muffins aren't good unless there are 'more blueberries than muffin'!" Great breakfast fare.

1/2 cup butter, softened
1 1/4 cups sugar
2 cups flour
2 teaspoons baking powder
1/2 teaspoon salt
2 eggs
1/2 cup milk
2 1/2 cups blueberries

Cream butter and sugar together. Add all other ingredients except blueberries and stir until just mixed. Fold in blueberries and spoon into paper-lined muffin tins. Bake at 350° for 15-20 minutes. *Makes 1-2 dozen.*

HAWTHORNE INN
Concord, Massachusetts

BERRY-BANANA MUFFINS

Mildly sweet with an appealingly different texture. Vary the berry to find your favorite flavor.

2 eggs
1/4 cup oil
3/4 cup milk
1/3 cup honey
1 mashed banana
3/4 cup blueberries or raspberries
3/4 teaspoon salt
2 teaspoons baking powder
2 cups flour
3/4 cup almonds

Beat together eggs, oil, milk, honey, banana, and berries. Add salt, baking powder, flour, and almonds, stirring just enough to moisten. Bake in greased muffin tins at 350° for 20-25 minutes.

Makes 1 dozen.

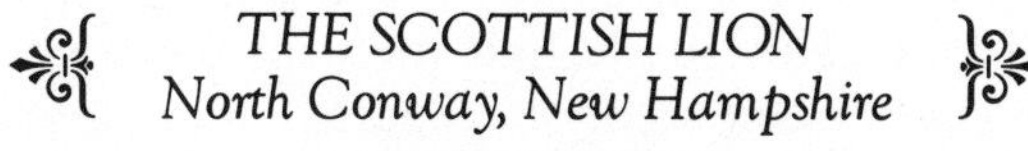

THE SCOTTISH LION
North Conway, New Hampshire

SCOTTISH LION OATCAKES

Hearty, wholesome, and habit-forming. Serve warm with butter and your favorite jam or preserves.

1 cup sifted flour
1 tablespoon sugar
1 teaspoon baking powder
1/2 teaspoon salt
2 cups quick rolled oats
1/2 cup softened butter
1/2 cup milk

Sift flour, sugar, baking powder, and salt together. Mix in rolled oats, cut in butter thoroughly, and gradually add milk, stirring until dough is formed. Roll dough on lightly floured surface to 1/8-inch thickness and cut out with cookie cutter. Place on greased baking sheet and bake at 375° for 12-15 minutes or until slightly browned.

Makes 18 three-inch cakes.

TEA SCONES

"This is our New England version of Scottish scones. They are a delectable accompaniment to a light luncheon."

¾ cup all-purpose flour
¾ cup whole-wheat flour
½ cup toasted wheat germ
4 teaspoons baking powder
¼ cup sugar
½ teaspoon salt
½ cup butter
2 eggs, beaten
⅓ cup milk
¼ cup golden seedless raisins

Stir flours, wheat germ, baking powder, sugar, and salt together. Cut butter into flour mixture. Add eggs and milk, beaten together. Add raisins. Turn out onto lightly floured board and knead 7 or 8 times. Roll into 2 half-inch-thick 8-inch rounds. Cut each into 8 pie-shaped wedges. Separate with sharp knife and place on greased and floured cookie sheets. Bake in a 400° preheated oven for 12-15 minutes. Split and serve warm with jam and butter. *Makes 16.*

STONE HOUSE INN
North Thetford, Vermont

SCOTTISH OAT SCONES

Light golden and buttery-rich. These can be whipped up in a matter of minutes and are at their very best while warm, drizzled with honey or spread with jam.

2/3 cup butter or margarine, melted
1/3 cup milk
1 egg
1 1/2 cups flour
1 1/4 cups uncooked oats
1/4 cup sugar
1 tablespoon baking powder
1 teaspoon cream of tartar
1/2 teaspoon salt
1/2 cup raisins or currants

Add cooled butter, milk, and eggs to combined dry ingredients; mix just until moistened. Stir in raisins. Shape dough into ball and pat out onto floured surface to form an 8-inch circle. (You may have to add a little flour to your hands and the dough for easier handling.) Cut circle into 12 wedges and bake on greased baking sheet at 425° for 12-15 minutes or until light golden brown. *Makes 1 dozen.*

APPETIZERS

West Dover Inn, West Dover, Vermont

THE RAM IN THE THICKET
Wilton, New Hampshire

CAROLINA SHRIMP BUTTER

Serve with crackers, on sliced cucumbers, or as stuffing for cherry tomatoes.

1 pound cream cheese, softened
2 ounces butter, softened
1 tablespoon dry sherry
1½ teaspoons lemon juice
¼ teaspoon mace
¼ teaspoon dry mustard
½ teaspoon cayenne (or to taste)
½ teaspoon salt
¼ teaspoon white pepper
¼ pound shrimp, cooked and minced

Beat all ingredients with electric mixer until well blended. For best flavor, store overnight or for several hours in refrigerator. *Serves 10-12.*

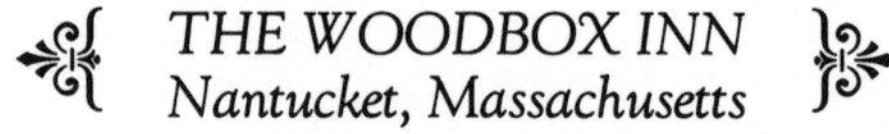

THE WOODBOX INN
Nantucket, Massachusetts

CRAB TINA

This simple and tasty appetizer is best with an unsalted cracker.

¼ pound of both King and Snow crab
2 tablespoons lemon juice
3 tablespoons horseradish
1½ cups mayonnaise
½ cup crumbled fresh blue cheese
Pepper to taste

Mix all ingredients together. Chill and serve on lettuce bed with garnish of parsley, lemon, or tomato rose. *Serves 8-10.*

THE FOUR CHIMNEYS INN
Nantucket, Massachusetts

CLAM-CHEESE SPREAD

"Of all the things that we serve as a cocktail snack, this is by far the favorite and the recipe for which we receive the most requests. Makes about 2 pounds, so it's great for a group of 20 or so, with some left for another day."

1½ pounds cream cheese
2 sticks butter, melted
½ package dry leek soup mix
1 can smoked clams (oysters, etc., can be substituted)

Blend everything in a food processer, adding the clams last. This keeps very well in a refrigerator container and tastes even better the second day. Serve with Sea Rounds or Melba toast.

Makes 2 pounds.

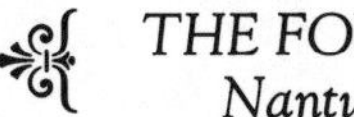

THE FOUR CHIMNEYS INN
Nantucket, Massachusetts

CAVIAR PIE

A luxurious dish for a fancy gathering.

6 hard-boiled eggs, chopped
½ cup butter, very soft
¼ cup mayonnaise
½ cup chopped green onions
1 teaspoon lemon juice
Salt
White pepper
½ cup sour cream
1 to 2 spoonfuls each of red and black caviar

Combine all but last 2 ingredients and mix well. Line a bowl with plastic wrap and pack mixture firmly into bowl. Chill overnight. Then unmold onto a plate, frost with sour cream, and decorate with caviar. Serve with party rye.

Serves 4-6.

THE CAPTAIN JEFFERDS INN 
Kennebunkport, Maine

CAPTAIN JEFFERDS HOUSE PÂTÉ

"This is a rather simple but very tasty appetizer which I like to serve at cocktail time in a fancy pedestal dish with plain crackers."

3 cloves garlic, crushed
1/2 stick butter
1 pound chicken livers
1/4 cup sliced onion
1/4 cup heavy cream
2 tablespoons dry sherry
1/2 teaspoon salt
1/2 teaspoon celery salt
1/4 teaspoon pepper
2 hard-cooked eggs

Sauté crushed garlic in butter. Then add chicken livers and continue to sauté until just tender and no longer pink inside. Add onion a few minutes before livers are cooked. Cool. Transfer all ingredients except eggs to blender or food processor and purée until smooth. Add eggs and continue to blend until smooth. This can be frozen. *Serves 12.*

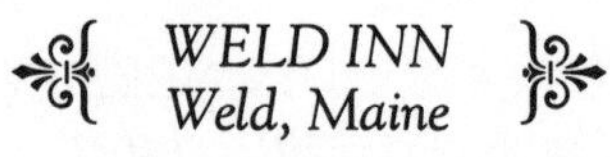

WELD INN
Weld, Maine

CHEESE BALL

"We serve this at our special Holidays Evening, just before Christmas. The ball tastes better made a day ahead."

2 packages (8 ounces each) cream cheese, softened
8 ounces shredded cheddar cheese
1 teaspoon lemon juice
2 teaspoons Worcestershire sauce
1 tablespoon finely minced pimiento
1 tablespoon grated onion
1 tablespoon minced green pepper
Grated walnuts

Combine all but last ingredient and put into freezer for 20 minutes. Remove, shape into a ball, and roll in grated walnuts. Wrap in plastic wrap and put in refrigerator until ready to use.

Makes 1 large ball or 2 small ones.

HUMMUS

Middle Eastern in origin, this is a creamy mixture of puréed garbanzo beans, sesame seed paste, and garlic.

1 can (15½ ounces) garbanzo beans
¼ to ½ cup liquid from beans
3 tablespoons lemon juice
2 to 3 cloves garlic, crushed
½ teaspoon salt
½ teaspoon white pepper
¼ cup tahini (sesame seed paste, available at supermarkets and health food stores)
Olive oil
Paprika

Drain the beans and save the juice. In a food processor with metal blade or in a blender, purée the beans with all but last 2 ingredients. Taste for seasoning and refrigerate.

Serve at room temperature on a bed of lettuce with warmed pita bread. Drizzle olive oil on top of the hummus and add a dash of paprika. *Serves 8.*

WINDFLOWER INN
Great Barrington, Massachusetts

CURRIED DIP WITH CRUDITÉS

The kind of curry powder used will determine the amount of "zip" in this scrumptious dip. It's easy to make, colorful, and suitable for any occasion, but must be prepared at least a day ahead.

1 pint mayonnaise
3 tablespoons catsup
3 tablespoons honey
1/4 teaspoon salt
3 tablespoons grated onion
1 1/2 teaspoons lemon juice
7 to 9 drops Tabasco sauce
1 1/4 teaspoons curry powder

Mix all ingredients together and refrigerate for at least 1 day. Serve with fresh vegetables. *Makes 2 cups.*

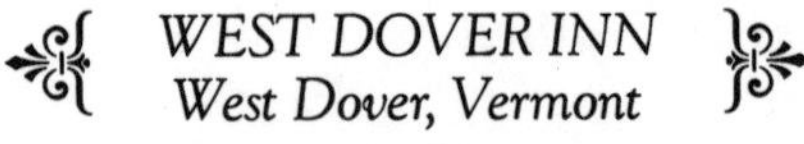

WEST DOVER INN
West Dover, Vermont

BROCCOLI-CAULIFLOWER MEDLEY

"Frequently, a guest requests this recipe. We serve it as an appetizer but with the addition of diced turkey, it makes an excellent luncheon salad."

1 pound cauliflower florets
1 pound broccoli spears (trimmed to 2 inches)
Seasoned salt and pepper to taste
1 teaspoon curry powder
1/4 teaspoon dry mustard
1 dash Tabasco sauce
1 cup mayonnaise
1 ounce French dressing (bottled)

Blanch vegetables and drain well. Add dry ingredients and Tabasco sauce to mayonnaise. Stir to blend. Beat in French dressing gradually until thoroughly mixed. Place vegetables in bowl, add dressing, and lightly toss. Refrigerate for at least 2 hours. At serving time place each individual serving on a bed of lettuce.

Serves 6-8.

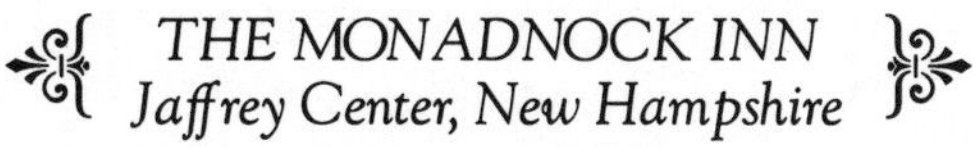

THE MONADNOCK INN
Jaffrey Center, New Hampshire

"QUICK" MARINATED MUSHROOMS

Ready in 15 minutes but tastes best when thoroughly chilled.

1 pound whole small mushrooms, washed
1 medium onion, sliced
2 cloves garlic, crushed
1/4 cup olive or salad oil
1/4 cup white wine
1/4 cup cider or red wine vinegar
Salt and pepper to taste

Sauté mushrooms, onion, and garlic in oil until mushrooms just start to color. Add white wine and simmer 1-2 minutes. Add vinegar, remove from heat, and chill. Adjust seasoning just before serving. Place on a bed of lettuce. *Serves 4-6.*

EDENCROFT MANOR
Littleton, New Hampshire

MUSHROOMS WITH CRAB

Fine finger food for a cocktail party. This can be prepared ahead of time and popped under the broiler at the last minute.

22 ounces crab meat (Snow)
1/4 teaspoon Tabasco sauce
1 tablespoon lemon juice
4 ounces mayonnaise
8 ounces bread crumbs
50 mushroom caps
1/2 to 3/4 pound clarified butter

Combine crab meat, Tabasco sauce, and lemon juice and mix in bowl. Evenly incorporate mayonnaise into mixture. Add bread crumbs to desired consistency. Mixture should be moist and full of crab meat. Mound mixture into mushroom caps, top with butter, and broil to brown. Serve on platter.

Makes 50 mushroom caps.

MOUNTAIN TOP INN
Chittenden, Vermont

STUFFED MUSHROOMS MOUNTAIN TOP

Don't let the number of ingredients discourage you from making this outstanding appetizer. It's sure to be a hit at any dinner or cocktail party.

6 cherrystone clams, or 4 to 6 ounces canned chopped clams, reserving juice
Water
1 lemon, cut in half
1/4 teaspoon salt
1 pound mushrooms
1 small onion, cut up
1 stalk celery, cut up
1 green pepper, cut up
3 strips raw bacon, cut up
1 tablespoon chopped pimiento
1/2 stick butter
2 eggs
1/4 cup bread crumbs
1 teaspoon garlic powder
1/2 teaspoon white pepper
1/2 teaspoon paprika
1 teaspoon lemon juice

If using fresh clams, wash thoroughly to remove grit and sand. Place in a large pot, cover with water, and add lemon halves and salt. Bring to a boil and cook until shells open. Remove clams and cool under running water; reserve 1/2 cup of the cooking liquid.

Wash mushrooms, remove stems and reserve, and place caps on a cookie sheet; set aside.

When clams have cooled, remove the usable portion from the shell, dice finely, and set aside. Purée onion, celery, green pepper, reserved mushroom stems, bacon, and pimiento using a grinder or food processor. Sauté this mixture in a skillet with butter and reserved clam broth on moderate heat until liquid is reduced. Set aside to cool.

Combine diced clams, puréed mixture, and remaining ingredients and mix by hand. If stuffing is too wet, add additional bread crumbs. Place stuffing in mushroom caps and bake at 350° for 20 minutes. *Serves 6-8.*

CRAB-STUFFED MUSHROOMS

Before serving, seat your guests at the table, where it will be easier for them to eat and enjoy this hors d'oeuvre.

1/2 cup King crab meat, chopped
1/4 cup finely crushed Ritz cracker crumbs
1 teaspoon grated Parmesan cheese
2 to 4 tablespoons melted butter
2 drops Tabasco sauce
2 drops Worcestershire sauce
15 to 20 jumbo mushroom caps
1 cup Mornay Sauce (recipe follows)
1/4 pound Gruyère cheese, sliced thin

Combine crab meat, cracker crumbs, and Parmesan cheese in bowl and mix well. Combine melted butter, Tabasco, and Worcestershire, stir to blend, and add to crab mixture — bit by bit — until stuffing is moist and binds together.

Place mushrooms in lightly greased casserole. Divide stuffing evenly among caps. Cover all caps with Mornay Sauce. Bake at 375° for 20 minutes, top with sliced Gruyère cheese, and continue baking until cheese is melted and golden brown.

Makes approximately 15-20 jumbo mushroom caps.

MORNAY SAUCE

1 cup milk
Dash each of salt, white pepper, and Tabasco sauce
2 tablespoons melted butter
2 tablespoons flour
1/4 pound Gruyère cheese, grated

Heat milk, salt, pepper, and Tabasco in double boiler. In saucepan, make a roux by combining melted butter and flour. Whisk roux, bit by bit, into milk until the consistency of a loose medium white sauce. Whisk in cheese, bit by bit, and cook 10 minutes, whisking occasionally. Proceed with recipe above.

THE BERNERHOF INN
Glen, New Hampshire

DÉLICE DE GRUYÈRE

Small cheese croquettes served as an appetizer, accompanied by a dab of spiced tomato. "This recipe has been a favorite of visitors of the Bernerhof since Claire Zumstein brought it here from Switzerland in the mid-1950s. Many food critics have commented upon it, and it was even featured in Gourmet *magazine many years ago."*

3 cups milk
4 ounces butter (1 stick)
Salt to taste
Freshly ground whole white pepper to taste
10 ounces sifted flour (white bleached)
½ pound Emmenthaler cheese, grated
½ pound Gruyère cheese, grated
6 egg yolks
4 eggs, beaten
3 cups dried bread crumbs
½ cup chopped onion
¼ cup chopped green pepper
1 teaspoon dried dill
2 tablespoons olive oil
1 can (28 ounces) stewed tomatoes
¼ cup finely chopped parsley
Butter for sautéing délice

Bring milk, 4 ounces butter, salt, and pepper to a boil, making sure butter is melted before removing from heat. Add flour and stir thoroughly until you achieve a mashed potato consistency. Immediately add the cheeses, mixing thoroughly to a smooth texture or until cheese has completely melted. Add egg yolks, again mixing until a smooth yellow hue is achieved.

Refrigerate for several hours or until firm enough to mold. Spreading mixture in a shallow pan (approximately 10x6x2 inches) will allow for faster chilling. Once mixture is firm, cut into 8 equal pieces, place on floured board, and roll into strips about 24 inches long and ½ inch in diameter. Cut each strip into 3-inch pieces, set pieces on a tray, and return to the refrigerator for about an hour or until firm again. Dip in beaten eggs and roll in dried bread crumbs. Lightly sauté onion, green pepper, and dill in olive oil. Combine with stewed tomatoes, breaking up if whole, and stir in parsley. Keep warm while cooking délice.

Melt ½ teaspoon butter in heavy 10-inch skillet until almost brown. Add about 6 délice, and sauté quickly until golden brown. Remove from skillet and repeat (using ½ teaspoon butter per 6 délice) until all délice are cooked. To serve, place 3 délice in a spoke arrangement on a small 8-inch plate with heated spiced tomato at the hub. Add a fresh parsley sprig for color.

Makes about 20 servings of 3 délice each.

 THE HARVEST AT THE VILLAGE INN
Lenox, Massachusetts 

DEEP-FRIED CAMEMBERT

"At the inn we serve this as a first course with a cucumber garnish and fresh parsley for color."

2 four-inch wheels Camembert cheese
½ cup flour
4 eggs, beaten
2 cups fine bread crumbs mixed with 1 tablespoon dried mixed herbs (thyme, basil, oregano, dill, etc.)
2 cups oil for deep-frying
Cucumber Garnish (recipe follows)

Cut each wheel of Camembert into 6 wedges and remove the rind from each wedge. Roll each wedge in flour, then dip in the egg, then the bread crumbs. Put on a platter and chill for at least 1 hour. When ready to serve, heat oil to 375° and fry 4 wedges at a time for 45 seconds or until well browned. Remove. Drain briefly on a paper towel. Put each serving on a separate plate, surround with cucumber slices, and add a sprig of parsley. Serve immediately.

Makes 12 wedges.

CUCUMBER GARNISH

½ cup red wine vinegar
1 tablespoon sugar
¼ teaspoon salt
½ teaspoon crushed fennel seed
½ teaspoon freshly ground pepper
1 cucumber

Combine vinegar, sugar, salt, fennel, and pepper. Slice cucumber into paper-thin slices and marinate in vinegar mixture.

MOUSSE OF SPINACH AND CARROT WITH LEMON SABAYON SAUCE

"The wonderful blendings of color — orange, dark green, and yellow — make this dish as beautiful to look at as it is delicious to eat. A very popular item at The Four Columns Inn and a good choice for a light appetizer."

CARROT MOUSSE

2 pounds carrots, peeled and cut into chunks
2 tablespoons unsalted butter
1/2 cup heavy cream
4 egg yolks plus 1 whole egg, lightly beaten
Salt and freshly ground pepper to taste
Pinch of cayenne pepper

Steam carrots 15-20 minutes (until tender). Drain well, put in food processor with butter, and process until smooth. Remove from processor, cool, and stir in remaining ingredients. Set aside while preparing spinach mixture.

SPINACH MOUSSE

3 pounds spinach, washed and drained well, with stems removed
2 tablespoons unsalted butter
1/2 cup heavy cream
3 egg yolks and 2 whole eggs, lightly beaten
Salt and freshly ground pepper to taste
Pinch of nutmeg

Steam the spinach until soft and wilted. Place in a food processor with the butter and process until smooth. Remove the purée from the processor and cool. Stir in remaining ingredients.

Preheat oven to 350°. Generously butter eight 6-ounce ramekins. Evenly divide the carrot mixture among the ramekins. Place equal amounts of spinach mixture over the carrot. Smooth the tops. Cover the ramekins with buttered wax paper, butter side down. Place them in baking pan and add boiling water to come halfway up the sides of the ramekins. Bake for 20-30 minutes or until firm to the touch. (May at this point be refrigerated, then reheated later for 10-15 minutes in a pan of boiling water on top of the stove.) Serve with Lemon Sabayon Sauce (recipe follows).

Serves 8.

LEMON SABAYON SAUCE

8 egg yolks
8 tablespoons water
4 tablespoons lemon juice
Salt

At the time of serving, place the yolks, water, and lemon juice in a double boiler over medium heat and beat until semi-thick. Add salt to taste. Spoon sauce on 8 plates and pop each mousse onto a plate.

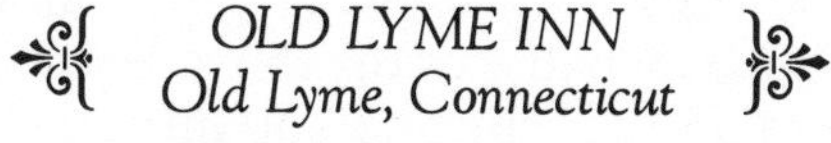

OLD LYME INN
Old Lyme, Connecticut

SCALLOPS STEAMED WITH SPINACH AND RED PEPPERS

Especially attractive served in a large scallop shell with lemon slice and parsley sprig as garnish.

5 teaspoons chopped shallots
9 tablespoons butter (reserve 1 to finish sauce)
12 ounces bay scallops (approximately)
3 tablespoons finely chopped pimientos
10 ounces fresh spinach, washed and dried thoroughly
6 tablespoons white wine
3 teaspoons chopped parsley
Salt and pepper to taste
8 rings of red pepper

Sweat shallots in 2 tablespoons butter just till tender. Add 6 tablespoons butter and rest of ingredients, cover, and steam until scallops are cooked, stirring occasionally. (Scallops do not take long to cook, so watch them closely.) Remove from heat, stir in remaining 1 tablespoon butter, and serve. *Serves 4.*

CRAB MOUSSE WITH THREE SAUCES

"This dish, created by Chef Thomas Pandiscio, won a first place award at the 1983 Crab Cooking Olympics in San Francisco."

8 ounces fresh crab meat, picked over
8 ounces fresh grey sole, cut in small pieces
4 medium egg yolks
2 medium eggs
1 cup milk
1¼ teaspoons salt
¼ teaspoon white pepper
¼ teaspoon cayenne pepper

Place crab and pieces of sole in a blender. Purée well. Mix yolks, eggs, milk, salt, and peppers and add to fish in the blender. Blend 2 minutes till perfectly smooth mix is achieved. Strain through a fine sieve. Lightly butter muffin tins (eighteen 1½-inch-diameter cups). Pour crab mixture almost to top, cover with aluminum foil, and place in roasting pan(s) along with enough boiling water to reach halfway up the sides of the muffin tins. Bake in preheated 350° oven for 20-30 minutes or until mixture has set. It is done when an inserted knife comes out clean. Remove from oven, allow to rest 5 minutes, invert on a large platter, and keep warm while making the sauces.

SORREL SAUCE

(May be made a day ahead, up to but not including the point when sorrel is added. When ready to use, gently reheat, add sorrel, and continue the recipe.)

1 large shallot, minced
1 cup fish fumet (concentrated cooking liquid)
¼ cup dry white wine
1¼ cups heavy cream
1 cup packed fresh sorrel, stems removed, cut in strips
Juice of half a lemon
Salt and white pepper
2 tablespoons butter

Place shallot, fumet, and wine in saucepan, and rapidly boil down to a syrupy glaze; add the cream and reduce till slightly thickened. Add sorrel, boil 30 seconds, and add lemon and salt and pepper to taste. Remove from heat and whisk in butter.

LOBSTER SAUCE

(May also be made the day before.)

1/4 cup olive oil
1 small cooked lobster, cut in several pieces
1 shallot, chopped
1 carrot, chopped
1 small onion, chopped
1 clove garlic, unpeeled
3 ripe tomatoes, chopped
1/4 cup cognac
1 cup dry white wine
3 cups fish fumet
1 tablespoon tomato paste
1 sprig each fresh thyme and tarragon
1 bay leaf
1 cup heavy cream
2 tablespoons butter

Heat oil till very hot in a large skillet. Add pieces of lobster and cook 1-2 minutes, till shells are bright red. Add shallot, carrot, onion, garlic, and tomatoes. Cook covered over medium heat for 5 minutes. Raise heat to high, add cognac, and cook 1 minute. Add wine and boil down till reduced by half. Remove lobster from skillet. Add fumet, paste, and herbs. Remove meat from shells of lobster and place shells back into stock. Gently simmer with a cover half on till stock is reduced by half. Strain and degrease. Boil down by half again, add cream, and reduce till thickened. Add lobster meat. Take off heat and whisk in butter.

WATERCRESS SAUCE

1 shallot, chopped
1/4 cup dry white wine
1/2 cup fish fumet
2 tablespoons port wine
1 bunch watercress, stems removed
1 cup heavy cream
Juice of half a lemon
Salt and white pepper

Place shallot and wine in small saucepan. Boil down till the wine has evaporated. Add fumet and reduce by half. Add port wine, cress leaves, and cream. Boil down till slightly thickened. Place in a blender and purée well. Add lemon juice and salt and white pepper to taste.

To serve:

Arrange 3 mousses on each plate. Top one with sorrel sauce, another with lobster sauce, and the third one with watercress sauce. Garnish center of each plate with a little chopped, peeled, and seeded tomato and a slice of truffle. *Serves* 6.

CRAB MEAT DÉLICE

During hot weather, it is helpful to refrigerate the mixture in the pan for about an hour before and after breading to facilitate handling.

½ pint milk
3 tablespoons butter
3 tablespoons flour
3 tablespoons white wine
1 cup finely diced scallions, blanched (or 1 cup finely diced fresh chives)
1 tablespoon chopped fresh tarragon, or ¼ teaspoon dried
1 teaspoon Worcestershire sauce
Salt and pepper
½ pound crab meat
1 pound Vermont cheddar cheese, grated
2 egg yolks
Flour
Egg wash (whole eggs beaten with a little water or milk)
Bread crumbs
Fat for deep-frying

Heat milk slowly. In another pan melt butter and add flour to make roux. Add white wine and hot milk. Cook slowly until roux thickens. Add blanched scallions (or fresh chives), tarragon, Worcestershire, and salt and pepper to taste. Stir in crab meat, cheddar cheese, and egg yolks. Turn into buttered 8-inch-square pan and cool. (Refrigerate for easier handling.) Cut into squares, dip into flour, then into egg wash, and coat with bread crumbs. Fry in deep fat (330°-350°) until golden brown. Place in 325° oven for a few minutes to finish heating through. When done, internal temperature should register between 130°-140°.

Serves 8-10.

THE INN'S SPECIAL

"Our Inn's Special is served as an appetizer. It may also be used as a dinner entrée over rice or toast points. The blend of clams, shrimp, and crab meat is enhanced by the rich cream sauce."

1 cup milk
9 tablespoons chopped clams and juice
8 large raw shrimp, shelled and deveined
1/2 pound crab meat
1/4 pound butter
1/2 cup all-purpose flour, sifted
1/3 cup heavy cream
2/3 cup grated Swiss cheese
1/4 teaspoon black pepper
1/8 teaspoon crushed red pepper
Salt
6-8 patty shells, prebaked
Grated Parmesan cheese
Buttered bread crumbs
Parsley

Pour milk and juice from clams into medium-size pot. Using knife blade on processor, grind clams, shrimp, and crab meat. Add to milk and clam juice and slowly bring to boil over low heat.

Melt butter in saucepan. Add sifted flour, stirring well. Cook roux for 3-4 minutes over low heat. Do not allow to scorch. Meanwhile, slowly heat cream and add grated Swiss cheese, blending until cheese is melted. Gradually add roux to cheese mixture. Whisk this into simmering seafood, blending thoroughly. Bring to boil, lower heat, and simmer for 20 minutes. Add peppers and salt to taste, if needed. Spoon approximately 4 tablespoons of mixture into baking shells. Sprinkle with Parmesan cheese and buttered bread crumbs. Place under broiler for a few minutes until topping is lightly browned and mixture is bubbling. Garnish with parsley. *Serves 6-8.*

BEE AND THISTLE INN
Old Lyme, Connecticut

BROILED CLAMS ON THE HALF SHELL

Prepare these for easy yet elegant entertaining.

3 tablespoons horseradish
1/4 bunch watercress, finely chopped
1/2 cup mayonnaise
1/2 cup sour cream
4 tablespoons lemon juice
3 dozen small cherrystone clams, shucked

Combine horseradish, watercress, mayonnaise, sour cream, and lemon juice. Arrange raw clams on a broiler pan and spread approximately 1 teaspoon of mixture on top of each clam. Broil until lightly browned; serve hot. *Serves 6.*

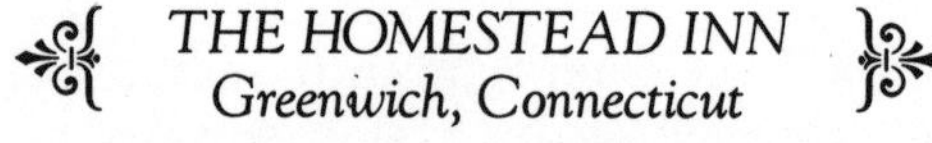

THE HOMESTEAD INN
Greenwich, Connecticut

CASSOLETTE D'ESCARGOTS

Food for the gods — and very special guests!

24 snails
5 ounces chanterelles
1 tablespoon butter
2 teaspoons chopped shallots
4 tablespoons garlic butter (garlic, shallots, parsley, salt, pepper)
1/2 cup heavy cream
1/2 teaspoon (splash) Pernod (optional)
Chopped fresh parsley

Sauté snails and chanterelles in butter with shallots. Add garlic butter, let melt, swirl. Add heavy cream and Pernod and let mixture reduce somewhat. Sprinkle with chopped parsley and serve at once. *Serves 4.*

MUSSELS CASINO

"The shores of Breezemere Farm abound with mussels. We always have clam rakes and hoes and baskets ready for the adventuresome guest who wants to try his hand at musseling and clamming. The guest arrives back at the inn covered with mud, with an aching back, but joyful as any fisherman showing off his catch."

4 to 5 pounds mussels in shells
2 small yellow onions, chopped
2 cloves garlic, chopped
2 sprigs parsley
Dash of freshly ground pepper
Dash of cayenne
1 cup dry white wine
½ bay leaf
½ teaspoon thyme
Garlic salt
Bottle of chili sauce
½ pound bacon, cut into 1-inch pieces

Wash and scrub mussels under cold running water. Yank out "beard" with fingers or pliers. Place mussels in large kettle with onions, garlic cloves, parsley, pepper, cayenne, wine, bay leaf, and thyme. Cover and bring to boil. Steam just until shells open, approximately 5 minutes. Drain mussels, reserving all the liquid. (Use in Billi-Bi Soup, page 101.) Discard top shells of mussels. Arrange mussels in bottom shells on cookie sheet. Sprinkle each with garlic salt, dab ½ teaspoon chili sauce on each mussel, and top with piece of raw bacon. Broil until bacon is crisp and serve immediately. *Serves 6.*

JARED COFFIN HOUSE
Nantucket, Massachusetts

STEAMED MUSSELS WITH HERB, WINE, AND CREAM SAUCE

The salt air on Nantucket Island gives such a boost to the appetite that the inn can serve this hearty dish as an appetizer.

4 dozen mussels, washed and cleaned well
1 cup dry white wine
1 teaspoon chopped garlic
1 teaspoon chopped parsley
Pinch of thyme
Pinch of dill
Salt and pepper to taste
1 cup heavy cream (do not use whipping cream)
Chopped fresh parsley

Steam mussels in white wine, garlic, and herbs until shells open. Remove. Add rest of ingredients and reduce until mixture coats back of a spoon. In soup bowl ladle sauce, arrange mussels on top, and sprinkle with chopped parsley. *Serves 4-6.*

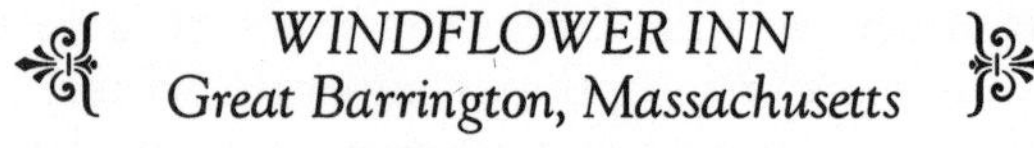

WINDFLOWER INN
Great Barrington, Massachusetts

HERRING IN CREAM SAUCE

At its best if refrigerated overnight so flavors meld and sauce thickens a bit.

Large jar (or two 8-ounce jars) herring in wine sauce
3/4 pint sour cream
4 tablespoons liquid from herring
1/4 cup heavy sweet cream
3 tablespoons sugar
1 Bermuda onion, thinly sliced

Drain herring, rinse, and pat dry, reserving liquid from jar. Blend together sour cream, 4 tablespoons reserved liquid, sweet cream, and sugar. Add onion and herring, stir to coat with sauce, and refrigerate until ready to serve. *Serves 8.*

LONGWOOD INN
Marlboro, Vermont

FETTUCCINI TOSSED WITH SMOKED NATIVE TROUT

"This dish uses our Vermont trout and is delicious as a first course or an entrée."

2 quarts salted water
1 pound fresh or packaged fettuccini
2 tablespoons butter
2 tablespoons olive oil
1 teaspoon capers
1 teaspoon chopped shallots
1 small jar (4 ounces) sliced roasted sweet peppers
1 small tomato, chopped
½ cup white wine
2 whole smoked trout, skinned, boned, and sliced into 1-inch strips
1 cup heavy cream
2 ounces pine nuts
Fresh grated black pepper
Fresh grated Parmesan cheese

Bring water to a boil and cook fettuccini as directed. In 12-inch sauté pan melt butter with olive oil; add capers, shallots, sweet peppers, tomato, and wine; sauté rapidly for 3-4 minutes. Add trout and heavy cream. Reduce heat and let simmer 4 minutes to slightly thicken. Toss with hot drained fettuccini, sprinkle with pine nuts, and serve on warm plates. Put pepper and cheese on right before serving. *Serves 6-8 as appetizer.*

SMOKED BLUEFISH

Absolutely wonderful! The inn uses hickory bark in its smoker, which is an 'Aqua-Char' model 4000 from L.L. Bean. A Weber Kettle barbecue also works well and any kettle charcoal cooker could probably be rigged to smoke this fish.

3 pounds freshly caught Atlantic bluefish, cleaned and split
Juice from 3 lemons
1 cup Tamari or soy sauce

Place raw fish neatly on bottom of shallow baking dish. Cut lemons into quarters and squeeze juice over fish (be sure to pick out seeds). Then pour Tamari or soy sauce over fish. Cover and marinate in refrigerator overnight.

Fill a quart-size pan with water and add a handful of hickory bark. Let stand until smoker is ready, then drain. Fill charcoal pan to capacity and light charcoal with starter. When coals are glowing hot, take the handful of drained hickory bark and place on top of hot coals. Then place water pan over charcoal pan. Place fish on grill skin-side down in single layers leaving spaces between if possible. Cover and smoke cook 2-3 hours (2 hours for moist fish, 3 hours till fish flakes with a fork). Serve with crackers.

Serves 8 as an hors d'oeuvre.

STEAK SLICES WITH HORSERADISH CREAM

"Makes a wonderful summer appetizer. We like to serve this on a glass plate with the horseradish cream in a small side dish."

STEAK SLICES

1 pound flank steak
1/3 cup soy sauce
1/3 cup white wine
2 tablespoons salad oil

Slice steak into 5-inch-wide strips. Combine soy sauce and wine in shallow dish. Add steak and marinate in refrigerator 24 hours. Brush steak with oil and broil without rack 6 inches from heat for 1 minute on each side. Then broil 5 minutes each side. Allow steak to cool. Brush with marinade juices and refrigerate. When cold cut into very thin diagonal slices. Serve with toothpicks for dipping into horseradish cream.

HORSERADISH CREAM

1 large garlic clove
1 1/2-ounce piece of fresh horseradish, peeled and cut in half (or 3 tablespoons prepared horseradish)
1 cup heavy cream
1 tablespoon wine vinegar
1 teaspoon Worcestershire sauce
1/2 teaspoon salt
3 drops Tabasco or hot sauce

In food processor with steel blade, and with motor running, drop garlic through feed tube and mince finely. Add horseradish and mince. With machine still running pour cream through feed tube in slow stream and process until thick and fluffy. Add vinegar, Worcestershire, salt, and Tabasco. Blend 5 seconds. Serve immediately with steak slices and plain crackers.

Serves 12 at cocktail party as appetizer, or 6 if served individually as appetizer.

FRESH MELON AND FRESH FIGS AND PROSCIUTTO

Sensational for a picnic as well as a cocktail party.

½ ripe melon (cantaloupe or honeydew)
1 bunch Italian parsley, finely chopped
5 to 6 slices prosciutto, cut into 1-inch strips
Freshly grated black pepper
1 dozen fresh figs

Peel and seed the melon. Cut into bite-sized cubes, coat each cube with freshly chopped parsley, wrap with a strip of prosciutto, and fasten with a toothpick. Grind a dusting of black pepper over prosciutto.

Wash the figs and slice in half lengthwise. Follow as for the melon, ending with a dusting of black pepper. *Serves 4-6.*

SOUPS & CHOWDERS

Snowvillage Inn, Snowville, New Hampshire

HOT SOUPS

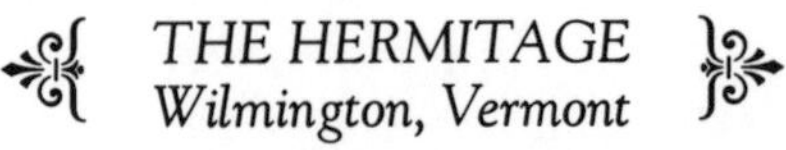

VERMONT CHEDDAR CHEESE SOUP

Either chicken or turkey stock can be used here. The wine and cheese blend beautifully, the cream smooths out the flavors, and the nutmeg tickles the palate.

1½ quarts richly flavored poultry stock
¾ cup dry white wine
¾ pound shredded cheddar cheese
Beurre manié
6 ounces heavy cream
Nutmeg

Simmer stock and wine for 10 minutes. Gradually add shredded cheese, stirring constantly until cheese is melted. Thicken with beurre manié and simmer 7 minutes, whisking constantly. Do not let soup boil. Stir in cream, add ground nutmeg to taste, and serve. *Serves 8.*

 THE BLACKBERRY RIVER INN
Norfolk, Connecticut 

FLEMISH CHEESE SOUP

Experiment with different kinds of beer to discover your own preference. For a more intense cheese flavor, add a little grated Parmesan.

3 tablespoons whole-wheat flour
3 tablespoons butter
½ cup puréed onion
½ cup puréed celery
2 cups chicken stock
1 bottle light beer
Salt and pepper to taste
1 cup grated cheddar cheese

Combine flour and butter in soup pot and cook 2-3 minutes, until mixture thickens. Add onion and celery and cook another 1-2 minutes. Add stock, beer, and salt and pepper and stir well. Cook until soup thickens, then add cheese, stirring until it melts. Adjust seasonings and serve. *Serves 4-6.*

 PUBLICK HOUSE
Sturbridge, Massachusetts 

NEW ENGLAND CLAM CHOWDER

This classic clam chowder doesn't use flour for thickening. Watch the potatoes carefully so they don't overcook.

¼ pound salt pork
1 large onion, finely diced
3 medium-sized potatoes, peeled and cubed
1½ cups water
1 quart chopped clams
3 cups light cream
⅛ pound butter (½ stick)
Salt and pepper to taste

Cut salt pork into small dice and render in saucepan. Reserve the cracklings. Use fat to cook onion until golden. In 2-quart pan cook potatoes in water for ten minutes. Drain liquid from potatoes into 4-quart pan, add clams, and cook for 25 minutes. Then add light cream, cracklings, potatoes, onion, butter, and salt and pepper to taste. Serve in soup bowls with Dot crackers. *Serves 8.*

THE GOSNOLD'S NEW ENGLAND CLAM CHOWDER

A thick and creamy clam chowder, which is actually best served the day after it is made. Reheat in a double boiler but don't let it boil.

3 cups medium-diced potatoes
2 ounces salt pork
2 ounces butter
6 ounces medium-diced onions
2 ounces flour
1/8 teaspoon white pepper
3 cups clam juice
2 cups light cream
2 cans (10 ounces each) sliced baby clams

Boil potatoes until tender but firm. Process salt pork in a food processor or blender to the consistency of soft butter.

In 4-quart saucepan melt salt pork and butter. Add onions and cook over medium heat until transparent. Add flour and white pepper and cook this roux for 2-3 minutes. Do not brown.

While roux is cooking, heat clam juice and cream, being careful not to boil. Slowly add this hot liquid to the roux, cooking until thickened. Do not allow to boil. Add potatoes and canned clams, including the broth clams are packed in, and simmer for 10 minutes. *Serves 6-8.*

KNOLL FARM VEGETABLE CHOWDER

"This is a good soup for lunch on cool days. We serve it in large bowls with Vermont soda crackers, broiled tomato/cheddar cheese sandwiches, and applesauce cake."

½ pound margarine
1 medium onion, cut up
1 cup cut up fresh mushrooms
2 carrots, peeled and thinly shaved with peeler
1 teaspoon basil
1 teaspoon celery salt
1 teaspoon dill weed
1 package onion soup mix (optional)
1 cup flour
3 quarts milk (can use skim)
Any amount of leftover vegetables (corn, broccoli, peas, etc.)
1 to 2 cups diced cooked potatoes or rice

Melt margarine in large pot. Add onion and mushrooms and braise over low heat. Add carrots, basil, celery salt, dill, and onion soup mix if desired, stirring well. Cook 2-3 minutes. Slowly stir in flour until margarine is all absorbed. Slowly add part of milk until there is enough liquid to make a cream sauce. Add rest of milk, leftover vegetables, and potatoes or rice. Simmer over low heat until thick, but do not boil. *Serves 6-8.*

SOUPE DE POISSONS LE DOMAINE

An exceptional fish and seafood soup, with an herb and white wine broth, and a spoonful of spiciness swirled in before serving.

4 pounds mussels
1 cup white wine for steaming
2 leeks, well washed and thinly sliced
2 onions, thinly sliced
1/4 cup olive oil
3 tomatoes, chopped
2 pounds striped bass, cut in 1 1/2-inch-thick slices
6 cups water
2 fennel branches, chopped, or 1 scant tablespoon fennel seed
1 cup dry white wine
3 two-inch pieces orange rind
2 large garlic cloves, minced
2 bay leaves
Salt and pepper
1/2 teaspoon crumbled saffron threads
1/2 pound lobster meat, cut into 1/2-inch pieces
1/2 pound crab meat, picked over
1/2 pound cooked spaghetti
1 to 2 teaspoons Rouille Le Domaine (recipe follows)

Clean mussels. Steam them in 1 cup white wine in a large saucepan, covered, over moderately high heat, shaking the pan once or twice for 5 minutes or until the shells have opened. Discard any unopened mussels. Transfer the mussels with a slotted spoon to a large bowl and shell them, removing the black rims if desired. Strain the cooking liquid through a fine sieve lined with a double thickness of rinsed and squeezed cheesecloth into a bowl and reserve it.

In a heavy stainless steel or enameled casserole, sauté leeks and onions in olive oil over moderately high heat, stirring occasionally, for 10 minutes or until they are golden. Stir in tomatoes, cook the mixture for 3 minutes, and add the reserved cooking liquid, striped bass, water, fennel, wine, orange rind, garlic cloves, bay leaves, and salt and pepper to taste. Bring the liquid to a boil over moderately high heat and boil the mixture, stirring occasionally, for 15 minutes.

With a slotted spoon, transfer the fish to a bowl, remove and discard the bones and skin, and return the fish to the casserole.

(continued)

Purée the mixture through a food mill into a large stainless steel or enameled saucepan and bring the purée to a simmer over moderately high heat. Add saffron threads and cook the purée for 5 minutes.

Stir in the mussels, lobster meat, crab meat, and more salt and pepper to taste and simmer the soup for 5 minutes. Divide spaghetti among 6 heated bowls and ladle the soup over it. Swirl Rouille Le Domaine onto each bowl. *Serves 6.*

ROUILLE LE DOMAINE

½ cup fresh bread crumbs
2 tablespoons milk
2 cloves garlic
2 small fresh red hot chili peppers or ½ teaspoon cayenne
2 to 3 tablespoons olive oil

In a small bowl let bread crumbs soak in milk. With a mortar and pestle crush garlic cloves with chili peppers or cayenne, add the bread crumbs, squeezed dry, and combine the mixture well. Add olive oil in a stream, beating, and beat the mixture until creamy.

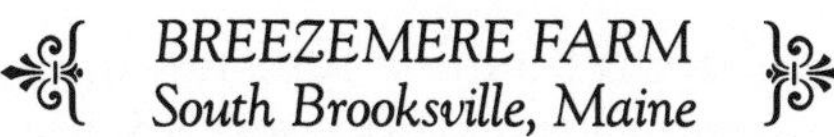

BILLI-BI SOUP

The cooking liquid from steamed mussels is the base for this soup. See Mussels Casino, page 89, for specific ingredients.

Mussel cooking liquid
All-purpose or heavy cream
1 egg yolk, lightly beaten
2 tablespoons butter

Strain mussel cooking liquid through double thickness of cheesecloth and measure. Add an equal amount of cream. Heat in soup kettle to point where film forms on top but do not allow liquid to boil. Remove from heat. Stir 1 tablespoon liquid into egg yolk to warm it, then add yolk and butter to kettle. Return to heat long enough for soup to slightly thicken, being careful not to boil. Serve immediately or refrigerate and serve cold. *Serves 4.*

THE FOUR COLUMNS INN
Newfane, Vermont

LOBSTER BISQUE

An outstanding bisque with rich lobster flavor and attractive color. The recipe requires a commitment of time and investment of money, but if you're an experienced (or adventurous!) cook, it will be well worth both.

4 live lobsters, 1 to 1¼ pounds each
Court bouillon (recipe follows)
3 tablespoons olive oil
2 carrots, chopped
1 cup chopped leeks (white part only)
2 stalks celery, chopped
4 tomatoes, chopped (seeds removed)
6 shallots, chopped
3 cloves garlic, minced
4 sprigs fresh tarragon, or pinch of dried
6 sprigs fresh thyme, or pinch of dried
4 tablespoons cognac
4 cups dry white wine
1 tablespoon tomato paste
1 bay leaf
8 cups fish stock (recipe follows)
Salt and pepper to taste
3 cups heavy cream, reduced to half its volume
Cognac
Lemon juice

Boil lobsters in court bouillon for 9 minutes. Refresh lobsters in ice water, then remove tails and reserve. Chop remaining lobster into 2-inch chunks (including shells). Add olive oil to heavy-bottomed pot and sauté lobster meat and shells until red. Add carrots, leeks, celery, tomatoes, shallots, garlic, tarragon, and thyme and continue to sauté 20 minutes longer. Flambé with 4 tablespoons cognac and then deglaze with the white wine.

Add tomato paste, bay leaf, and fish stock. Season with salt and pepper and simmer for 3 hours, skimming often.

Put all solid ingredients into a food processor and process thoroughly. Then strain the liquid through cheesecloth, squeezing and rendering as much liquid as possible. Return this to the pot and reduce by one quarter.

Add reduced cream and balance with more cognac and lemon juice to taste.

(continued)

Remove shell from lobster tails, cut meat into chunks, and add to bisque. *Serves 6-8.*

COURT BOUILLON

Combine 2 whole cloves, 1 onion, 6 cloves garlic, 4 fresh thyme sprigs, and 6 fresh parsley sprigs with 1 quart dry white wine and 3 quarts water.

FISH STOCK

Use any fresh fish bones except salmon. Cover with water, bring to a boil, then reduce heat and cook between a simmer and a boil for 8 hours, uncovered, skimming frequently.

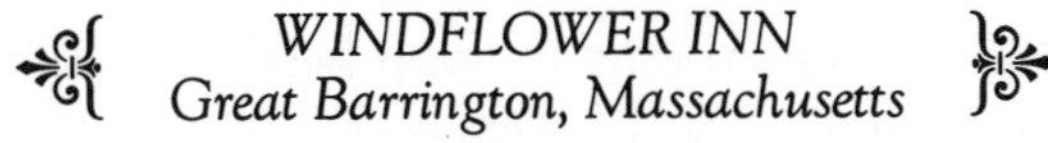

RED POTATO, LEEK, AND SORREL SOUP

Spinach substitutes well for the sorrel in this versatile soup, which can be served hot or chilled as an unusual vichyssoise.

3 to 4 cups sliced red potatoes
1 large onion, thinly sliced
2 ounces sorrel or spinach, washed well and shredded
4 leeks, washed well and thinly sliced (white and tender green parts)
1 quart chicken stock
2 cups white wine
1 cup heavy cream or half-and-half
Salt and pepper to taste
Drop each of Tabasco and sherry (optional)

Simmer vegetables in stock and wine until soft. Purée in blender or food processor, add cream, season to taste, and if desired, add Tabasco and sherry. *Serves 6-8.*

PHILADELPHIA PEPPERPOT SOUP

"The secret to this soup, as with any other, is a very strong stock. I use no beef bouillon or MSG."

2 quarts very strong veal or beef stock (recipe follows)
1 medium onion, diced
2 medium carrots, diced
½ cup diced celery
Broccoli, zucchini, or other garden vegetables (optional)
1 tablespoon salt
½ tablespoon freshly ground black pepper
1 medium tomato, diced
1 cup crushed tomatoes or purée

Combine all ingredients in soup kettle and simmer for approximately 1 hour or until vegetables are cooked as you like them.
Serves 8.

VEAL OR BEEF STOCK

1 pound lean beef or veal knuckle
3 to 4 quarts cold water
½ teaspoon sweet basil
½ cup chopped parsley
⅓ cup chopped onion
⅓ cup chopped carrots
2 stalks celery
¼ teaspoon chopped garlic
½ teaspoon each oregano, thyme, and tarragon

Bring all ingredients to a rolling boil, then simmer on very low heat until stock is reduced by half. Strain through a very fine sieve and use as directed for Pepperpot Soup.

SENEGALESE SOUP

Wonderfully delicate curried soup that goes well with a fish or chicken entrée.

1½ quarts chicken stock (6 cups)
1 large potato, peeled and cubed
2 large cloves garlic, diced
½ pound fresh or frozen peas
2 tablespoons curry powder
1 cup whipping cream
1 tablespoon minced lemon balm (or lemongrass)
1 tablespoon minced fresh basil

Combine stock, potato, and garlic in large saucepan or Dutch oven and bring to boil over medium-high heat. Reduce heat, cover, and simmer until potato is soft, about 20 minutes. Remove from heat and add peas and curry. Let stand, covered, 10 minutes.

Transfer mixture to food processor or blender in batches and purée. Strain through fine sieve, pressing with back of wooden spoon to extract as much liquid as possible.

Return mixture to saucepan, place over low heat, and stir in cream and herbs. Increase heat and simmer 5 minutes; do not let soup boil. Serve either hot or cold. *Serves* 6.

HANOVER INN'S CREAM OF BROCCOLI SOUP

You can substitute a number of other vegetables for the broccoli used here to create your own favorite cream of vegetable soup.

1 cup chopped onions
1 cup chopped raw potatoes
½ cup chopped celery
1 cup chopped leeks, white part
2 cups finely chopped broccoli (including stems and leaves)
1 cup butter
2 cups water
2 chicken bouillon cubes
2 cups hot milk
Salt and pepper

Sauté vegetables in butter until butter starts to brown. Add water and chicken bouillon cubes (or equivalent) and cook until tender. Put through food mill, then add hot milk and salt and pepper to taste. *Serves 8.*

THE RED LION INN
Stockbridge, Massachusetts

CREAM OF BROCCOLI SOUP

Velvety-smooth texture, delicate broccoli flavor, and lovely appearance — ideal dinner-party fare.

3 tablespoons butter
1/3 cup diced leeks
1/3 cup diced onion
1/3 cup diced celery
1 cup diced broccoli
3 tablespoons flour
3 cups chicken stock
Salt, pepper, and thyme to taste
1/3 cup white wine
1 cup light cream

Melt butter in saucepan and add leeks, onion, celery, and broccoli. Sauté about 5 minutes over low heat so butter won't brown. Blend in flour, then add chicken stock. Cook till boiling. Add salt, pepper, thyme, and wine. Let simmer till vegetables are tender (about 20 minutes). Purée in blender. Return to low heat and add cream just before serving. *Serves 4-6.*

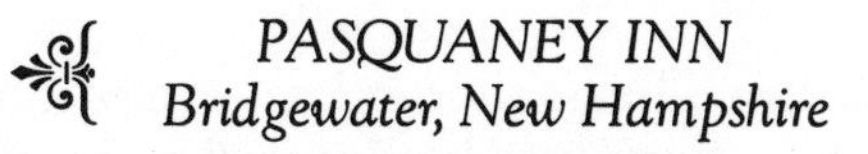

PASQUANEY INN
Bridgewater, New Hampshire

DILL PICKLE SOUP

"One way to start conversations among our guests in the dining room is to serve unusual sounding recipes, and this soup is a perfect example!"

8 cups chicken stock
5 tablespoons dill pickle juice
2 carrots, diced
1 stalk celery, diced
3 medium-size dill pickles, diced
1/2 cup cooked rice
Salt and pepper
Sour cream for garnish

Combine stock and pickle juice. Mix together carrots, celery, and pickles and cook in small amount of stock until vegetables are tender. Add vegetables and rice to the stock and bring to a boil. Simmer slowly for 40 minutes. Add salt and pepper to taste. Serve in individual soup bowls with a large dab of sour cream on top of each. *Serves 8.*

SPINACH AND GARLIC SOUP

A robust and flavorful winter or summer soup. Serve it with cheese and Italian bread for lunch or supper.

1 cup olive oil
9 cloves garlic, peeled and chopped fine
1 large onion, chopped
2 carrots, peeled and diced
2 stalks celery, chopped
2 teaspoons chopped dry basil
8 cups chicken stock
2 pounds fresh spinach, chopped
3 potatoes, diced in half-inch cubes
Grated Parmesan cheese

In heavy saucepan, heat olive oil over medium heat. Add garlic, onion, carrots, celery, and basil. Stir 4 to 5 minutes, taking care not to let garlic brown. Add chicken stock, spinach, and potatoes, and boil gently until potatoes are done.

Serve topped with grated Parmesan. *Serves 8-10.*

CREAM OF SPINACH SOUP

"Our special soup always receives favorable comment. It makes a fine accompaniment for a vegetarian platter."

1 pound spinach, washed, tough stems removed
2 cups water
2 teaspoons salt
1 large Spanish onion, finely chopped
2 tablespoons butter
2 tablespoons flour
1 teaspoon nutmeg
1/4 teaspoon freshly ground pepper
2 cups half-and-half
1 cup sour cream

Steam spinach briefly in salted water. Reserve liquid. Chop spinach fine in food processor or blender. Set aside. Sauté onion in butter, then blend in flour. Stir in reserved liquid, chopped spinach, nutmeg, and pepper. Simmer 10 minutes. Add half-and-half. Heat but do not boil. Add sour cream and serve immediately.

Serves 4.

CREAM OF SWISS CHARD SOUP

"Made from our home-grown Swiss chard, this is the most popular soup served at the inn. Use fresh lettuce, spinach, or broccoli when Swiss chard is not available."

1¾ quarts hot chicken stock
¾ pound Swiss chard, chopped
3 ounces diced onion
1 bay leaf
3 ounces butter
3 ounces flour
1 pint hot milk
½ pint hot light cream
Salt and pepper to taste
¼ teaspoon nutmeg

Heat stock in large pot. Add Swiss chard, onion, and bay leaf. Simmer 1 hour. (This stock can be put in containers and frozen, then used when needed.) In another large pot, melt butter and stir in flour to make roux. Cook over low heat for 8 minutes. Do not brown. Add stock to roux gradually, stirring until slightly thickened and smooth. Simmer 30 minutes. Pass through food mill or blender; add heated milk and cream. Season and serve.

Serves 6-8.

WINE MERCHANT SOUP

Light but filling. Excellent served with a bean salad and good crusty bread. The broth should have a shiny appearance from the cornstarch.

6 cups beef broth
1 cup chopped onions
1 cup chopped celery
1 cup chopped carrots
2 tablespoons butter
2 tablespoons oil
1 cup sliced mushrooms
1 cup Burgundy wine
1 tablespoon cornstarch
½ cup cold water

Heat beef broth in large kettle. Sauté onions, celery, and carrots in butter and oil until *just* tender. Transfer with slotted spoon to broth and simmer. Use same oil and butter to sauté mushrooms. When done pour mushrooms and liquid into soup. Add wine and bring to a boil. Combine cornstarch and cold water, then add to soup. Heat until slightly thickened and serve.

Serves 6.

THE INN AT MANCHESTER
Manchester, Vermont

FRESH TOMATO SOUP

"A great favorite at our inn and a marvelous way to utilize the abundance of tomatoes from the garden. The recipe was given to me by the chef at a charming inn in Shepton Mallet, England. A soupspoon of Port may be added, but it is not necessary."

2 pounds ripe tomatoes (do not use canned)
1 onion
1 carrot
2 tablespoons butter
2 tablespoons flour
2 pints chicken stock
Bouquet garni
Salt and freshly ground pepper
2 tablespoons cream

Dice tomatoes; slice onion and carrot. Melt butter in a saucepan, add the vegetables, and cook gently for 5 minutes. Remove from heat, add flour, and stir in stock. Add bouquet garni (parsley, basil, thyme) and season to taste. Strain the soup, but save some of the carrots. Mash the carrots, add to soup, reheat, and add cream. *Serves 4-5.*

SUGAR HILL INN
Franconia, New Hampshire

TOMATO BISQUE

Herbs, spices, and wine contribute admirably to this chunky bisque.

1/4 pound bacon
4 large garlic cloves, minced
6 celery stalks, finely chopped
1 1/2 onions, finely chopped
1 bay leaf
1 teaspoon thyme
1 can (28 ounces) tomatoes, diced (reserve juice)
1 can (6 ounces) tomato paste
2 tablespoons butter (1/4 stick)
3 tablespoons flour
1 quart whipping cream at room temperature (or half-and-half)
1/2 onion, finely chopped
1 small bay leaf
2 whole cloves
Salt and freshly ground pepper to taste
4 fresh tomatoes, peeled, seeded, and chopped
1/2 cup white wine

Cook bacon in skillet until fat is rendered; remove meat and use as desired. Add garlic to fat and sauté until lightly browned. Add celery, 1 1/2 onions, bay leaf, and thyme and sauté until onions are transparent. Add canned tomatoes with juice and tomato paste and bring to boil, stirring occasionally. Reduce heat, cover, and simmer for 30 minutes.

Begin white sauce by heating butter in saucepan. Stir in flour and bring to boil, stirring constantly. Remove from heat and slowly add cream, then add 1/2 onion, small bay leaf, and cloves. Place over medium heat and cook uncovered for 45 minutes, stirring occasionally. Pour through fine strainer into tomato mixture and add salt and pepper. Cover and simmer for about 15 minutes, stirring occasionally. Add fresh tomatoes and wine just before serving.

Serves 8-10.

SNOWVILLAGE INN
Snowville, New Hampshire

TOMATO SOUP WITH COGNAC

A thick, full-bodied soup with subtle sweetness. Suitable for lunch or fancy dinner.

3 pounds ripe tomatoes or canned whole tomatoes
1 large onion
3 ounces butter
1 teaspoon sweet basil leaves
1 pint rich cream
1 teaspoon brown sugar
4 to 5 tablespoons cognac (or other brandy)
Salt and pepper to taste

Scald tomatoes and slip them out of their skins. Cut them coarsely and chop the onion. Melt butter in large soup pot. Sauté onions till brown, add tomatoes and basil, and simmer for 1 hour. Heat cream in another pot with the sugar until it is ready to boil. Stirring quickly, pour the cream into the tomatoes. Add cognac, season well, and serve. *Serves 6-8.*

WEEKAPAUG INN
Weekapaug, Rhode Island

ZUCCHINI SOUP

Rich and colorful — a fine start for a sophisticated meal. The saltiness of the chicken stock will determine how much additional salt is needed, so taste before adding.

1/2 cup butter
1 medium onion, quartered
1 1/2 to 2 pounds zucchini, washed and trimmed
2 1/2 cups chicken stock
1 teaspoon basil
1 teaspoon salt, or to taste
1/2 teaspoon nutmeg
Freshly ground black pepper
1 cup heavy cream

In a large pan melt butter, add onion, and cook until limp. Cut zucchini in small pieces and put into blender. Add chicken stock and purée. Combine with onions and simmer for 15 minutes. Then add basil, salt, nutmeg, black pepper to taste, and heavy cream. Mix well. Simmer for 30 minutes. *Serves 4-6.*

OLD TOWN FARM LODGE
Gassetts, Vermont

ZUCCHINI SOUP

Equally good served hot or chilled, this soup freezes well if the milk or cream is omitted and added later when reheating.

1 chicken bouillon cube
3 tablespoons water
3 to 4 cups zucchini, cut in 1-inch pieces
1/2 small onion, cut up
Milk or cream

Put bouillon cube, water, zucchini, and onion in saucepan on medium heat. Cook till tender, stirring constantly. Pour into blender and liquefy 1 minute. Add equal amounts of milk or cream to zucchini mixture, heat thoroughly, and serve. *Serves 4.*

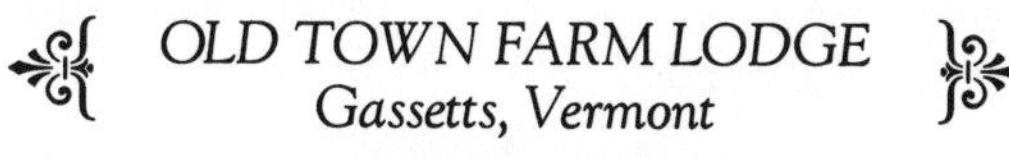

OLD TOWN FARM LODGE
Gassetts, Vermont

CARROT SOUP

Simple ingredients joined in just the right proportions make this a splendid soup — thick and smooth, with a hint of sweetness.

3 tablespoons butter
6 large carrots, peeled and sliced
2 medium onions, chopped
1 large potato, peeled and diced
4 cups beef broth
1/2 teaspoon sugar
Salt and pepper to taste
Parsley or chervil

In heavy soup kettle melt butter, add carrots, onions, and potato, and cook over medium-high heat, stirring occasionally until lightly browned — about 15 minutes. Add beef broth, then sugar and salt and pepper to taste. Bring to a boil, reduce heat to low, cover, and cook 15 minutes or till vegetables are tender. Purée in blender till smooth. Return to kettle, reheat, and serve garnished with parsley or chervil. *Serves 6-8.*

CREAM OF CARROT SOUP

Enhanced with herbs and cashews, enriched with sour cream, with an appealing texture and attractive color. Although the herb flavor is more apparent when served hot, this also makes a refreshing chilled soup.

2 pounds carrots, scrubbed or peeled and chopped
4 cups rich chicken stock
1½ teaspoons salt
1 cup chopped onions
2 cloves garlic, chopped
⅓ cup chopped cashews
4 tablespoons butter
3 cups half-and-half
1 teaspoon each thyme, marjoram, and basil
Sour cream

Combine carrots, stock, and salt in soup pot, bring to a boil, reduce heat, and simmer, covered, for 15 minutes. Sauté onions, garlic, and cashews in butter until onions are transparent. Purée carrots and stock with sautéed mixture in food processor until smooth. Return to soup pot, whisk in half-and-half, and add herbs, stirring until heated through. Serve garnished with dollop of sour cream. *Serves 6.*

CARROT-TOMATO BISQUE

If you prefer a thinner consistency, add some chicken stock, tomato juice, water, milk, or a combination.

1½ large Spanish onions, roughly chopped
1½ tablespoons finely chopped fresh garlic
1 tablespoon basil
¼ tablespoon black pepper
¾ cup melted butter
1 cup flour
1 pound carrots, coarsely chopped
½ can (#10) peeled tomatoes in juice
¼ cup Parmesan cheese
½ cup cooking sherry

Sauté onions, garlic, basil, and black pepper in butter in large heavy sauté pan. Stir continuously until onions are transparent. Add flour and lower flame; let cook for 5 to 7 minutes. Add carrots and tomatoes with juice and stir. Let mixture cook for 30 minutes, stirring occasionally. Add Parmesan and sherry. Pour hot soup into blender or food processor in small amounts and purée. Thin with additional liquid, season to taste, and serve.

Serves 12.

PUMPKIN SOUP

"Made from potatoes and pumpkin picked fresh from the garden. We serve it as 'mystery soup' and let the guests try to guess what kind it is." Perfect with Thanksgiving dinner because it isn't sweet and won't destroy the appetite. The potatoes add body, the chicken broth complements the pumpkin, and the spices give extra flavor.

1 pound fresh pumpkin, peeled and cut into chunks
2 potatoes, peeled and cut up (or 1½ cups mashed potatoes)
3 cups chicken broth
3 cups milk
¾ teaspoon salt
½ teaspoon nutmeg
½ teaspoon ginger
Pepper to taste
Paprika to taste

In separate pans, cook pumpkin and potatoes in water until done. Drain and place in food processor. Add some chicken broth and process 30-45 seconds. Transfer to large saucepan and add all remaining ingredients except paprika. Simmer 5 minutes and garnish with a dash of paprika. Serve with crackers. *Serves 8.*

THE RAM IN THE THICKET
Wilton, New Hampshire

SWEET-SOUR VEGETABLE SOUP

The gingersnaps add spicy sweetness.

1 head (2 pounds) cabbage, shredded
9 cups water
1/2 cup chopped onions
1/2 cup chopped carrots
1/2 cup chopped celery
1 can (28 ounces) tomatoes, chopped
3/4 cup granulated sugar
1/4 cup brown sugar
2 teaspoons salt or to taste
1/2 teaspoon celery salt
1/2 teaspoon dried dill
1/3 cup lemon juice
8 to 10 gingersnaps, crumbled (or 8 graham crackers, crumbled and mixed with 1 teaspoon ginger and 2 tablespoons molasses)

Combine all ingredients in large kettle, bring to a boil, reduce heat, and simmer, covered, 2 hours. *Serves 10.*

SAUSAGE AND CABBAGE SOUP

Serve for lunch with rye bread and a dark beer — ideal after a morning of cross-country skiing, snowshoeing, or wood-cutting. The recipe makes a lot, but it freezes well. To save space in the freezer, use only half the water for the portion you are freezing, then add remainder of water when ready to reheat and serve.

½ pound pure pork sausage (breakfast type)
1 large onion, chopped
1 medium head cabbage, chopped
2 teaspoons salt
1 teaspoon pepper
2 tablespoons oregano
2 tablespoons sugar
2 tablespoons powdered chicken bouillon, or more to taste
5 quarts water

In large kettle over medium heat, fry sausage, breaking into small bits. When nearly cooked, add onion and continue to cook and stir until onion is translucent. Do not pour off fat. Add cabbage. Cook, stirring occasionally, for about 20 minutes or until cabbage is limp. Add salt, pepper, oregano, sugar, and bouillon, mixing well. Add water, bring almost to a boil, and cook over low heat for at least 1½ hours. *Serves 20.*

SHOREHAM INN
Shoreham, Vermont

RUSSIAN CABBAGE SOUP

Steaming hot mugs of this mixture will take the chill off the coldest winter's day.

1 can (48 ounces) V8 juice
48 ounces water
1 medium-sized onion, chopped
1 medium-sized head cabbage, cut into small pieces
8 ounces brown sugar
1 cup raisins
Granulated garlic and pepper to taste

Combine all ingredients in soup kettle and simmer over low heat until cabbage is soft — about 1½ hours. *Serves 12-15.*

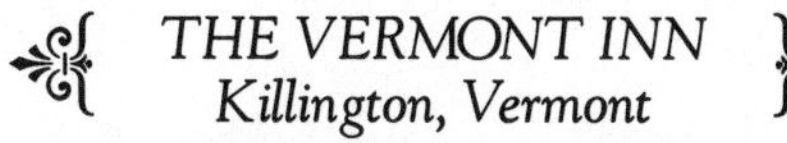

THE VERMONT INN
Killington, Vermont

FRENCH MUSHROOM SOUP

Substantial and flavorful, with lots of mushrooms in a warm-hued broth.

2 pounds fresh mushrooms, sliced
4 ounces butter
½ cup flour
½ gallon milk
1 tablespoon basil
1 teaspoon rosemary
1 can beef consommé or 1 bouillon cube plus 1 cup water
Worcestershire sauce to taste
Sherry wine to taste
Salt and pepper to taste
Sour cream for garnish

Sauté mushrooms in butter, add flour, and boil. Add milk and boil. Stir in herbs, consommé, Worcestershire, sherry, and salt and pepper. Serve with dollop of sour cream. *Serves 8.*

HUNGARIAN MUSHROOM SOUP

Best made with spicy Hungarian paprika, but the milder kind works fine, too. Don't skimp on the dill — it's just the right amount.

2 cups chopped onions
4 tablespoons butter
12 ounces fresh mushrooms, sliced
2 teaspoons dill weed
2 cups stock
1 tablespoon Tamari (soy sauce)
1 tablespoon Hungarian paprika
3 tablespoons flour
1 cup milk
½ cup sour cream
2 teaspoons lemon juice
1 teaspoon salt
Black pepper to taste
¼ cup chopped fresh parsley

Sauté onions in 2 tablespoons butter. A few minutes later add mushrooms, dill, ½ cup stock, Tamari, and paprika. Simmer covered for 15 minutes. Melt remaining butter in pan and whisk in flour. Add milk and cook for 10 minutes, stirring frequently. Add mushroom mixture and remaining stock. Cover and simmer for 10 minutes. Just before serving add a little stock to sour cream to liquefy. Pour into soup along with the lemon juice, salt, and pepper. Garnish with parsley. *Serves 4-6.*

FRESH MUSHROOM SOUP

A mushroom soup that is clear rather than creamy. The Tamari enriches the taste as well as the appearance.

9 cups chicken stock
1/4 cup Tamari (soy sauce)
2 bay leaves
1/4 cup vinegar
1/4 teaspoon thyme
1 teaspoon parsley
1/4 cup butter
4 medium onions, chopped
2 pounds fresh mushrooms, sliced
1/4 cup flour
Salt and pepper, if necessary
1/4 cup rice
Chives

Simmer together stock, Tamari, bay leaves, vinegar, thyme, and parsley. Meanwhile, in a large pot, melt butter and sauté onions until transparent. Add mushrooms, cook briefly, and stir in flour, blending well. Strain the stock and add to onion and mushroom mixture, mixing well. Season to taste with salt and pepper. Bring to a boil, then reduce heat, add rice, and simmer for 25 minutes. Garnish with chives. *Serves 8.*

ANGELA'S CREAM OF ALMOND SOUP

Sliced almonds, almond liqueur, and light cream create a most unusual soup that can be served either hot or cold.

1¼ cups sliced almonds
½ cup butter
1 small can artichoke hearts (for a rich soup) or 3 to 4 large stalks celery
6 to 8 tablespoons flour
1 cup chicken broth
4 cups light cream
1 cup almond liqueur
Salt and pepper to taste
Parsley flakes for garnish

Sauté almonds in butter until golden brown. Set aside ¼ cup almonds for garnish and put remaining cup in blender with artichoke hearts or celery and purée. Pour butter used for sautéing into saucepan and bring to a boil. Add flour to make a roux, then add chicken broth and light cream. Stir constantly so that it does not stick. Add contents of blender and almond liqueur. Season with salt and pepper and garnish with reserved almonds and parsley flakes. *Serves 6.*

CHILLED SOUPS

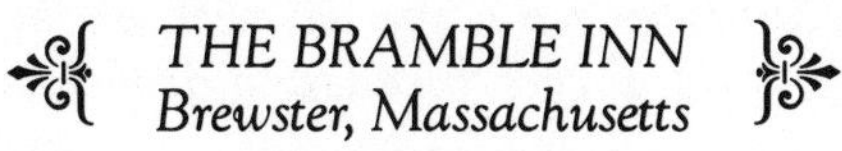

COLD CUCUMBER SOUP

"On a hot summer's day, there is nothing quite as appealing as a chilled soup made of the freshest produce right from the garden!"

1 cucumber, peeled, sliced, and seeded
1/2 cup water
1 slice of onion
1/8 teaspoon salt
Dash white pepper
2 tablespoons flour
1 cup chicken stock
1/4 bay leaf
6 tablespoons sour cream
1 1/2 teaspoons dill
Salt and pepper to taste

Cook first 5 ingredients till very soft; put through fine sieve. Blend flour and stock. Add to cucumber mixture with bay leaf. Simmer 2 minutes, strain, and chill, covered. Add and stir in sour cream, dill, and salt and pepper to taste. Serve very cold, garnished with dill. *Serves 4.*

TOMATO-CUCUMBER BISQUE WITH AVOCADO

Serve as an appetizer for a special meal, or for lunch or supper accompanied by a salad, French bread, and dry white wine. Also good heated.

2 tablespoons butter
2 cloves garlic, coarsely chopped
1 small onion, chopped
3 cucumbers, peeled, seeded, and cut into half-inch pieces
4 cups canned tomatoes in juice
2 cups chicken broth
1 tablespoon chopped fresh dill or 1 teaspoon dried dill
1 cup heavy cream
Salt and freshly ground pepper to taste
2 avocados, peeled and diced

Melt butter in 2-quart saucepan. Add garlic, onion, and cucumber pieces and gently sauté for 15 minutes. Do not allow to brown. Add tomatoes, chicken broth, and dill, and simmer for 45 minutes. Remove from heat and purée in a food processor or blender. Add the cream and salt and pepper to taste. Stir in the diced avocados. If the soup is to be served cold, chill for at least 4 hours. *Serves 6-8.*

WINDHAM HILL INN
West Townshend, Vermont

REFRESHING TOMATO SOUP

An excellent recipe that belongs in everyone's repertoire. Incredibly easy to make. Those who are calorie conscious might want to substitute yogurt for the sour cream.

3 cups tomato juice
2 tablespoons tomato paste
4 scallions, minced
Zest of 1/2 lemon
2 tablespoons fresh lemon juice
1 cup sour cream
2 teaspoons superfine sugar
1/8 teaspoon powdered thyme
1/2 teaspoon curry powder
Salt and freshly ground pepper to taste
Fresh chopped chives

Whisk all ingredients together in large stainless steel or glass bowl. Chill thoroughly. Ladle into chilled individual bowls and garnish with fresh chopped chives. *Serves 4-6.*

GREENHURST INN
Bethel, Vermont

COLD AVOCADO SOUP

"It has been claimed that this soup is an aphrodisiac. Not so. It is merely fattening."

1 large avocado
2 cups milk
Lemon juice (to taste)
Salt (to taste)

Remove avocado flesh from seed in such a way that 4 thin rings of avocado may be sliced. Purée remaining avocado and milk in blender. Add lemon juice and salt to taste. If too thick, add more milk. Pour into soup bowls and gently lay avocado rings on top. *Serves 4.*

COLD BISQUE OF FRESH SPINACH, NOILLY PRAT

Pretty and refreshing — with lots of pizzazz from the generous amount of vermouth.

1 shallot, chopped
1 tablespoon butter
1 pound fresh spinach, washed
1½ quarts cream of chicken base (or equal amount of canned cream of chicken soup, diluted)
1 cup light cream
1 cup Noilly Prat Dry Vermouth
Sour cream

Sauté shallot in butter, add spinach, cover, and cook only until tender. Combine with chicken base and thoroughly mix in blender. Stir in cream and chill, then add French vermouth. Serve in chilled cups, with a spoonful of sour cream on each.

Serves 10-12.

CHILLED ZUCCHINI SOUP

"This is a great favorite with our guests and we serve it during the winter season, too, as it can be served hot by substituting cream for the sour cream."

½ cup minced onions or scallions
3 tablespoons butter
1½ pounds zucchini, cut into chunks
6 cups liquid (either water or chicken broth or a combination of both)
1½ teaspoons white wine vinegar
¾ teaspoon dried dill
4 tablespoons quick-cooking Cream of Wheat
1 cup sour cream

Cook onions slowly in butter until soft. Add zucchini, liquid, vinegar, and dill and bring to a rolling boil. Add Cream of Wheat and cook, partially covered, about 20 to 25 minutes. Cool and put through food mill or blender. Add sour cream and blend well. Serve well chilled, with a sprinkling of chopped fresh dill if desired or a dollop of sour cream sprinkled with fresh dill.

Serves 8.

WOODSTOCK INN APPLE AND GINGER BISQUE

Sweet and filling — and well received at the inn during foliage season. Use a tart, flavorful apple like a McIntosh or Granny Smith and serve for lunch along with a sandwich or salad.

1 cup chopped almonds
1 cup chopped walnuts
2 tablespoons walnut oil
3/4 pound celery, cleaned and chopped
3/4 pound carrots, cleaned and chopped
1 1/2 onions, quartered
1/2 pound butter
1/2 pound flour
4 apples, peeled, cored, and diced
1/2 gallon cider
1 quart chicken stock
2 teaspoons cinnamon
1 tablespoon nutmeg
1 cup applesauce
1 tablespoon white pepper
2 tablespoons thyme
2 bay leaves
1/2 cup Vermont maple syrup
1/2 cup brown sugar
2 ounces vanilla
3 ounces freshly grated ginger
1/2 cup applejack brandy
1/2 quart heavy cream
Grated or powdered ginger

Run the nuts through a food chopper with the walnut oil. Then run through the celery, carrots, and onions. Sauté the vegetables in a heavy pot in butter. Add nuts and sweat for approximately 5 minutes. Add flour to make a roux. Stir in remaining ingredients except for heavy cream and grated or powdered ginger. All or part of the diced apples may also be reserved for garnishing. Simmer for about 10-15 minutes, adjust seasonings, if necessary, and finish soup by topping with whipped heavy cream, grated or powdered ginger, and diced apples. Serve hot or chill and serve cold. *Serves 16.*

OLD LYME INN
Old Lyme, Connecticut

COLD APPLE BISQUE

Applejack makes this an adult's soup. Perfect in the fall for a picnic or a football tailgate party.

9 apples, peeled, cored, and quartered
1 pint heavy cream
1 cup applejack
1½ cups sugar
1 pint apple cider

Cook apples in minimal amount of water until soft. Purée and then cool. Add cream and applejack and blend. Caramelize sugar and dissolve with apple cider. Combine both mixtures and chill overnight. Serve garnished with apple slices.

Makes about 1 gallon.

THE MIDDLEBURY INN
Middlebury, Vermont

CHILLED FRUIT SOUP

A refreshing start to any summer meal. Creamy-smooth texture with an appealing color. Any seasonal fruit could be used.

1 pint fresh blueberries or strawberries
1 cup sour cream
Sugar to taste
3 tablespoons brandy
2 cups coffee cream

Chop berries in a blender. Add sour cream, sugar, and brandy. Blend until smooth, then mix in the coffee cream. Chill and serve.

Serves 6.

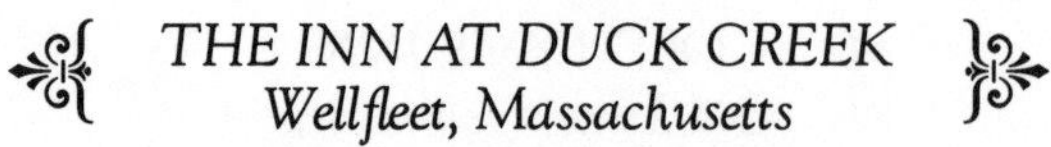

THE INN AT DUCK CREEK
Wellfleet, Massachusetts

CHILLED STRAWBERRY SOUP

"One of our most requested recipes. Some of our customers even order it for dessert on hot July evenings."

3 pints strawberries
1 cup water
½ cup sugar
¼ cup flour
2 cups Burgundy wine
2 cups orange juice
3 cups sour cream
1 cup milk or light cream

Wash, hull, and halve strawberries. Cook in water for 10 minutes. Combine sugar and flour in a separate saucepan and stir in wine and orange juice. Stir or whisk constantly until mixture boils (about 10 minutes). Add to strawberries and cool.

Purée in blender in batches, then add sour cream and milk or light cream. Chill thoroughly. Serve garnished with sliced strawberry and mint leaf. *Serves 10-12.*

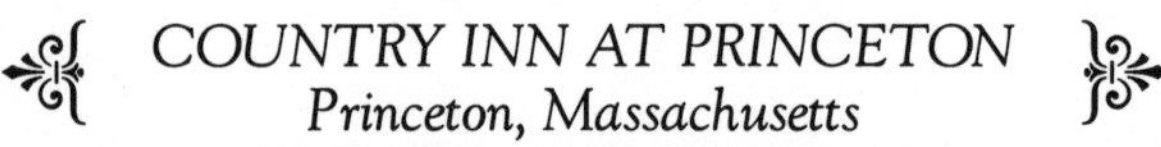

COUNTRY INN AT PRINCETON
Princeton, Massachusetts

STRAWBERRY SOUR-CREAM SOUP

Heavenly... The hardest part of this simple soup is waiting to eat it. Allow at least 3 to 4 hours for chilling — preferably 24.

2 cups fresh strawberries
½ cup sour cream
½ cup dry red wine
½ cup sugar

Hull and wash strawberries. Place in blender with sour cream; purée. While blender is running, add red wine and sugar. Chill thoroughly and serve in chilled bowls. *Serves 4-5.*

COLD STRAWBERRY SOUP

This sweet, rich, and irresistible soup can be made entirely with fresh strawberries by using 4 parts strawberries to 1 part sugar. Cut up strawberries, add sugar, and let sit until juicy. Then proceed with recipe.

3¼ pounds frozen strawberries (in syrup) and 1½ pounds fresh, hulled and cut up (reserve some for garnish)
½ teaspoon cinnamon
½ teaspoon salt
8 ounces frozen orange juice concentrate, undiluted
¼ cup red Burgundy wine
5 whole cloves (remove after cooking)
4 tablespoons cornstarch
½ cup cold water
2½ pounds vanilla ice cream
1 quart light cream

In heavy pot heat strawberries, cinnamon, salt, orange juice concentrate, wine, and cloves. Dissolve cornstarch in cold water and add to pot; cook until thickened. Remove from heat and let sit until cooled. Stir in ice cream and light cream, blending well. Refrigerate 1 hour or until thoroughly chilled. Garnish with fresh diced strawberries. *Serves 12.*

CHILLED CRANBERRY SOUP

"We start serving our very popular chilled soups over the Memorial Day weekend and continue through foliage season. However, we have been known to offer them in the winter, too, particularly this favorite."

2 oranges
1 tablespoon butter
1¼ cups sugar
1 cup sherry
1 pound cranberries
1 cup dry sauterne
1 cup light cream
1 cup club soda
1 cup sour cream
16 pecan halves

Squeeze juice from oranges and set aside. Julienne the rinds and sauté in butter, but do not let brown. Add sugar, sherry, and reserved orange juice. Boil 2 minutes. Add cranberries, cover, and boil 2 minutes longer. Uncover and continue boiling for 3 additional minutes. Chill overnight. Place in blender and add sauterne and light cream. Blend at moderate speed for 1 minute. Strain and chill well. Before serving add club soda and mix well. Garnish individual servings with a dollop of sour cream and 2 pecan halves. *Serves 8.*

THE GOVERNOR'S INN
Ludlow, Vermont

CHRISTMAS CHERRY

"Before settling in to wait for Santa by our crackling fire, guests at the Governor's Inn enjoy a wonderful Christmas Eve dinner. Six courses are presented in the inn's two dining rooms, which glow with candlelight and holiday cheer. Traditionally the chilled potage is Christmas Cherry served in a glass icer and garnished with a lemon wheel and a dollop of softly whipped cream. This beautiful soup will keep refrigerated at least 2 weeks."

3 cans (1 pound each) pitted tart red cherries (packed in water)
2 sticks cinnamon
6 whole cloves
6 whole allspice berries
½ lemon
½ cup sugar
Pinch of salt
1 pint heavy cream
1 tablespoon flour
½ bottle dry red French Medoc wine
Lemon wheels for garnish
Whipped cream for garnish

Combine in large pot juice and fruit from 2 cans tart red cherries and juice only from the third can, reserving the cherries. Add 1 can of water, the spices, lemon, sugar, and salt. Bring to boil. In a separate smaller pan scald the cream and whisk in flour. Cool scalded mixture slightly and strain into cherry mixture. Add wine and bring mixture just to the boiling point. Do not boil. Strain out solids and cool. Add reserved can of cherries and refrigerate overnight. Serve in beautiful glass containers — a champagne glass, icer, brandy snifter, or compote dish. Garnish each with lemon wheel and a dollop of whipped cream. Merry Christmas! *Serves 12.*

SALADS & SALAD DRESSINGS

The Red Lion Inn, Stockbridge, Massachusetts

LOBSTER SALAD VICTORIAN

This salad is a surprise because the butter sauce is served warm.

5 bay leaves
1/4 cup lemon juice
3 two-pound lobsters (about 1 1/2 cups of meat)
1/2 cup brandy
1 tablespoon fennel seed, crushed
1 1/2 tablespoons tarragon leaves
1/2 pound butter, softened at room temperature
1/2 teaspoon saffron threads
Avocado and mushrooms for garnish

To a deep kettle of rapidly boiling water add bay leaves and lemon juice. Plunge lobsters head first into boiling water. Bring back to boiling and cook 10 minutes. Remove from water, let cool, and remove meat from claws and tail. Discard body and shells. Cut meat into bite-sized chunks.

Place brandy, fennel seed, and 1 tablespoon of the tarragon in saucepan. Bring to boil and flambé until flame goes out. Remove from heat. Strain into softened butter. Discard solids. Add remaining tarragon and saffron. Place back on stove and boil briefly. Mound lobster meat on bed of shredded lettuce. Garnish with avocados and mushrooms. Pour butter sauce over dish and serve at once.

Serves 6.

MARINATED VEGETABLE SALAD AND SALMON

For an extra-special effect, steam and marinate the vegetables separately and arrange them separately around the salmon.

4 stalks celery
3 large carrots
2 large zucchini
2 cups broccoli florets
1 clove garlic, pressed
1/2 cup vegetable oil
1/4 cup minced onion
2 tablespoons red wine vinegar
2 tablespoons lemon juice
1 tablespoon honey
1 teaspoon dill weed, crumbled
1 teaspoon prepared mustard
1/2 teaspoon salt
2 cups fresh cooked salmon, or 1 can (15 1/2 ounces)
Crisp salad greens
1 large tomato, quartered

Thinly slice celery, carrots, and zucchini on the diagonal. Steam celery, carrots, zucchini, and broccoli 3 minutes or until crisp-tender. Place in a 3-quart casserole dish. Combine garlic, oil, onion, vinegar, lemon juice, honey, dill weed, mustard, and salt in screwtop jar. Shake well. Pour over vegetables; refrigerate at least 1 hour or overnight. Drain and bone salmon and place on crisp salad greens in center of platter. Arrange marinated vegetables and tomato pieces around salmon and pour any remaining dressing over it. *Serves 4.*

THE RAM IN THE THICKET
Wilton, New Hampshire

COPPER PENNIES

A colorful, sweet salad that can be served either hot or cold. It gets better the longer it marinates and will keep well in the refrigerator for a number of days.

5 pounds carrots, peeled, sliced, and cooked al dente
1 cup chopped onions, uncooked
1 cup chopped green peppers, uncooked
2 cups salad oil
1 cup vinegar
2 cups tomato juice or catsup or tomato paste (or a combination)
1½ cups sugar
1 tablespoon Worcestershire sauce
1 tablespoon prepared mustard

Toss carrots, onions, and green peppers together in a glass or stainless steel bowl. Combine remaining ingredients in a blender, pour over vegetables, and marinate. *Serves 15-20.*

THE RAM IN THE THICKET
Wilton, New Hampshire

MARINATED LIMA BEANS

A tongue-tingling way to enjoy lima beans. Serve them on a bed of lettuce surrounded by cucumber slices, tomato wedges, and mixed olives, with a sprinkling of chopped parsley and green onions on top.

1 package frozen baby limas
½ cup olive oil
¼ cup wine vinegar
1 teaspoon water
¼ teaspoon red pepper flakes (or to taste)
½ teaspoon oregano
1 teaspoon fresh mint
½ teaspoon sugar
Salt and pepper to taste

Cook limas until barely tender. Combine remaining ingredients in blender and process until well blended. Pour over drained limas and refrigerate for at least 2 hours, preferably longer, stirring occasionally. *Serves 4-6.*

CENTER LOVELL INN
Center Lovell, Maine

CAULIFLOWER VINAIGRETTE

A pleasant addition to salad plates. Replace cauliflower with 1 medium bunch broccoli for a change of color.

1 medium head cauliflower
2 cups white wine vinegar
1 clove garlic, minced
1 tablespoon chopped fresh basil
4 tablespoons olive oil
1 teaspoon chopped chives
1 teaspoon chopped parsley
½ teaspoon salt
¼ teaspoon crushed black pepper

Wash and separate cauliflower into small florets. Cook in boiling salted water for 5 minutes. Drain, place in enamel saucepan with vinegar and garlic, and bring to a boil. Drain immediately, mix with remaining ingredients, cover and let cool, then chill.

Serves 6.

THE RED LION INN
Stockbridge, Massachusetts

RED LION CRANBERRY SALAD

Full of "goodies," this easy salad does not require dressing. Great for buffets. Do not use fresh pineapple as it will interfere with gelling.

1 cup chopped and cored McIntosh apples
1 cup raw cranberries
1 cup sugar
1 package lemon Jello
1 cup boiling water
1 cup canned pineapple juice
½ cup Tokay grapes
¼ cup chopped walnuts
1 cup canned crushed pineapple

Grind apples and cranberries in food grinder. Add sugar and set aside. In a 1½- to 2-quart dish, dissolve Jello in boiling water and add pineapple juice. When Jello is softly set, add apple and cranberry mixture, grapes, walnuts, and crushed pineapple.

Serves 8-10.

JARED COFFIN HOUSE
Nantucket, Massachusetts

JARED'S CRANBERRY SALAD

Sweet, crunchy, and refreshing. Prepare in advance and refrigerate to give it plenty of time to set up.

1 cup cranberries
2 ounces sugar
1 cup mandarin orange segments
2 ounces chopped celery
2 ounces chopped walnuts
Pinch of salt
3 ounces mayonnaise
3 ounces heavy cream, whipped

Marinate cranberries in sugar for 1 hour in a stainless steel bowl. Add mandarin orange segments, celery, nuts, and salt. Fold in mayonnaise and whipped cream. Refrigerate until set. Serve on a bed of lettuce garnished with orange segments and chopped nuts. *Serves 8.*

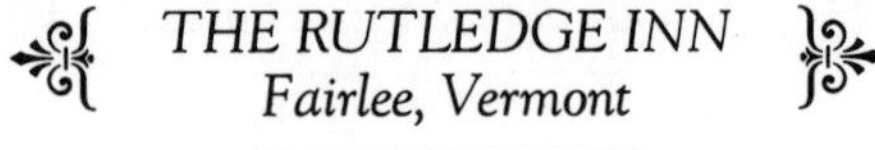

THE RUTLEDGE INN
Fairlee, Vermont

MOLDED 7-UP SALAD

A tangy salad that could also serve as an appetizer.

1 cup applesauce
1/2 cup raspberry Jello
1/3 cup crushed and drained pineapple
Rind of 1 orange
Juice of 1 orange
7-Up to make 1 cup with the orange juice

Bring applesauce to boiling (be sure it is not just bubbling). Add Jello and stir to fully dissolve. Add pineapple and orange rind. Stir in the orange juice combined with 7-Up, mix thoroughly, and chill in individual molds or one large mold. Serve on a bed of lettuce with mayonnaise and parsley for garnish. *Serves 6.*

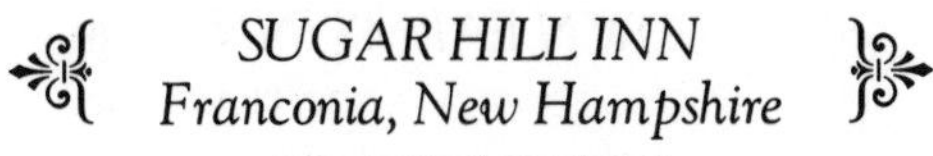

SUGAR HILL INN
Franconia, New Hampshire

CREAMY GARLIC DRESSING

"This recipe actually came from The Italian Village Restaurant in Chicago, where we obtained it from the chef about 15 years ago. The amounts given are reduced from the original."

2 cups sour cream
2/3 cup mayonnaise
3/4 teaspoon garlic powder (or to taste)
1/8 teaspoon cider vinegar
2 1/2 tablespoons sugar
Salt and pepper to taste
Chives (optional)

Mix all ingredients together in an appropriate size bowl, stirring well. The dressing's flavor improves with age — don't use it for at least 3 days. Keeps for a month refrigerated in a covered plastic container. *Makes 2 2/3 cups.*

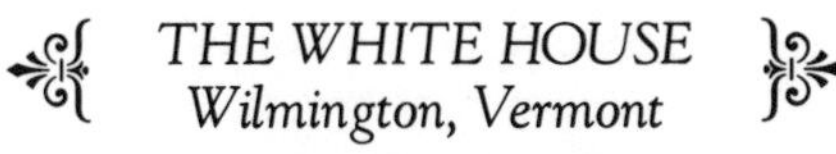

THE WHITE HOUSE
Wilmington, Vermont

WHITE HOUSE SALAD DRESSING

Keep refrigerated in a tightly capped container and the dressing will last 3 weeks without spoilage.

1 cup buttermilk
2 pints heavy mayonnaise
1 1/2 tablespoons dry mustard
1 clove garlic, crushed
2 tablespoons celery seed
Salt and pepper to taste

Put buttermilk in saucepan and heat until it simmers. Let cool. Place mayonnaise, mustard, garlic, celery seed, and salt and pepper in large bowl. Whisk together. When buttermilk is cool, add to mayonnaise mixture. Pour mixture into tightly capped container and refrigerate. *Makes 5 cups.*

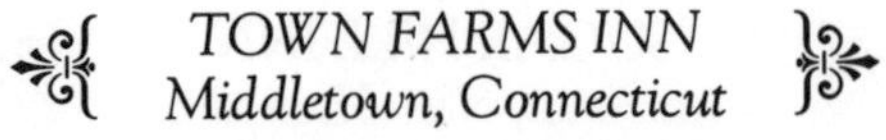

TOWN FARMS INN
Middletown, Connecticut

PEPPERCREAM DRESSING

Wonderful on tossed salads but also great on steamed vegetables or baked potatoes. It must sit for at least 24 hours before using.

1/2 gallon heavy mayonnaise
1/6 cup cider vinegar
2 1/2 tablespoons Accent
4 ounces grated Parmesan cheese
1/2 teaspoon salt
1/2 teaspoon ground black pepper
1/2 teaspoon garlic oil
1/4 small onion
1/8 cup whole peppercorns
Juice from 1/2 lemon

Combine first 7 ingredients in large container. Purée onion, peppercorns, and lemon juice and stir into mayonnaise mixture, blending well. Cover and refrigerate 24 hours.

Makes about 8 cups.

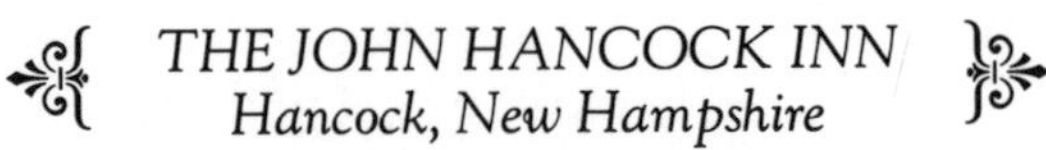

THE JOHN HANCOCK INN
Hancock, New Hampshire

HANCOCK DRESSING

"So many guests enjoy the mild anchovy flavor of this, our house dressing. Makes enough to share as a special gift to a friend. It stores well, covered, in the refrigerator."

4 eggs
3 cups salad oil
1/2 cup vinegar
1 teaspoon salt
1 teaspoon white pepper
1/2 teaspoon garlic powder
1/2 teaspoon oregano
Juice of 1 lemon
1/2 cup grated Parmesan cheese
2 ounces anchovies, finely chopped

Using a mixer or hand blender, whip eggs until light and frothy. Slowly add the oil. Combine remaining ingredients and then add slowly to oil mixture. *Makes 1 quart.*

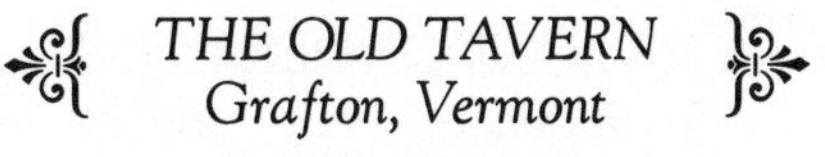

THE OLD TAVERN
Grafton, Vermont

OLD TAVERN HOUSE DRESSING

"We have been asked for this recipe hundreds of times but it has never been given out before. Eggs, oil, and mixer parts must be at room temperature. If a blender is used, substitute whole eggs for the yolks."

2 egg yolks
1 teaspoon dry mustard
1 teaspoon salt
1 teaspoon lemon juice
2 tablespoons confectioners sugar
1 cup light salad oil (divided)
2 tablespoons vinegar
4 tablespoons lemon juice
1 tablespoon freshly minced onion
1 clove garlic, minced
2 teaspoons celery seed
Dash Tabasco

Beat egg yolks until lemon color, then add next 4 ingredients. Beat in ½ cup salad oil *very* slowly until mixture begins to thicken. Mix vinegar and lemon juice together and alternate adding, drop by drop, with second ½ cup of oil. Add the onion, garlic, celery seed, and Tabasco, stirring. Thin dressing, if necessary, with light cream. *Makes 1½ cups.*

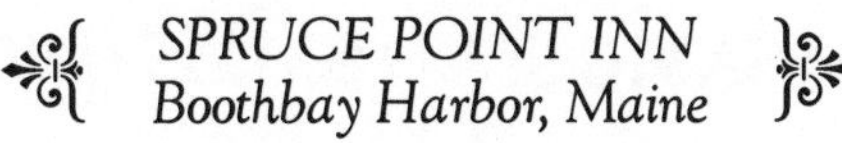

SPRUCE POINT INN
Boothbay Harbor, Maine

SALAD DRESSING

Excellent flavor. Suitable for fresh fruits as well as tossed green salads.

1 cup Mazola cooking oil
½ cup sugar
1 teaspoon dry mustard
1 teaspoon salt
½ onion, minced
¼ cup vinegar
1 tablespoon celery seed

Combine all ingredients and beat thoroughly.
Makes about 1½ cups.

THE LONDONDERRY INN
South Londonderry, Vermont

DON'S HOUSE SALAD DRESSING

Light green and cucumbery. Be careful not to overbeat the egg whites.

6 egg whites
1 cup olive oil
1/4 cup cider vinegar
1/2 teaspoon salt
1 clove garlic
Dash of cayenne
1 teaspoon chervil
1/4 teaspoon white pepper
2 tablespoons chopped parsley
1 tablespoon fresh chives
1 teaspoon mustard powder
3 tablespoons sour cream
1 teaspoon chopped capers
1 cucumber, puréed in blender

Whip egg whites until medium stiff (soft peaks), add oil and vinegar *alternately*, then add remaining ingredients. Mix for 2 minutes. *Makes 1 quart.*

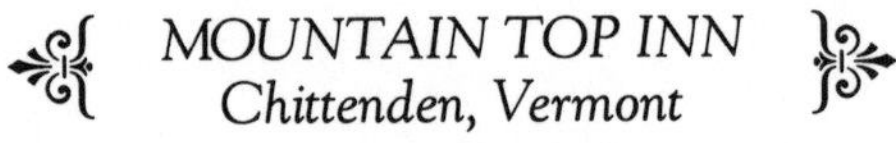

MOUNTAIN TOP INN
Chittenden, Vermont

LIME-SESAME SEED SALAD DRESSING

"This is one of our most popular dressings at the inn. It requires little preparation time and keeps well when refrigerated."

2 tablespoons whole sesame seeds
2 to 3 tablespoons fresh lime juice
1 cup salad oil
1/4 cup red wine vinegar
2 tablespoons honey

Spread sesame seeds on a baking pan and place in a 300° oven. Bake until lightly toasted (about 8 minutes). Combine with rest of ingredients and blend together with an electric mixer or blender. *Makes about 1½ cups.*

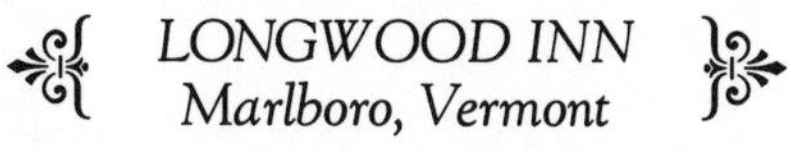

LONGWOOD INN
Marlboro, Vermont

CUCUMBER-MINT SALAD DRESSING

"A refreshing warm-weather dressing which is best when made in a food processor. Serve it over chilled romaine and cherry tomatoes."

2 medium cucumbers
½ cup fresh mint leaves
1 large clove garlic
Juice of half a lemon
½ cup mayonnaise
2 cups sour cream
⅓ cup red-wine vinegar
Fresh black pepper

Peel cucumbers, slice in half lengthwise, and scoop out seeds with a spoon. In processor purée mint leaves, garlic, cucumber, and lemon juice till very fine. In large bowl mix this together with mayonnaise, sour cream, and vinegar. Add a few twists of black pepper. *Makes 4 cups.*

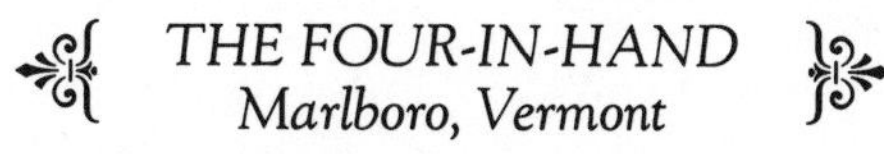

THE FOUR-IN-HAND
Marlboro, Vermont

RASPBERRY VINAIGRETTE

Look for raspberry vinegar in gourmet food shops. It is expensive but deserving of the splurge. For a real treat, serve this on salad with endive.

1 clove garlic
½ teaspoon salt
½ teaspoon fresh black pepper
2 tablespoons raspberry vinegar
7 tablespoons good Spanish olive oil

Mash garlic clove in a bowl with salt and pepper until a paste is formed. Add vinegar and blend well. Slowly incorporate the olive oil into the vinegar mixture, whisking well continuously. It will become nice and thick. *Makes about ½ cup.*

ENTRÉES

Avon Old Farms Inn, Avon, Connecticut

POULTRY

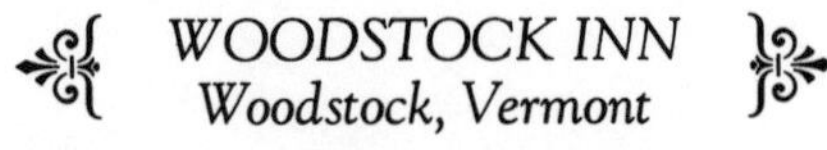

SAUTÉED CHICKEN VERMONT STYLE

Tender breasts of chicken in a creamy sauce spiked with applejack brandy.

2 whole chicken breasts, boned, skinned, and halved
Flour
1/2 cup butter
8 ounces fresh blanched morels
1 cup blanched almonds
3/8 cup applejack brandy
2 teaspoons tarragon vinegar
1 cup heavy cream
Chopped fresh parsley

Dredge chicken breasts in flour and sauté in butter, browning slightly on both sides. Add morels and almonds, sautéing at low temperature so as not to darken. Remove chicken and deglaze with applejack brandy. Add vinegar and cream, reduce to smooth consistency, and return chicken to pan just long enough to heat through. Garnish with parsley. *Serves 4.*

CHICKEN MARQUIS

"This is one of our most popular dishes at The Darby Field. For something really special, try it with shrimp instead of chicken . . . it's outstanding!"

16 ounces boneless, skinless breast of chicken
Flour
2 tablespoons clarified butter or olive oil
2 cloves garlic, sliced
4 cups thinly sliced mushrooms
3 tablespoons Tamari (soy sauce)
4 tablespoons dry white wine
3 tablespoons fresh lemon juice
2 to 3 tablespoons chicken stock
1½ cups fresh cubed tomatoes
¼ cup sliced scallions

Lightly flatten the chicken with the side of a meat mallet or heavy cleaver and slice into bite-sized pieces. Assemble all the other ingredients as this dish is very quick to cook. Dredge the chicken in flour and lightly shake the excess flour off. Have a large frying pan or cast iron skillet ready on the stove and add the clarified butter or oil, garlic, and chicken and sauté on a medium flame until the chicken is browned on one side. Flip the chicken and add the mushrooms, stirring with a wooden spoon until the mushrooms begin to darken. Then add the liquid ingredients and stir while the pan sauce thickens (about 2 minutes). Add the tomatoes and scallions, stir briefly, and serve. *Serves 4.*

POULET À LA CRÈME

"An adaptation of a dish served in a restaurant owned by the producers of Mercier champagne. You can try it with champagne, but cream sherry is better."

4 half chicken breasts, boned and skinned
Flour
1/2 pound butter
8 ounces mushrooms, thinly sliced
1/2 pint whipping cream
1/4 cup cream sherry
1/8 teaspoon tarragon, rubbed

Dredge chicken in flour and brown in half the butter. Remove chicken to oven pan and bake in 300° oven for 1 hour. Meanwhile, cook mushrooms in remaining half of butter. Add whipping cream, sherry, and tarragon. Simmer until consistency is that of medium-thick gravy (flour can be used to hasten thickening). Serve chicken on bed of boiled rice, with sauce spooned on top. More chicken may be used in the recipe, but the sauce is only enough for 4 people. *Serves 4.*

BEE AND THISTLE INN
Old Lyme, Connecticut

CHICKEN CAPIELLO

A most unusual blend of flavors, and the chunks of plump, tender chicken combined with sweet, crisp, sliced onion create a delightful contrast in texture. An added bonus to this piquant dish is that it's ready in a matter of minutes!

4 chicken breasts (8 ounces each), boned and skinned
Butter to coat bottom of a large sauté pan (about 2 tablespoons)
1 large Spanish onion, sliced
1½ teaspoons minced garlic
2 tablespoons Dijon mustard
½ cup dry white cooking wine
¼ cup grated Parmesan cheese

Cut chicken breasts into chunks. Sauté in butter until flesh of chicken has turned white. Add onions and toss while cooking. Add garlic and cook approximately 2 minutes more (until the aroma is apparent). Add mustard and white wine and blend together. Turn heat down and gently simmer for 5 minutes. Toss in Parmesan cheese and serve over rice pilaf. *Serves 4.*

CHICKEN BREASTS WITH PESTO

Similar to Chicken Kiev, but not as rich and much easier to prepare.

6 double-breasted chicken cutlets, boned and skinned
Pesto (recipe follows)
Flour
2 eggs, beaten, for egg wash
Bread crumbs
Oil for frying

Pound chicken flat and dry. Cover one side with thin layer of pesto. Roll up and secure with toothpicks. Dust with flour, dip in egg wash, and roll in bread crumbs. Refrigerate at least ½ hour.

In skillet, heat ½ inch oil and brown breasts on all sides. Remove and put into greased ovenproof dish. Bake at 400° for 10 minutes. *Serves 6.*

PESTO

1 cup fresh parsley, stems removed
1 cup fresh basil leaves or 1 tablespoon dried basil
¼ cup olive oil
1 garlic clove
½ cup freshly grated Parmesan cheese
1 tablespoon butter

Combine all ingredients in processor and process until fairly smooth.

CHICKEN À LA WEST DOVER

The garnish of seedless green grapes adds color as well as a complementary flavor.

6 boneless chicken breasts (8 ounces each)
Fresh bread crumbs
1 teaspoon tarragon leaves
1/8 teaspoon chopped chives
1/2 teaspoon salt
1/4 teaspoon freshly ground pepper
1/2 cup butter
3 tablespoons minced shallots
3/4 cup sliced mushrooms
2/3 cup chicken stock
2/3 cup dry white wine
Green seedless grapes

Preheat oven to 375°. Between sheets of waxed paper, flatten chicken breasts to 1/4-inch thickness. Combine bread crumbs, tarragon, chives, salt, and pepper. Coat chicken breasts evenly with crumb mixture.

Melt 1/4 cup butter in heavy skillet over medium heat. Lightly brown chicken on both sides. Remove from pan and place in a shallow baking dish. Add remaining butter to skillet and lightly sauté shallots and mushrooms for 3 minutes. Add chicken stock and wine to skillet. Bring to boil, stirring constantly. Pour mixture over chicken. Tent dish with foil and bake 10 minutes. Remove foil and add green grapes. Bake for another 5 minutes.

At serving time, place 1 breast of chicken on each plate and spoon some of the mushrooms, shallots, and broth atop. Garnish with green grapes. Serve with rice or baked potato and a vegetable.

Serves 6.

POMMERY CHICKEN BREASTS

Serve with brown rice and a fresh, lightly cooked green vegetable.

4 boneless chicken breasts (8 ounces each), trimmed of fat but with skin left on
Flour
2 tablespoons butter
2 tablespoons brandy
1 tablespoon chopped garlic
2 tablespoons chopped shallots
1/4 pound sliced mushrooms
1/2 cup heavy cream
2 tablespoons Pommery mustard
2 tablespoons chopped fresh parsley
Salt

Dust chicken breasts with flour and brown skin side down in butter in large skillet. When skin is brown and crisp turn over and cook on other side until barely done — about 10 minutes in all. Pour brandy over chicken and ignite. When flames die down, remove chicken to platter and keep warm in low oven. Add garlic and shallots to pan and sauté briefly. Add sliced mushrooms and sauté about 3 minutes. Add heavy cream, mustard, and parsley. Cook over high heat stirring constantly until reduced and thickened. Season with salt to taste and serve over chicken breasts.

Serves 4.

DRUNKEN BIRD

"We sell a lot of chicken at the inn and this peculiar bird outsells all others two-to-one. In fact, we have a couple in their late thirties who come every Saturday night at 6:00. He has always ordered this dish except for one night. This has been for five years."

6 ounces honey
6 ounces dry sherry
6 ounces chopped walnuts
4 boneless chicken breasts (about 8 ounces each)
Garlic powder
Leaf oregano
12 ounces extra sharp cheddar cheese
1 seedless orange (cut into twists)

Mix the honey and sherry until well blended, add walnuts, and set aside. Preheat oven to 350°. Spread out breasts and sprinkle with garlic powder and oregano. Wrap each breast around 1½ ounces of thickly sliced cheddar cheese and place in individual casserole dishes unseasoned side up. Sprinkle again with garlic and oregano and top with 1½ ounces cheese. Bake for approximately 30 minutes. When chicken breasts are cooked thoroughly, remove from oven and top each dish with 3 ounces of honey, sherry, and nut mixture. Return to oven and heat for another 2 to 4 minutes. Top each dish with an orange twist. *Serves 4.*

SNOWVILLAGE INN
Snowville, New Hampshire

CURRIED CHICKEN WITH PEACHES

"This is a curry everyone can enjoy. Serve it with white rice."

4 chicken breasts (1 pound each)
2 tablespoons olive oil or butter
1 medium onion, chopped fine
1½ tablespoons curry powder
1 teaspoon flour (or more if needed to thicken)
2 cups chicken stock
1 clove garlic, crushed
½ cup coconut milk
1 tablespoon red currant jelly or juice of half a lemon mixed with 2 teaspoons sugar
3 to 4 tablespoons heavy cream
1 teaspoon arrowroot mixed to a paste with 1 tablespoon stock
2 ripe peaches, peeled and halved

Skin breasts and cut in half. Brown slowly in casserole dish in half the oil. When brown on all sides remove from casserole and keep warm. Heat remaining oil or butter in the casserole, add onion, and gently cook until brown. Stir in curry powder and cook 3 minutes. Sprinkle in flour and cook 1 minute. Remove from heat and pour in stock. Add garlic, bring to boil, and simmer 20 minutes. Return chicken to casserole, cover, and cook for 45 minutes or until tender. Transfer chicken to a platter and keep warm. Strain sauce into a pan, add coconut milk and jelly or lemon juice and simmer 3 minutes. Stir in heavy cream and thicken if needed with arrowroot. Add peaches, heat, and pour over chicken on platter. *Serves 4.*

THE VICTORIAN
Whitinsville, Massachusetts

SUPRÊMES DE VOLAILLE EMBALLÉ

" 'Emballé' is a French word meaning 'giftwrapped' or 'wrapped like a package.' The fillings can be changed to suit your individual taste."

3 medium leeks, roots and heavy green tops removed
1/2 pound mushrooms, washed
2 tablespoons butter
2 cups apple juice
2 teaspoons thyme leaves
1/4 cup heavy cream
Salt and pepper
3 large boneless whole breasts of chicken
1 package filo dough (used for baklava — found in freezer section at the supermarket)
1/2 cup melted butter
2 eggs, beaten

Preheat oven to 450°. Wash leeks carefully and then roughly chop them. Roughly chop mushrooms. Melt butter in a large heavy skillet over medium high heat. Add mushrooms and leeks and sauté 10 minutes. Add apple juice and thyme, continue cooking till liquid is evaporated, then stir in cream. Add salt and pepper to taste. Let cool. Cut breasts in half and pound flat and even with a rolling pin. Spread mushroom and leek filling evenly on one side of each breast and roll into a cylinder. Roll all 6 pieces and place in refrigerator for 10 minutes. Then open filo dough (don't leave it open too long, because it dries very quickly), take 1 layer, and place it on a clean counter top. Brush with melted butter, and then place another sheet of dough right on top of the first. Brush this with melted butter also, and repeat till you have 3 sheets stacked one on top of the other. Place chicken on short end and roll up half way. Fold sides toward center and complete rolling. Brush with beaten egg. Wrap other chicken breasts the same way. Place completed "emballés" on cookie sheet and bake till golden brown (about 15 minutes). Serve with a chicken gravy, hollandaise, or any other compatible sauce. *Serves* 6.

THE COMBES FAMILY INN
Ludlow, Vermont

CHICKEN PICCATA

"This is our most popular entrée. I usually serve it with rice pilaf, fresh broccoli, and zucchini nut bread."

8 boneless chicken breasts (4 whole breasts halved)
2 eggs
2 tablespoons milk
3½ cups fresh bread crumbs (8 slices of bread)
¾ cup butter
2 medium lemons
1½ cups water
2 teaspoons powdered chicken bouillon
½ teaspoon salt
Parsley sprig for garnish

On a cutting board lightly pound the chicken breasts; set aside. In pie plate with fork, beat eggs with milk. On wax paper, place bread crumbs. Dip chicken in egg mixture, then in crumbs to coat both sides. Melt butter in electric skillet on medium-high heat; brown breasts, 4 at a time, on both sides, adding more butter if needed. Remove breasts to a platter and keep warm in low oven. Reduce heat in the skillet to low, squeeze juice of 1 lemon into drippings, and stir in water, bouillon, and salt. Scrape to loosen brown bits from bottom of pan. Return chicken to pan, cover, and simmer 15 minutes or until breasts are tender. To serve, thinly slice remaining lemon and arrange chicken on platter with lemon slices. Pour sauce in skillet over chicken. Garnish with parsley.

Serves 8.

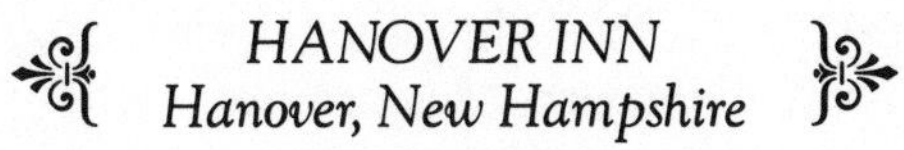

HANOVER INN
Hanover, New Hampshire

BONELESS BREAST OF CHICKEN WITH HERBS

Low calorie, low cholesterol, and delicate flavor.

1 chicken breast, boneless, per serving
1 cup white wine
Juice from one lemon (about 2 tablespoons)
Pinch of each: oregano, thyme leaves, marjoram, basil, garlic powder, salt, pepper, curry

Put chicken in a pan with wine and lemon juice. In a bowl combine the herbs and seasonings. Sprinkle on breast, cover with foil, bake in 350° oven for 20 minutes, uncover, and bake about 5 more minutes or until done. Remove from pan and thicken juice. Serve on a platter with rice pilaf. *Serves 1.*

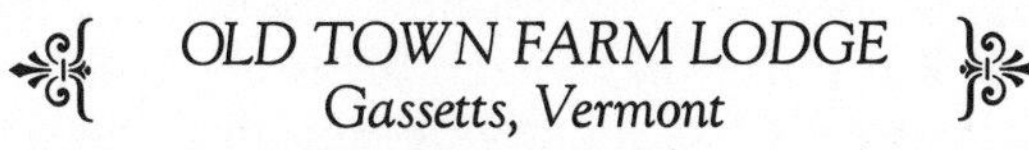

OLD TOWN FARM LODGE
Gassetts, Vermont

CRANBERRY GLAZED CHICKEN BREAST QUARTERS

The glaze is so good, you might want to bake the chicken right in it.

6 chicken breast quarters
Salt and pepper
1 can (8 ounces) jellied cranberry sauce
1/4 cup soy sauce
1/2 cup packed brown sugar
1 teaspoon salt
1 teaspoon dry mustard
1 teaspoon ground ginger
1 clove garlic, crushed
2 tablespoons lemon juice

In a broiling pan place chicken breast quarters. Salt and pepper slightly. Cook 1 1/2 hours at 325° in top of oven. Meanwhile, combine remaining ingredients for glaze; heat to dissolve sugar and liquefy cranberry sauce. Baste chicken with cranberry glaze mixture during last half hour of cooking. *Serves 6.*

CHICKEN CRANBERRY KIEV

Chicken breasts wrapped around a sweet-tart filling of cranberries and maple syrup.

4 boneless chicken breasts (6 ounces each)
2 tablespoons butter
4 teaspoons pure maple syrup
½ cup sliced frozen cranberries
1 tablespoon chopped chives
1 cup evaporated milk
1 pound fresh bread crumbs
Hot fat for frying

Take skin off chicken and pound breasts out to about ¼-inch thickness. Put in center of each breast ½ tablespoon butter and 1 teaspoon maple syrup; divide amongst the chicken the cranberries and chives. Roll up each breast and shape so ingredients stay inside. Put in freezer till hard enough to handle. Dip in milk and coat with bread crumbs, making sure ingredients are sealed inside. Fry in 350° fat till lightly browned. Bake in 350° oven 15-20 minutes or until done. *Serves 4.*

CHICKEN BREASTS À LA SNOWVILLE

Don't boil the mandarin oranges in the sauce; just toss them in at the last minute.

4 whole chicken breasts, halved, boned, and skinned
Salt
2 tablespoons butter
1/2 teaspoon tarragon
1/2 cup white wine
1 1/2 tablespoons orange marmalade
1/2 cup whipping cream
2 teaspoons cornstarch
1 1/2 cups drained mandarin oranges

Sprinkle chicken breasts lightly with salt. Melt butter in a wide frying pan over medium heat. Add breasts and brown lightly on each side. Blend tarragon, wine, and marmalade and combine with chicken. Cover frying pan and simmer very gently for 20 minutes. Transfer breasts to another pan and keep warm. To pan juices add the whipping cream and bring to a quick boil. Blend the cornstarch with a little water and stir into sauce; return to boil to thicken. Remove from heat, stir in mandarin oranges, then immediately pour sauce over chicken and serve. *Serves 4.*

BREAST OF CHICKEN MONT D'OR

"Serve with plain white rice that has been cooked with 2 or 3 threads of saffron in it, a plainly steamed and slightly undercooked green vegetable, and a tomato and onion salad."

4 chicken breasts, boned and skinned
Salt and freshly ground black pepper
Flour
1/3 cup Spanish olive oil (best quality)
Butter size of a walnut
2/3 cup coarsely chopped shallots
1/2 cup fresh lemon juice
1/2 cup dry sherry
1 cup heavy cream

Trim breasts of any skin or fat. Sprinkle with a liberal amount of salt and freshly ground pepper. Pat this well into the flesh. Dredge lightly in flour.

In a heavy skillet heat olive oil. Add to this the lump of butter. When the oil and butter are very hot put the chicken breasts in and sauté them until they are golden brown and just a tiny bit less than perfectly done. Remove them from the pan and place on a clean towel on a platter. Put aside where it is warm.

If the pan is too hot, allow it to cool a bit before adding the chopped shallots. Sauté until translucent. Now add fresh lemon juice and stir until just slightly reduced. Add sherry (Tio Pepe or something similarly dry and of a comparable thinness), stirring and cooking until liquid has been reduced by half.

When there is a nice mélange remaining in the pan, add the heavy cream. Again, stir and reduce for about 10 minutes over a moderate flame. Taste as you go and amend with salt and fresh pepper if you so desire. When the sauce is as you like it, return the chicken breasts to the pan and let them stay in the sauce, covered, over a very low heat until ready to serve.

Remove chicken and sauce to a heated platter or serving dish. Garnish with thin slices of lemon and fresh greens.

Serves 4.

OVEN-BAKED VERMONT CHICKEN

An old-fashioned dish that evokes memories of Sunday dinners at Grandmother's house. Include hot biscuits, greens, and relish to complete the picture.

- **1 broiler/fryer (about 3 pounds), cut into serving pieces**
- **½ cup finely crushed dry bread crumbs**
- **1 teaspoon seasoned salt**
- **1 egg plus 1 tablespoon water or use milk instead of egg mixture**
- **½ cup margarine or butter**
- **¼ cup fat from baking pan**
- **½ cup flour**
- **2 cups warm milk**
- **½ cup chopped parsley**

Remove the skin from as much of the chicken as possible and remove bones from breasts. Dip each piece of chicken into bread crumbs that have been combined with seasoned salt. Shake off loose crumbs. Then dip into egg beaten with water or milk. Drain chicken and redip in bread crumbs. Place pieces of chicken in well-greased casserole or baking pan. Bake uncovered in moderate oven (350°) 45-60 minutes or until tender. Baste frequently with butter. Remove chicken and keep warm. Make gravy with ¼ cup fat left in baking pan, flour, and warm milk. Season to taste and add parsley. Put chicken on platter and pour gravy over chicken. Sprinkle a little parsley on top. *Serves 4.*

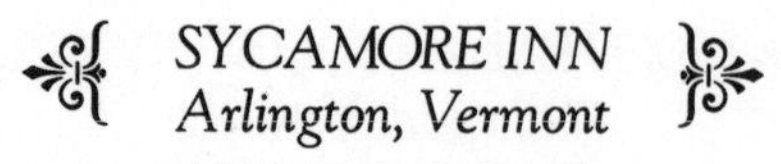

MUSTARD CHICKEN

Spoon out the crumb coating that falls to the bottom of the pan and serve alongside the chicken.

½ stick butter or margarine
2 tablespoons Dijon-style mustard
1 cup bread crumbs
⅓ cup grated Parmesan cheese
1 teaspoon tarragon
1 cut-up chicken (about 3½ pounds)

In small saucepan, melt butter and mustard. In small bowl, combine bread crumbs, grated cheese, and tarragon. Place chicken, skin side up, in baking pan. Generously brush with butter mixture; then sprinkle with half the crumbs. Turn chicken pieces over and repeat. Cover pan and place in 375° oven. Bake for 30 minutes. Remove cover, turn pieces over, and bake uncovered for another 30 minutes. *Serves 4.*

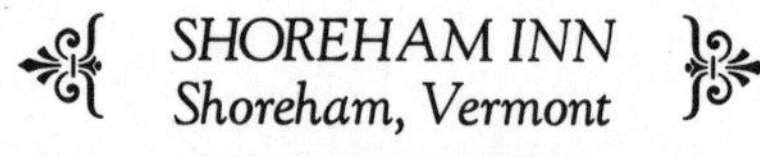

FRUITED CHICKEN

Chicken pieces marinated in a pineapple sauce, then slowly roasted to a golden brown.

3 chickens (2½-pound fryers), cut into eighths
½ large onion, finely chopped
20 ounces crushed pineapple
1½ tablespoons vinegar
Granulated garlic and pepper to taste

Cut, skin, and wash chickens. Place on bed of chopped onion in a large roasting pan. Mix crushed pineapple, vinegar, garlic, and pepper, and pour over chicken. Marinate for at least 3 hours. Roast in a 300° oven for about 1½ hours, turning pieces every 30 minutes. Cook to a golden brown. *Serves 8.*

POLYNESIAN CHICKEN

Beautiful blend of flavors and colorful mixture of ingredients.

1 fryer (about 3½ pounds), cut up
¼ cup oil
1 large white onion, quartered and separated into layers
1 green pepper, cut into strips
1 can (1 pound, 13 ounces) cling peach slices
1 tablespoon cornstarch
1 tablespoon soy sauce
3 tablespoons vinegar
2 medium-sized tomatoes, cut into sixths

In large skillet, brown fryer in oil, cover, and cook until tender (about 15-20 minutes). Drain off excess fat. Cook onion and pepper with chicken until onion is transparent. Drain peaches, reserving syrup. Into 1 cup peach syrup, stir cornstarch, soy sauce, and vinegar. Pour over chicken and cook until clear and slightly thickened. Add peach slices and tomatoes. Heat 5 minutes longer. Serve with hot rice. *Serves 4-6.*

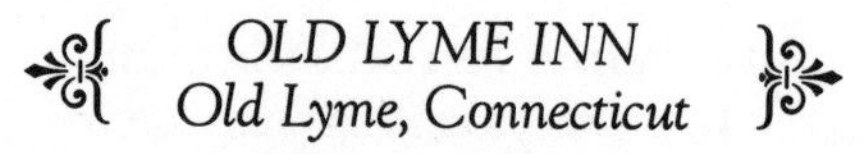

OLD LYME INN
Old Lyme, Connecticut

POULET AUTOMNE DE JOSEPH KLIM

Be sure to read this rather complicated recipe thoroughly and prepare it with the time and care that it deserves. You'll be rewarded with an exquisite entrée, guaranteed to bring you rave reviews.

4 chickens (3 pounds each)
1 egg
1/8 teaspoon salt
Pinch white pepper
1/8 teaspoon chervil
2 ounces applejack
4 ounces heavy cream
1/4 cup seedless grapes
3/4 cup chopped mixed dried fruits
2 tablespoons butter

To make stuffing, remove legs from 2 chickens. Remove bones, skin, and white tendons from legs and cut meat into small pieces. Mix in food processor with egg, salt, pepper, chervil, and applejack. Purée thoroughly and refrigerate mixture for 30 minutes in food processor bowl. Return to unit and add heavy cream. Do not overmix. Remove mixture to bowl and add fruits. Refrigerate until ready to use.

Remove the breast meat from the 4 chickens (the remaining parts of the chickens {legs, thighs, backs, etc.} are not needed for this recipe, so you could use them for something else) leaving the wing bones on. Remove skin and cut off tip ends of the wings. Remove only the filets from the breasts and gently pound thin between layers of plastic film or wax paper. Lay each breast, wing bone pointing away, in front of you and butterfly it open. Take 1/8 of the stuffing and place it down the center of each breast. Lay the flattened filet over stuffing and fold ends of breast over filet and stuffing. Turn over, so folds are on bottom, brush with butter, and bake at 350° for approximately 30 minutes. Serve with Cider Sauce (recipe follows). *Serves 8.*

CIDER SAUCE

1 pint cider
2 ounces brandy
1 cup heavy cream

Over medium heat reduce cider by one half. Add brandy and simmer 5 minutes. Add cream and simmer until mixture coats the back of a spoon. Place a small amount on each plate. Slice breasts into 4 or 5 pieces and lay on top of sauce with slices overlapping each other, like cards fanned open. Serve with white rice mixed with orzo and broccoli.

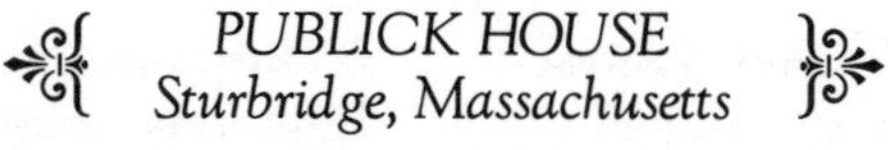

PUBLICK HOUSE
Sturbridge, Massachusetts

OLD-FASHIONED CHICKEN PIE IN BROWN GRAVY

There's no bottom crust and no vegetables baked in this pie — just tender pieces of chicken surrounded by a rich brown gravy, topped with a pastry cover, and baked until bubbling hot and golden brown.

1 chicken (about 5 pounds)
Onion
Celery
Carrot
Salt and pepper
6 cups chicken stock
6 tablespoons margarine
6 tablespoons flour
2 tablespoons Chablis
Kitchen Bouquet
3 cups pastry flour
1½ cups shortening
1 teaspoon salt
Milk

Cook chicken until tender with enough water to cover, onion, celery, carrot, salt, and pepper. When cooked remove chicken meat from bones and cut into large pieces. Place in 13x9-inch baking dish.

Make gravy by bringing to a boil 6 cups chicken stock. Melt margarine, add 6 tablespoons flour, and stir to blend. Add hot stock and cook until thickened. Add wine, season with salt and pepper, and darken with Kitchen Bouquet. Pour gravy over chicken in baking dish.

Make pastry cover by combining pastry flour, shortening, and 1 teaspoon salt. Add enough milk for proper consistency, roll out on floured board, and place over chicken. Bake at 375° until chicken and gravy are sizzling hot and pastry is nicely browned.

Individual casseroles may be used in place of a single larger baking dish. *Serves 6.*

STAFFORD'S IN THE FIELD
Chocorua, New Hampshire

POULET FINE CHAMPAGNE

"This is an easy dish — roasted chicken with a very special sauce. The sauce itself can be made ahead and reheated at serving time so that you have time to do other things while the chicken is roasting."

1 roasting chicken (about 3½ pounds), trussed
Salt and pepper
½ cup butter, softened
Fine Champagne Sauce (recipe follows)

Sprinkle chicken with salt and pepper and rub all over with the softened butter. Place on its side in a roasting pan and roast in a preheated 400° oven for 15 minutes, basting occasionally. Turn on the other side and roast another 15 minutes. Turn breast side up and roast 15-20 minutes longer, still basting. Remove the trussing string, place chicken on a platter, and keep warm.

Pour off the fat that has accumulated in the roasting pan. Deglaze the pan with 1 cup of water. Melt all the solidified juices and pour into a saucepan through a fine strainer. Allow the liquid to reduce until it is as thick as jam. This is a meat glaze. Keep warm while you make the sauce.

FINE CHAMPAGNE SAUCE

2 cups chicken stock, homemade or canned
½ cup diced onion
½ teaspoon whole black peppercorns
8 to 10 sprigs parsley, coarsely chopped
¼ cup flour
3 tablespoons butter
¾ cup champagne (or dry white wine)
1 cup heavy cream
¼ cup good cognac

Combine the first 4 ingredients in a saucepan and reduce by half. Mix the flour and butter together, add to the sauce, bit by bit, beating constantly with a wire whisk, then simmer slowly for 10 minutes. Add the champagne and bring to a boil; reduce for another 3-4 minutes and stir in the cream. Cook over medium heat for 5 minutes, strain the sauce, correct the seasonings, and stir in the cognac. To serve, coat the chicken with the sauce and drizzle the meat glaze over the top. *Serves 4-6.*

CORNISH HENS DIABLE

Handsomely browned Cornish game hens with the pungent flavor of mustard.

4 fresh Cornish game hens
1/2 teaspoon salt
1/4 teaspoon pepper
1/2 cup oil
1 medium clove garlic, minced
1/4 teaspoon rosemary, crushed
1/4 teaspoon thyme, crushed
1/4 cup Dijon-style mustard
1 cup fine dry bread crumbs

Cut hens in half, remove backbones, and wash and pat dry. Season with salt and pepper. Combine oil, garlic, rosemary, and thyme. Arrange hens in a shallow dish and pour oil mixture over them. Cover, let marinate 30 minutes or refrigerate overnight. Arrange hens on broiler rack, brush with marinade, and broil 4 inches from heat for 20 minutes or until done, turning several times and brushing with marinade. Remove hens. With skin side up, spread with mustard, sprinkle with bread crumbs, and broil 2 minutes or until bread crumbs are golden. *Serves 4.*

CORNISH HENS WITH SPINACH, FETA CHEESE, AND RICE STUFFING

Simple yet sensational.

6 fresh Cornish game hens
1/2 cup minced onion
2 tablespoons oil
2 packages (10 ounces each) frozen chopped spinach, thawed and drained
1/2 teaspoon salt
1/2 teaspoon thyme
1/8 teaspoon pepper
1 cup cooked rice
1/2 cup crumbled feta cheese
1 1/4 cups dry white wine
1/4 cup Marsala wine
Juice of 1 lemon (2 tablespoons)
1/4 cup butter, melted
1 teaspoon crushed tarragon

Wash hens, pat dry. Chop giblets. In skillet, sauté onion in oil. Add giblets; sauté 4 minutes. Add spinach, salt, thyme, and pepper. Cook 5 minutes, stirring often. Remove from heat. Add rice, cheese, 1/4 cup white wine, and Marsala. Spoon into hens. Fold back wings and tie legs. Place on rack in shallow pan. Cover loosely with foil. Bake 30 minutes at 350°. Uncover. Blend remaining cup of white wine with lemon juice, butter, and tarragon. Spoon over hens. Bake 30 minutes more or until done, basting occasionally. Serve with marinade from pan. *Serves* 6.

MOUNTAIN VIEW INN
Norfolk, Connecticut

DUCK À L'ORANGE

Roast duckling cooked to crisp brown perfection, with a not-too-sweet orange sauce.

3 ducklings (5 to 6 pounds total)
Salt
Pepper
Celery stalks
2 oranges
1 lemon
2 ounces sugar
2 ounces vinegar
1 cup orange juice
1 pint brown sauce
½ cup white wine

Season duck cavities with salt and pepper. Place necks and giblets in bottom of pan with celery stalks so ducks will stay out of cooking grease. Roast in preheated oven at 400° for 1½-2 hours.

Peel zest from fruit; squeeze juices and reserve. Cut zest in thin matchstrip shapes and blanch in boiling water for 5 minutes.

Caramelize sugar in saucepan. Add vinegar, 1 cup orange juice, reserved juice from oranges and lemon, and brown sauce. Hold over low heat.

When ducks are done remove from oven, split in half, and place on platters. Remove excess fat, vegetables, and giblets and necks from roasting pan. Add wine to pan and deglaze over low heat, stirring to remove all drippings. Strain, add to sauce, and pour over ducks when ready to serve. *Serves* 6.

BEACH PLUM'S ROAST DUCK WITH HONEY CURRY SAUCE

Magnificent! Both the duck and sauce can be made in advance. The final glazing is best done about 30 minutes before serving.

2 ducks (4½ to 5 pounds each)
2 teaspoons coarse (kosher) salt
1 cup fresh orange juice (from 2 to 3 oranges)
2 tablespoons fresh lemon juice
½ cup dry white wine
1 large clove garlic, minced
2 teaspoons curry powder, or to taste
1½ cups honey
⅛ teaspoon hot pepper sauce
Salt and freshly ground pepper
1 bunch watercress, for garnish

Preheat oven to 425°. Rinse the ducks inside and out, drain, and pat dry. Tie the legs together. Place the ducks side by side on a large rack in a large, deep roasting pan. Using a sharp fork, prick the skin about ¼ inch deep all over. Sprinkle each duck with 1 teaspoon of the coarse salt. Roast on the center rack of the oven for 20 minutes. Reduce the heat to 350° and continue to roast for 1 hour, 35 minutes, removing excess fat as it collects. Remove from the oven and let cool.

Meanwhile, in a small saucepan, combine the orange juice, lemon juice, wine, and garlic. Cook over moderate heat until reduced by half, about 15 minutes. Stir in the curry powder, honey, and hot pepper sauce; continue to cook until the sauce is reduced by about one-third to the consistency of a thick syrup, about 25 minutes. Strain into a clean saucepan and season to taste with salt and pepper. Thirty minutes before serving, preheat the oven to 425°. Reheat the sauce. Split the ducks in half lengthwise and arrange skin side up in a large baking pan. Brush the ducks with ⅓ cup of the warm sauce and roast, basting often, until the skin is crisp and the juices run clear, about 15 minutes. Carve the ducks into smaller serving pieces and arrange on a serving platter. Garnish with watercress. Pass the remaining sauce separately.

Serves 6.

THE HERMITAGE
Wilmington, Vermont

ROAST PARTRIDGE HERMITAGE

"One hundred years ago, game was a significant and necessary part of an innkeeper's larder. The Hermitage continues to maintain this tradition. We raise thousands of game birds and serve them most every night to our guests."

Salt and pepper
2 partridges, dressed whole
2 bay leaves
1 medium onion, peeled and quartered
Melted butter
6 strips raw bacon
4 ounces dry, white wine
2 ounces heavy cream
Chopped parsley

Lightly salt and pepper the cavity of each bird. Place 1 bay leaf and 2 onion quarters in each cavity. Lay each partridge on a separate sheet of aluminum foil, bringing the corners up loosely. Baste each bird with melted butter and arrange 3 strips bacon on top of each. Pour wine over birds and seal the foil envelopes. Place in pie pans and roast for 30 minutes in 375° oven. Remove pans from oven and slowly open the foil to expose the birds and bacon, being careful not to spill cooking liquids. Baste each bird with juices in foil envelope and return to oven with the top of the birds and bacon now exposed to direct heat. Roast 10 minutes more or until bacon starts to crisp. Then remove from oven, place birds in serving dish, and keep warm. Pour juices from foil into a sauté pan and quickly reduce over high heat. Add heavy cream and finish sauce. Adjust seasonings and pour over birds. Garnish with parsley.

Serves 2.

FISH AND SEAFOOD

 *THE INN AT DUCK CREEK*
Wellfleet, Massachusetts 

POACHED HADDOCK WITH LEEKS AND MUSSELS AND A JULIENNE OF VEGETABLES

"This is a popular combination of local fish and mussels with a touch of color."

½ cup each fine julienne strips of celery, carrots, and zucchini (1½ inches by ¼ inch)
1 cup water (reserved from cooking vegetables)
2 pounds haddock or cod
4 dozen mussels
1 cup dry white wine
½ cup finely sliced leeks or scallions
½ cup heavy cream
¼ teaspoon nutmeg
2 tablespoons freshly chopped parsley
Salt and pepper to taste
¼ cup butter

In a saucepan cook the julienne vegetables in water to cover. Cook till tender but still firm. Strain, reserving 1 cup of water to poach the fish.

Portion fish. Scrub and de-beard mussels. Bring water, wine, and sliced leeks to a simmer. Add mussels, cover, and steam 5 minutes until they have opened. Remove mussels from shells. Save some shells for garnish. Strain liquid into a large skillet and add fish. Cover and gently simmer for 8-10 minutes or until fish is flaky. Transfer to an oven-proof casserole and keep warm in the oven.

Reduce liquid quickly to ½ cup. Add cream, seasonings, and butter in small pieces, whisking constantly. Add the mussels and parsley and heat through. Pour sauce over fish. Top with julienne of carrots, celery, and zucchini and garnish with mussel shells.

Serves 6.

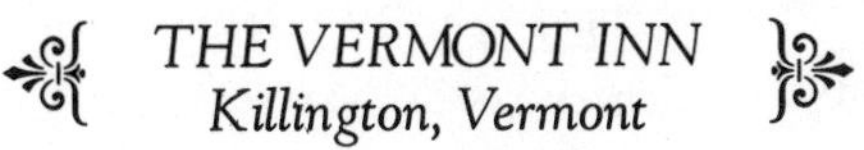

THE VERMONT INN
Killington, Vermont

FRESH BOSTON SCROD À LA MAISON

An outstanding way to prepare fish fillets — coated with buttermilk batter and bread crumbs, then baked until golden and slightly crisp.

1 cup heavy mayonnaise
1 cup buttermilk
1 cup lemon juice
1 teaspoon granulated garlic
Salt and pepper to taste
8 filets of fresh Boston scrod (6 ounces each)
2 cups bread crumbs
Lemon garnish

Mix first 5 ingredients to form a batter; coat fish filets with batter and then with bread crumbs; bake at 450° for 12-15 minutes on greased baking sheet. Serve with lemon garnish. *Serves 8.*

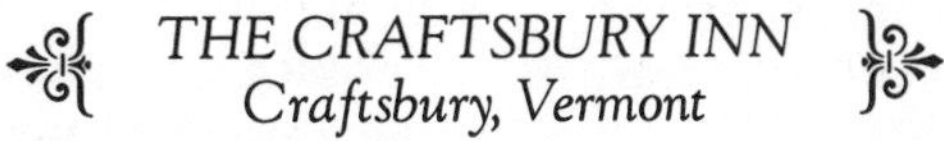

THE CRAFTSBURY INN
Craftsbury, Vermont

CRAFTSBURY INN FILET OF SOLE

A fine company dish but easy enough to make anytime.

1 stick sweet butter
½ cup sliced fresh mushrooms
½ cup chopped fresh tomato, skin and seeds removed
¼ cup diced shallots
1 clove garlic, minced
2 teaspoons capers
6 filets of sole (6 ounces each)
Juice of ½ lemon
Flour
1 egg beaten with 2 tablespoons cream
¼ stick butter

Make sauce by melting 1 stick butter in skillet, then adding mushrooms, tomato, shallots, garlic, and capers. Sauté for 3-4 minutes and keep warm while preparing fish.

Sprinkle filets with lemon juice and dust with flour. Dip in egg mixture. Heat ¼ stick butter in pan and brown fish for about 1½ minutes on each side. Place filets on serving dish, cover with sauce, and serve with lemon wedges. *Serves 6.*

SOLE SUCCESSO CENTER LOVELL INN

Fresh vegetables cooked tender-crisp, topped with sautéed filet of sole, and garnished with herbs from the garden.

1 cup butter
2 sweet red peppers, cut into strips (seeds and membrane removed)
1 small onion, chopped
2 cups Italian green beans, cut into 2-inch pieces
1/2 teaspoon rosemary
1/2 pound small zucchini, sliced
1 clove garlic, minced
4 tomatoes, peeled, seeded, drained, and chopped
Salt and pepper to taste
6 small sole filets (or 2 to 3 large filets, cut into 6 servings)
Flour
1 tablespoon chopped parsley
1 teaspoon chopped basil

Sauté separately each of the following in 2 tablespoons of butter until tender-crisp: pepper strips, onion, Italian green beans with rosemary, zucchini with garlic. Remove to casserole and keep warm. Then melt 1 tablespoon butter, add tomatoes, season with salt and pepper, and cook for about 10 minutes. Dust filets with flour and melt remaining butter in large frying pan until it is browned (nut colored). Sauté filets over fairly high heat, approximately 3 minutes on each side. Mix all hot vegetables on serving platter, arrange filets over the top, and garnish with fresh parsley and basil.

Serves 6.

SPRUCE POINT INN
Boothbay Harbor, Maine

FILET OF SOLE

Good and simple.

1 medium onion, minced
1 stick oleo or butter
1 roll Ritz crackers, crumbled
2 tablespoons water
1 pound filet of sole
1 can cream of celery soup
½ pint sour cream

Sauté onion in butter and pour over cracker crumbs. Add water to hold mixture together. Spread on filets, roll up, and pin each with toothpick. Put in baking dish. Cover with cream of celery soup combined with sour cream. Bake at 350° for 30 minutes.

Serves 4.

THE BLACKBERRY RIVER INN
Norfolk, Connecticut

SOLE DIJONNAISE

Sautèed fish filets topped with a mustard and wine sauce.

2½ pounds filet of sole
3 eggs, beaten with ¼ cup water
Flour
5 ounces butter
4 ounces leeks, sliced
5 ounces water chestnuts, sliced
6 ounces artichoke hearts, sliced
2½ ounces white wine
1 tablespoon Dijon mustard

Dip fish into egg wash, then flour. Heat 4 ounces butter in large sautè pan. When butter bubbles, place fish in pan; remove when golden brown on both sides. In same pan sautè leeks, water chestnuts, and artichoke hearts until golden. Add wine and reduce liquid by one third; add remaining 1 tablespoon butter and mustard. Pour over fish.

Serves 4-6.

CHEZ PIERRE'S POACHED FLOUNDER WITH SPINACH CREAM SAUCE

It takes some time (and an assortment of pots and pans) to make this, but your efforts will not be in vain.

2 pounds spinach
4 cups heavy cream
Salt and pepper
6 very large white mushrooms (Pennsylvania-type)
4 pounds filet of flounder (or other white-flesh fish such as sole)
6 scallions, julienne
2 to 3 cups dry white vermouth (just enough to come halfway up sides of fish)
4 shallots, coarsely chopped
Puff pastry crescents (optional)

Clean spinach. Steam in a small amount of water, drain, and purée. Set aside and keep warm. In a pan, bring heavy cream to a soft boil and allow to reduce in volume by half. (This may take a while.) Gradually add reduced cream to spinach purée until desired thickness and color of sauce is obtained. (Keep in mind that sauce will thin out when fish is added.) Add salt and pepper to taste and keep warm. Slice each mushroom individually in thin slices (about 8 slices) and place in order of slicing down the entire length of each filet of fish. Top each filet with julienne scallions.

In a large pan, bring vermouth and shallots to a simmer (thyme, parsley, and a slice of onion may be added to enhance the poaching liquid). Place fish filets in simmering liquid, cover, and cook at about 180° (liquid should be "trembling," not actually simmering) until fish is just cooked through, about 3-5 minutes depending on thickness. Ladle spinach cream sauce onto individual warmed plates. Carefully remove each filet with slotted spatula, tipping against a paper towel to drain excess moisture. Then lay gently on the spinach sauce. Garnish with puff pastry crescent if desired. Serve immediately. *Serves 6.*

SEABASS WITH FRESH DILL SAUCE

Fish baked in white wine and sauced with dill cream.

1 tablespoon chopped shallots
1 seabass filet (6 ounces)
½ cup white wine
Salt
Pepper

Sprinkle shallots in ovenproof pan, place salted and peppered fish in pan, pour on white wine, and place in 400° oven, uncovered, for 6-8 minutes.

DILL SAUCE

¼ cup fish stock
½ cup white wine
2 cups heavy cream
1 tablespoon butter
2 tablespoons fresh dill
Salt and pepper to taste

Reduce stock and wine in saucepan by half. Add half the cream and reduce till thickened. Add remaining cream and reduce to sauce consistency. Whisk in butter, add fresh dill and salt and pepper to taste, and spoon over fish. *Serves 1.*

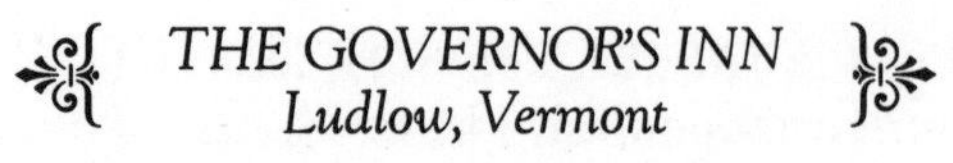

THE GOVERNOR'S INN
Ludlow, Vermont

BLUEFISH FLAMBÉ WITH GIN

"When bluefish is available, the kitchen at The Governor's Inn virtually hums with new ideas for presenting this lovely fish. Gin gives it a splendid flavor."

4 bluefish filets (about 1/2 pound each)
4 tablespoons unsalted butter, melted
3 tablespoons minced onion
1/2 teaspoon salt
1/4 teaspoon freshly ground pepper
7 tablespoons gin

Grease a broiler pan that is just large enough to accommodate the filets and place them in the pan side by side. Pour half the melted butter over the fish and sprinkle with the onion, salt, and pepper. Place the pan 3 inches below broiler and let the fish start to brown. Meanwhile mix gin with remaining butter and heat until warm. When fish is "just done" remove pan from broiler. Pour warmed gin-butter mixture over fish and ignite. Serve when flame has died. *Serves 4.*

THE INN ON LAKE WARAMAUG
New Preston, Connecticut

TROUT CLEOPATRA

A superior dish that can be prepared in less than 15 minutes.

6 small trout
Milk
Flour
1/4 pound butter (1 stick)
3 lemons
4 ounces bay shrimp
4 tablespoons capers
Chopped parsley

Dip trout in milk and then in flour and fry them in lightly browned butter, using about 2/3 of a stick. Squeeze juice of 1 lemon over trout. In separate pan, put rest of butter, trimmed wedges of 2 lemons, shrimp, and capers and cook until butter is lightly browned. Pour over trout, sprinkle with chopped parsley, and serve. *Serves 6.*

CHEZ PIERRE AT THE CHARLOTTE INN 
Edgartown (Martha's Vineyard), Massachusetts

CHEZ PIERRE'S LOBSTER À LA CRÈME

You will savor every mouthful of this elaborate dish. Make it for an anniversary celebration or small dinner party.

2 lobsters (1½ pounds each)
6 tablespoons unsalted butter
½ cup white wine
¼ cup cognac
2 cups heavy cream, brought to a soft boil and reduced in volume to 1 cup
Cayenne pepper

Drop lobsters in boiling water just until cracker claw turns red. Remove from water and cool. Separate tail, claws, and joints of lobsters. Turn tails over to expose undersides and by placing a large, sharp knife between the sections, cut each tail into 4 medallion-like sections, using sudden, cleaver-like motions. With poultry shears, cut underside of each claw and remove enough of the shell so that meat is well exposed.

In a skillet, heat the butter and wine, then add lobster sections, larger pieces first, smaller last for even cooking. Sauté until lobster turns bright red and flesh is white. (One dozen scrubbed and de-bearded mussels may also be added. They will open when cooked and then should be used as a garnish on either side of lobster.)

Remove skillet from heat source, add cognac, and light with a match. Flambé until flame extinguishes. Return to heat only briefly and gently. Shake pan to incorporate flavors. Remove lobster and keep warm.

Add reduced cream to the pan and season with a dash of cayenne pepper. Reduce by half or until a light golden color.

To serve, arrange each lobster attractively on a heated dinner plate. Strive to reassemble lobster as much as possible. Tail sections should be replaced in order, with joints on either side, ending in claws, which are placed with the exposed part on the bottom. Serve with sauce on the side or in individual ramekins; place parsley sprig in each claw and serve immediately. *Serves 2.*

COONAMESSETT LOBSTER PIE

Extremely rich and undeniably delicious. Serve with a dry white wine and tossed salad.

1 tablespoon finely chopped shallots
1/2 pound fresh mushrooms, sliced
3 ounces butter
6 ounces sherry
1 1/2 pounds cooked fresh lobster meat, cut in 1-inch chunks
2 ounces brandy
1/2 teaspoon dry mustard
1/4 tablespoon lobster base (available from gourmet food shops and some seafood markets)
1/4 teaspoon Worcestershire sauce
2 drops Tabasco sauce
1 quart heavy cream sauce (made from 1 quart milk, 1/4 pound butter, and 1/4 pound flour)
1 pound crushed potato chips, moistened with drawn butter

Sauté shallots and mushrooms in butter until tender. Add sherry and lobster meat and cook 3 minutes. Add brandy and flame. Stir in remaining ingredients, except potato chips, and bring to boil. Cook 5 minutes. Pour into deep casserole dish, cover with 1/4-inch-thick layer of moistened potato chips, and bake in 350° oven for 15-20 minutes or until brown and bubbly.

Serves 6-8.

PUBLICK HOUSE INDIVIDUAL LOBSTER PIE

Excellent! Beautiful color and just the right thickness. Accompany with rice.

8 tablespoons melted butter
4 tablespoons flour
1 pint hot milk
1 pint light cream
1 pound lobster meat
1/2 teaspoon paprika
1/3 cup sherry wine
Pinch cayenne pepper
1 teaspoon salt
4 egg yolks
Topping (recipe follows)

Combine 4 tablespoons melted butter with flour in saucepan. Cook over low heat (do not brown). Add hot milk, then slowly add light cream; cook 15 minutes stirring often. Strain and set aside. Sauté lobster meat in paprika and remaining butter. Add 1/4 cup sherry and cook for another 3 minutes. Add the cayenne pepper and salt and the thin cream sauce. Blend 4 tablespoons of the sauce into the egg yolks, then stir this back into the whole mixture. Stir until the Newburg bubbles and thickens, take off the fire, and stir in the remaining sherry.

Spoon the Newburg into casseroles, making sure to distribute the lobster meat evenly. Sprinkle with topping and brown in 400° oven. *Serves 6.*

TOPPING

3/4 cup grated fresh bread crumbs
3/4 teaspoon paprika
3 tablespoons crushed potato chips
1 tablespoon Parmesan cheese
5 tablespoons melted butter

Mix together until well blended.

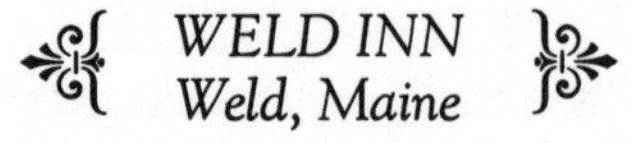

WELD INN
Weld, Maine

SAUTÉED SCALLOPS

"One of our most popular dishes. We serve it winter or summer."

1½ pounds scallops
1 cup flour
¼ teaspoon garlic powder
½ teaspoon paprika
¼ cup melted butter
½ cup white wine

Dredge scallops in flour mixed with seasonings. (Scallops should be dry so flour will stick to them.) Sauté in butter for about 3 minutes or until nicely brown. Add wine, cover, and simmer 3-5 minutes. *Serves 4.*

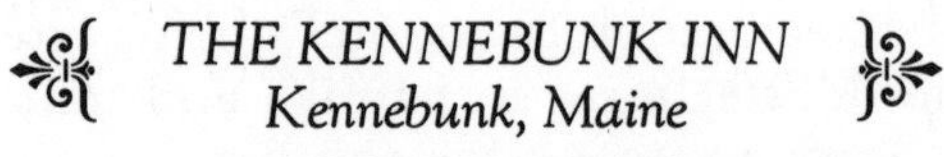

THE KENNEBUNK INN
Kennebunk, Maine

ALAN'S COQUILLES PÊCHE ROYALE

A house specialty that unites the subtle flavor of scallops with the sweetness of peaches and a touch of spice.

1 medium onion, chopped fine
¼ pound butter (1 stick)
1 pound fresh scallops
⅛ teaspoon garlic
Parsley flakes
⅛ teaspoon cinnamon
8 canned peach halves (reserve juice)
Ritz cracker crumbs

Sauté onion in butter until clear and light brown, 2-3 minutes. Add scallops and sauté until just mixed with onion. Add garlic, parsley, cinnamon, and juice from peaches.

In a 2-quart casserole (or four individual casseroles), place the peach halves (2 per individual dish), cut side up, and cover with scallop mixture. Top with Ritz cracker crumbs and bake at 350° until liquid bubbles and crumbs are golden brown.

Serves 4.

AUBERGINE
Camden, Maine

SCALLOPS WITH GINGER AND VEGETABLES

Be careful that you don't overcook the scallops or allow the vegetables to lose color as the visual quality will be diminished.

1 pound fresh sea or bay scallops
1 cup broccoli florets, blanched
1/2 pound baby carrots, peeled, halved, and blanched
1/2 cup asparagus spears, blanched
2 tablespoons finely chopped fresh ginger
3 tablespoons chopped fresh parsley, chives, lemon balm, or a combination
3 tablespoons clarified butter
1 cup fish stock or bottled clam juice
1/2 to 1 pint whipping cream
Salt and pepper

Clean scallops of muscle or grit and set aside. Prepare blanched vegetables and chopped fresh ginger and fresh herbs. Put clarified butter in 10-inch sauté pan and heat until smoking. (If butter burns too quickly, add 1-2 tablespoons good olive oil and try again.) Add scallops and allow to brown before shaking pan. After well browned add chopped ginger and allow to cook for 1-2 minutes. Add fish stock and let reduce slightly. Add cream, vegetables, salt and pepper, and herbs and continue cooking until heated and slightly reduced. Serve with pasta or risotto.

Serves 4.

NORWICH INN SCALLOPS

Ready to serve in about half an hour, this makes entertaining seem effortless. The dash of allspice adds a unique touch.

1 pound baby sea scallops or bay scallops
20 Ritz crackers
Salt
Pepper
Allspice
1 teaspoon minced red Italian onion
1 teaspoon minced green top of leek or scallion
½ clove garlic, minced
1 teaspoon lemon juice
¼ cup butter, at room temperature
¼ cup dry sherry
Lemon wedges

Preheat oven to 350°. Wash scallops and dry on paper towels. If large sea scallops are used, cut them in thirds. In a blender or food processor pulverize crackers to a fine powder. Empty onto a plate and stir in pinches of salt, pepper, and allspice. With a spoon or the fingers, knead minced onion, leek or scallion, garlic, and lemon juice into the butter. Roll scallops in powdered crackers until thoroughly coated. Shake off excess and place scallops in a casserole. Dot with the prepared butter and add sherry. Place in oven and bake just until tender, 15-20 minutes. Whisk under broiler about half a minute to lightly brown scallop tops. Serve with lemon wedges. *Serves 4.*

SCALLOPS SCAMPI WITH LEMON RICE

Don't skimp on the garlic for it's important to the balance of flavors and is not at all overwhelming.

1 cup rice
1½ cups water
Juice and grated peel of 1 lemon
½ teaspoon salt
1 tablespoon salad oil
1½ pounds bay scallops, or cut-up sea scallops
¼ pound butter
4 cloves garlic, crushed
Lemon wedges for garnish
Fresh parsley

Cook rice in water, lemon juice, salt, and oil. When liquid is absorbed, remove rice from heat and add grated lemon peel. Hold the rice in a warm dish until scallops are done.

Sauté scallops in butter with garlic until tender. Remove garlic and pour scallops and butter over cooked lemon rice. Serve with garnish of lemon wedges and sprigs of fresh parsley.

Serves 5-6.

SAUTÉ OF SCALLOPS AND CHANTERELLES

This can be prepared in advance, with the cream added just before serving. It makes an impressive entrée or appetizer.

1/4 cup butter
2 tablespoons chopped shallots
1 pound bay scallops
1/2 pound chanterelles
2 tablespoons flour
1/4 cup dry sherry
1/4 cup hot water
1 tablespoon seasoning mix (recipe follows)
1/4 cup medium cream

In a large frying pan melt butter over medium flame. Add shallots and brown lightly. Add scallops and chanterelles and cook until scallops are almost done. Add flour, stirring to blend well. Add sherry and flame. Stir in water and seasoning mix and blend well. Add cream and heat thoroughly. Serve hot in scallop shells and garnish with fresh parsley. *Serves 4-6.*

SEASONING MIX

1 cup salt
1 cup monosodium glutamate
2 tablespoons white pepper
1 tablespoon garlic powder
1 tablespoon onion powder

Mix well and store in a sealed jar.

SUGAR HILL INN
Franconia, New Hampshire

GARLIC AND WINE SCALLOPS

Broiled scallops with a buttery cracker-crumb topping.

1½ pounds scallops
2 to 3 cloves garlic, split
4 tablespoons butter
2 tablespoons minced scallions or green onions
2 tablespoons chopped parsley
½ teaspoon salt
¼ teaspoon pepper
¼ cup dry white wine
8 to 10 Ritz crackers, crumbled

Wash and dry scallops. Brown garlic in half the butter (2 tablespoons), then remove garlic and discard. Add onions, parsley, and seasonings. Place scallops in shallow baking dish and pour seasoned butter over them. Let stand in refrigerator until just before serving time. Then add wine and broil 3-4 minutes. Turn and broil for same length of time on other side. A minute before scallops are done, add crumbled Ritz crackers that have been sautéed in the remaining 2 tablespoons butter. Broil until topping is browned. *Serves 6.*

CHEZ PIERRE AT THE CHARLOTTE INN
Edgartown (Martha's Vineyard), Massachusetts

FRESH SEAFOOD MARINADE CHEZ PIERRE

This tastes wonderful no matter how it's presented, but arranging it artistically on each plate is half the fun and turns it into a spectacular-looking dish.

1 medium-sized filet of flounder
6 oysters, shucked
24 bay scallops (or 12 sea scallops, sliced in half)
Juice of 6 limes
Juice of 2 lemons
6 small shallots, coarsely chopped
Salt and freshly ground pepper to taste
Mustard Sauce (recipe follows)
Scallions and radishes for garnish

Slice flounder into 1-inch strips. Line bottom of glass or ceramic dish with fish and seafood. (It is important that the pieces not overlap or crowd each other.) Pour lime and lemon juice over fish and seafood (juices should come half way up the thickest piece). Sprinkle with chopped shallots, season with salt and pepper, cover, and refrigerate 1½ hours. Turn pieces over, cover, and refrigerate 1½ hours more. To serve, divide fish and seafood evenly among 6 small chilled plates and arrange attractively by fanning out strips of fish and creating a design with oysters and scallops. Add 1 teaspoon Mustard Sauce to one side of each plate and garnish with very thin strips of scallions and with radish slices. Discard juice. *Serves* 6.

MUSTARD SAUCE

¼ cup heavy cream
⅓ cup sour cream
2 tablespoons Dijon-style mustard

Whip heavy cream until soft peaks form. Combine with sour cream and mustard and stir until smooth and well mixed. Cover and chill until needed. (These portions will make more sauce than is necessary for 6 servings, but it is difficult to make it in smaller quantities. Extra sauce may be used over vegetables or salad.)

BROILED SEAFOOD KABOB

Parboiling the vegetables first is the secret step in this popular entrée.

12 ounces sea scallops
8 shrimp, peeled but leaving tail shells on
12 ounces haddock
16 chunks onion (parboiled 2 minutes)
16 chunks green peppers (parboiled 2 minutes)

On each of 8 bamboo or stainless steel skewers place 1½ ounces each scallops and haddock, 1 shrimp, and 2 chunks each onion and green pepper, alternating seafood and vegetables on the skewer.

MARINADE

12 ounces beer
½ cup salad oil
1 large clove garlic, minced
4 ounces onion, chopped very fine
¼ cup fresh lemon juice
1 teaspoon salt
½ teaspoon fresh ground pepper
1 teaspoon mustard powder

Combine all ingredients, mix well, and pour over kabobs. Marinate for at least 3 hours.

When ready to cook kabobs remove them from marinade and place on a broiler rack with a drip pan under it. Broil 10-12 minutes, turning once. While broiling, baste with butter. Serve 2 skewers on a bed of your favorite rice with drawn butter. Spoon drippings over each kabob. *Serves 4.*

TROPICAL SEAFOOD AND MELON BROCHETTES

"This dish can be done under the broiler but is also a great treat at summer barbecues. It leaves the creativity and quantity of seafood and fruit to the cook as it is assembled on skewers, and it's interesting to vary the arrangements." Use wooden skewers that have been soaked in water.

8 ounces butter
1 cup finely chopped scallions
Juice of 1 lemon and 1 lime
1 tablespoon chopped fresh parsley
1 teaspoon each of oregano, basil, thyme, garlic, nutmeg, and black pepper
1/4 cup Augo or Sambucca
1/2 swordfish steak per person, cut in chunks
Scallops and shrimp
Honeydew and cantaloupe balls
Mango, pineapple, and green pepper cut in chunks

Melt butter in small saucepan. Remove from heat and stir in the scallions, lemon and lime juices, herbs and spices, and liqueur. Place seafood in a glass or ceramic bowl and cover with marinade. Marinate for at least 1 hour before cooking. During this period, soak the wooden skewers in water to keep them from burning while cooking.

To assemble brochettes, alternate marinated seafood with fruits and green pepper. Baste brochettes with marinade during broiling or barbecueing. Fish will be done when firm but tender.

Quantity is determined by the cook.

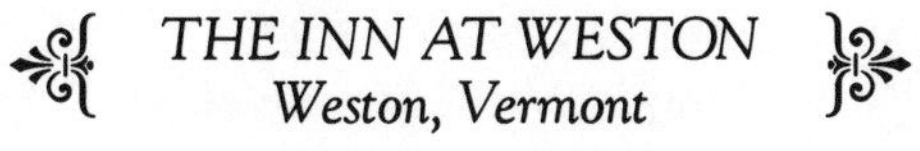
THE INN AT WESTON
Weston, Vermont

FLORENTINE DE MER

Attractive little packages of browned pastry filled with a spinach and seafood combination that appeals to children as well as adults.

¾ pound filet of scrod
½ pound sea scallops
Poaching liquid (recipe follows)
1½ cups chopped cooked spinach
2 shallots, minced
4 tablespoons heavy cream
1 tablespoon lemon juice
Dash nutmeg
¼ teaspoon each salt and pepper
1 package filo pastry
Melted butter

Place seafood in poaching liquid and bring to boil. Reduce heat and simmer 3 minutes. Remove seafood. Cut into 1-inch pieces. Combine with spinach, shallots, cream, lemon juice, nutmeg, and salt and pepper. Lay out 2 sheets of filo dough and brush with melted butter. Top with 2 more sheets, brushing with butter. Cut in half. Place ¼ of filling on each half. Bring in sides and roll up sheet to make a small packet. Place on buttered baking sheet. Repeat process with remaining filo. Bake at 400° till brown (10-15 minutes). Lower heat to 325°. Bake 5-10 minutes. Top with hollandaise, if desired. *Serves 4.*

POACHING LIQUID

1 cup water
½ cup dry white wine
¼ onion, chopped
1 sprig parsley
1 celery top
1 bay leaf
Pinch thyme

Combine ingredients and proceed as described above.

SHRIMP PARMESAN

This makes an elegant presentation. Somewhat similar to scampi, with a few more herbs to boot. Accompany with glazed carrots and French bread.

1 cup vegetable oil
1 cup dry white wine
2 cloves garlic, crushed
1 teaspoon parsley flakes
1 teaspoon tarragon
1 teaspoon oregano leaves
1 teaspoon lemon juice
Dash Worcestershire sauce
1/2 teaspoon salt
1/4 teaspoon fresh ground pepper
1 1/2 pounds large shrimp (18 to 22), peeled
1/2 stick butter
1/3 cup bread crumbs
8 ounces cooked spinach linguine noodles
1/2 cup grated Parmesan cheese

Prepare marinade of oil, wine, garlic, parsley flakes, tarragon, oregano, lemon juice, Worcestershire sauce, salt, and pepper. Marinate peeled shrimp at least 4 hours in refrigerator. Remove shrimp to shallow 12x9-inch baking dish, fitting them in a single layer as tightly together as possible. Spoon about 1/4 of the marinade over the shrimp and dot the top with pats of butter. Sprinkle bread crumbs lightly over the top. Bake in preheated 500° oven 15-25 minutes or until crumbs are nicely browned. Sprinkle Parmesan cheese over individual servings of spinach linguine and place shrimp and a little cooked marinade over each. *Serves 4.*

PASQUANEY SHRIMP

This has a light, delicate taste so do not be tempted to add cheese! If using frozen shrimp, cook them according to package directions, drain, and add along with the herbs and seasonings.

1/4 cup each thin julienne strips of carrots, celery, and green or red peppers
2 tablespoons butter
1/2 cup dry white wine
2 pounds fresh, unfrozen shrimp
1 teaspoon finely chopped parsley
1 teaspoon finely chopped fresh basil leaves, or 1/2 teaspoon dried
1 large clove garlic, crushed
1/4 teaspoon salt
1/8 teaspoon pepper
1 teaspoon all-purpose flour
1 tablespoon soft butter
1/2 cup heavy cream
6 puff pastry shells
Parsley

Stir-fry vegetables in a fry pan in 2 tablespoons butter for 1 minute. Add wine and shrimp and simmer for 3 minutes; stir in herbs and seasonings. (If using cooked frozen shrimp, add now.) Blend together flour and soft butter. Push shrimp and vegetables to the side of the pan and whisk in butter-flour mixture. Cook and stir until slightly thickened, then stir in the cream and mix in shrimp and vegetables. Spoon into puff pastry shells and lightly sprinkle with parsley. *Serves* 6.

SHRIMP MEDITERRANEAN

Festive, exotic, and aromatic. The delicate sauce is flavorful but does not overpower the shrimp. This recipe can easily be increased to yield more servings.

2 ounces corn oil
7 medium-sized shrimp, peeled, deveined, tails removed
1/4 cup flour
1/2 teaspoon capers
1/2 tomato, cut into large dice
3 artichoke hearts, cut in half
1/4 teaspoon Herbs de Provence
Dash lemon juice
Dash Tabasco sauce
1 ounce sauterne
1 1/2 ounces butter

In a medium-sized pan, heat oil. Coat shrimp with flour, shake off excess, and sauté shrimp only until they are just cooked (approximately 3 minutes). Remove from heat, drain off oil, and add capers, tomato, artichoke hearts, herbs, lemon juice, and Tabasco sauce. Place over high heat, add the sauterne, and allow to boil. Add butter to the pan, moving on the heat constantly until the butter becomes creamy. Place in a small dish and serve at once. Sprinkle with chopped parsley. *Serves 1.*

BAKED STUFFED SHRIMP

"The secret to this entrée is in the crumbs, which are made from our homemade croutons. We prepare them in large batches for they are also marvelous with soups and salads."

16 to 20 jumbo shrimp
1 1/3 cups crab meat
Buttered fine bread crumbs, made from croutons (recipe follows)

Place shrimp in 4 individual casserole dishes with the tails up. Place crab meat in center of shrimp. Use as much of the bread crumbs as necessary to cover the crab meat and part of the shrimp (scant 1/4 cup per serving). Bake in preheated 350° oven 15 minutes or until brown. *Serves 4.*

CROUTONS

Cubed white bread (1 loaf)
Garlic powder to taste
Paprika
Melted butter to moisten
Parmesan cheese to taste

Mix all but last ingredient together and bake in 350° oven for 5 minutes. When toasted, toss with Parmesan cheese.

SEAFOOD STROGANOFF

A nice change of pace for a buffet dinner or a special luncheon. Cut-up cooked chicken may be substituted to create an elegant chicken à la king.

- **1/4 cup butter or margarine**
- **3 tablespoons flour**
- **1 clove garlic, minced**
- **1/2 cup chopped onion**
- **1 1/2 cups chicken broth**
- **1 teaspoon Worcestershire sauce**
- **1/8 teaspoon Tabasco (optional)**
- **1/4 teaspoon salt**
- **2 tablespoons chopped parsley**
- **1 cup commercial sour cream**
- **1/2 pound cooked shrimp or crab or a combination**
- **1 can (4 ounces) chopped mushrooms**

Melt butter in top of double boiler. Stir in flour, garlic, and onion. Add chicken broth and seasonings and cook until thickened. Just before serving add sour cream, seafood, and mushrooms. Serve on patty shells or over rice or noodles. *Serves 5.*

AUBERGINE
Camden, Maine

PASTA WITH SAFFRON AND CRAB AUBERGINE

Fettuccini tossed with a sumptuous sauce. Cooking down the 4 cups of heavy cream takes some time so don't prepare this if you're in a hurry.

2 tablespoons dry vermouth
1/4 teaspoon crushed saffron threads
1 cup dry white wine
1/2 cup minced shallots
2 cloves garlic, sliced thin
2 tablespoons dried basil
1 teaspoon dried tarragon
4 cups heavy cream
3 tablespoons each minced fresh parsley and fresh basil
Salt and pepper to taste
1 pound lump crab meat, picked over
3/4 pound fettuccini, cooked

In a small bowl combine dry vermouth and crushed saffron threads. In a stainless steel or enameled saucepan combine dry white wine, shallots, garlic, dried basil, and dried tarragon and bring to a boil; reduce over high heat until almost completely evaporated. Add heavy cream and simmer the mixture, stirring occasionally, until it is reduced to about 2½ cups (this may take awhile). Strain mixture through a fine sieve into another stainless steel or enameled saucepan, bring to a boil over moderate heat, and stir in the saffron mixture, parsley, basil, and salt and pepper to taste. Add crab meat and simmer the mixture until the crab meat is heated through. In a heated serving bowl toss the sauce with the fettuccini. *Serves 6 as a main course.*

COLBY HILL INN
Henniker, New Hampshire

CRAB IMPERIAL

Simple, colorful, and quick — perfect for a dinner party.

1 pound lump crab meat
4 tablespoons mayonnaise
½ cup chopped green pepper, sautéed in butter
1 teaspoon salt
½ cup pimiento
1 teaspoon Worcestershire sauce
½ cup bread crumbs (fresh or dry)
Cayenne to taste

Place all ingredients in large mixing bowl and mix thoroughly. Fill ceramic crab shells with mixture and bake at 350° for 30 minutes. *Serves 4.*

LINCOLN HOUSE COUNTRY INN
Dennysville, Maine

CLAMS PENNAMAQUAN

"The coast of Maine is rich in clams, one of the best areas being the Pennamaquan River and the Cobscook Bay. Folks here can tell by looking at a clam from which bay it was dug and during which recent tide!"

1 pound Monterey Jack cheese, shredded
1 pound clams, shucked and chopped
2 tablespoons parsley
2 tablespoons chives
2 cloves garlic, finely minced
Dash ground cayenne pepper
Dash freshly ground black pepper
6 slices pumpernickel bread

Combine cheese, clams, parsley, chives, garlic, and peppers and mix until well blended. For each serving, place bread slice in 6-ounce au gratin dish. Divide clam mixture among dishes. Broil until golden brown and bubbly or bake at 425° for 10 minutes or until golden brown and bubbly. Serve immediately. *Serves 6.*

BEEF AND VEAL

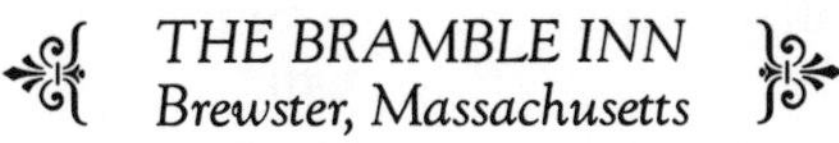

THE BRAMBLE INN
Brewster, Massachusetts

CARBONNADE DE BOEUF BOURGUIGNON

One of the specialties of The Bramble Inn. At its best if cooked a day in advance.

3 pounds beef rump, cut in 2-inch cubes
1 cup red Burgundy wine
2 whole cloves
1 large bay leaf
8 peppercorns, crushed
1 teaspoon salt
1 clove garlic
4 slices bacon, cut small
1 small clove garlic
2 cups beef stock
2 bouquets garnis
4 carrots, sliced
4 onions, sliced
¾ pound mushrooms, sliced
1 medium turnip, cut bite-sized

Marinate meat cubes in mixture of wine, cloves, bay leaf, peppercorns, salt, and 1 clove garlic for 1 hour in refrigerator, stirring occasionally. Fry bacon over low heat. Drain meat, save marinade, and add meat to bacon with 1 small garlic clove. Sear meat over high heat till well browned. Put meat and bacon fat into flameproof 4-quart casserole. Add marinade, heated to boiling point, beef stock, and bouquets garnis. Boil mixture for 10 minutes. Lower heat and simmer for 30 minutes. Add carrots, onions, mushrooms, and turnip. Bake covered in 350° oven for 1½ hours. Discard bouquets garnis and bay leaf and garnish with chopped parsley. *Serves* 6.

TENDERLOIN FILET AU POIVRE

The filets are sautéed because the pan in which they are cooked is vital to the making of the sauce.

¼ cup crushed black peppercorns (coarse)
4 tenderloin filets (8 ounces each), bound with a strip of lean bacon
4 ounces clarified butter
½ cup brandy
1 cup chicken velouté (recipe follows)
1 cup crème fraîche (recipe follows)
⅓ cup chopped green onions
Salt

Work the crushed peppercorns into each side of the steaks; more or less may be used according to personal preference. Sauté filets in butter until cooked as desired. Remove and hold. Drain excess grease from pan, add brandy, and boil. Add velouté and crème fraîche and bring to simmer. Add green onions, salt to taste, and serve to accompany filets. *Serves 4.*

CHICKEN VELOUTÉ

6 teaspoons butter
6 teaspoons flour
4 cups white poultry stock

Melt the butter over low heat in a saucepan. Stir in the flour. Moisten with small amount of stock. Gradually add rest of the stock, stirring all the while. Simmer for about 19 minutes. Strain and hold. *Makes about 4 cups.*

CRÈME FRAÎCHE

4 ounces buttermilk
4 ounces heavy cream

Combine ingredients and heat in double boiler (stainless steel or glass) to lukewarm (85°); allow to stand at room temperature until thickened. Temperature should not go below 60° nor higher than 85°. In very hot weather it may thicken in as little as 6 hours; in cooler weather, it may take 36 hours. Crème fraîche can be stored in refrigerator for about 1 week. *Makes about 1 cup.*

TOURNEDOS HANOVER INN

Crispy, golden potato pancakes topped with mouth-watering filets of beef and accompanied by spicy apple chips.

POTATO PANCAKES

2 medium raw potatoes, grated and squeezed dry
1 small onion, grated
Salt and pepper
1 egg
Flour
Butter or oil for frying

Mix together potatoes, onion, seasonings, and egg. Add enough flour to bind and make a moist batter. Spoon into frying pan and fry to golden brown on both sides.

CINNAMON APPLE CHIPS

2 cups apple slices
1/4 cup sugar
1 tablespoon cinnamon
Butter

Toss apples with sugar and cinnamon and sauté in butter until tender.

TOURNEDOS

4 tenderloin beef filets (3 ounces each)
Butter

Sauté beef in butter to desired doneness.

To serve:

Arrange potato pancakes on platter and set tournedos on top with apple chips in center of platter. Serve with sour cream.

Serves 2.

YANKEE POT ROAST

This classic pot roast is an example of the traditional New England foods served at the Wayside Inn — "the oldest operating inn in the country."

1 bottom round roast (4 to 6 pounds)
½ cup oil
2 celery stalks
2 carrots
1 onion
1 can (1 pound) tomatoes
2 teaspoons salt
½ teaspoon black pepper
3 cups water
¼ cup flour
⅓ cup each cooked peas, cubed carrots, cut string beans
½ cup cooked, chopped celery

In Dutch oven, brown roast in oil with celery, carrots, and onions around meat. Add tomatoes, salt, and pepper and cover with water. Bring to boil and let simmer over low heat or in 350° oven for 2½ hours. Lift out roast; keep warm. Strain stock, discarding vegetables. Skim fat off stock, returning ¼ cup fat to Dutch oven; stir flour into fat and add 4 cups stock. Cook and stir until thickened. Check seasonings and add vegetables. Serve gravy with sliced beef.

Serves 12-15.

SPICY NEW ENGLAND POT ROAST

A spicy-sweet pot roast, perfect for dinner on a winter evening.

4 to 5 pounds beef roast (rump or round is good)
2 tablespoons vegetable oil or bacon grease
Flour
1/2 pound cranberries
1 cup water
1 cup sugar
1 large onion, chopped
2 cinnamon sticks (each 3 inches long), broken
1/2 cup red wine
1 1/2 cups beef broth
2 tablespoons horseradish

Place roast and oil in heavy Dutch oven. Brown well over medium heat. Pour off fat and combine with an equal amount of flour. Reserve. Combine cranberries, water, and sugar, bring to boil, and simmer 10 minutes. Stir in remaining ingredients and pour over roast. Simmer 3-4 hours. Strain liquid and combine with reserved fat and flour. Heat gently until sauce thickens. Serve with roast.

Serves 6-8.

THE INN ON LAKE WARAMAUG
New Preston, Connecticut

VEAL CHASSEUR

An entrée for holidays or special occasions. Make sure the veal is in thin escallops and use fresh, not dried, parsley.

Salt and pepper to taste
Flour
6 veal escallops (4 ounces each)
5 ounces clarified butter
1 small shallot, finely chopped
½ pound fresh mushrooms, sliced
¼ pint white wine
1 teaspoon tomato purée
¼ pint brown sauce
½ ounce butter
Chopped fresh parsley

Season and flour the veal and sauté in clarified butter. Remove from pan, sweat shallots in same pan, add mushrooms, and cook. Stir in wine and reduce by half. Add tomato purée and brown sauce. Bring to boil, add ½ ounce butter, stir to blend, and pour over veal. Sprinkle with parsley. *Serves 6.*

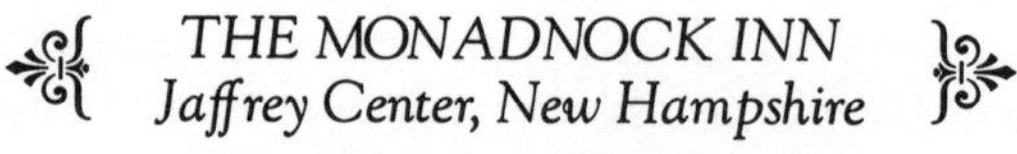

THE MONADNOCK INN
Jaffrey Center, New Hampshire

VEAL À L'INDIENNE

If you have a reliable source for veal, this is ideal for those spur-of-the-moment occasions that call for a touch of class.

2 tablespoons oil
1 pound veal cutlets, thinly sliced
1 cup flour
½ teaspoon curry powder
¼ cup chopped onion
½ cup white wine
½ cup heavy cream

Heat oil in large frying pan. Dredge cutlets in flour and sauté until lightly browned on one side. Turn cutlets over and sprinkle with curry powder. Brown second side, remove from pan, and keep warm. Drain oil from pan, return to heat, and add onions. Cook for 1 minute, then add white wine. Continue cooking until liquid is reduced to 1 tablespoon. Stir in heavy cream and cook 1-2 minutes longer until sauce thickens. Serve cutlets on a bed of rice and coat with sauce. *Serves 4.*

VEAL PICCATA

Lightly seasoned veal cutlets cooked to perfection — and they make a spectacular presentation!

4 leg veal cutlets (4 ounces each)
1 egg
2 tablespoons milk
1½ cups ground Ritz crackers
½ cup unseasoned bread crumbs
Dash each of black pepper, garlic salt, onion salt, seasoned salt, chives, oregano, chopped parsley, grated Parmesan cheese
Flour
½ cup clarified butter
2 lemons (1 quartered, 1 cut into 8 slices)
White wine
Parsley

Pound the cutlets until thin and cut each serving into 3 uniform slices. Beat together egg and milk. Mix together Ritz crackers, bread crumbs, spices, and Parmesan cheese. Dredge each individual slice of veal thoroughly in flour, shake off excess, dip in egg wash, and then dredge in bread crumb mixture. Heat butter in 1 or 2 large sauté pans on medium heat and slowly sauté veal until golden brown on each side. While veal is cooking, squeeze the lemon quarters over it (1 wedge for every 3 slices), then splash with white wine. When veal is almost done, arrange lemon slices on the outer edge of sauté pan, so they will be warm but not overcooked. To serve, alternate veal (3 slices per person) and lemon slices on each plate. Sprinkle with parsley and serve immediately.

Serves 4.

VEAL OSCAR WITH HOLLANDAISE SAUCE

Any leftover sauce will keep refrigerated for 2 to 3 days. To serve again, stir in a little hot water over low heat until heated through.

4 slices of veal (5 ounces each)
Flour seasoned with salt and pepper
4 tablespoons butter
1/4 cup crab meat
12 asparagus spears, cooked
Hollandaise Sauce (recipe follows)

Pound veal thin (or have your butcher do it), dredge in seasoned flour, and sauté in butter. Remove to serving platter. Place crab meat on top of veal and top each serving with 3 asparagus spears. Serve with Hollandaise Sauce. *Serves 4.*

HOLLANDAISE SAUCE

4 egg yolks, unbeaten
4 1/2 tablespoons fresh lemon juice
12 tablespoons frozen clarified butter
Salt and cayenne to taste
1/4 teaspoon Worcestershire sauce

Place egg yolks, lemon juice, and 6 tablespoons butter in small saucepan. Cook over low heat stirring continuously with wooden spoon. When butter has melted, add the remaining 6 tablespoons butter and stir until sauce thickens. Add salt, cayenne, and Worcestershire sauce. Serve over Veal Oscar or your favorite recipe. *Makes 1 1/2 cups.*

THE WHITE HOUSE
Wilmington, Vermont

WHITE HOUSE SALTIMBOCCA

Out of this world! You'll feel like a gourmet chef when you prepare (and consume) this entrée. The veal is cooked so briefly that it is moist and succulent and makes the perfect base for the flavors of prosciutto and nutty Swiss cheese.

Veal medallions (5 ounces total)
Prosciutto, thinly sliced
2 ounces Swiss cheese, grated
4 ounces fresh mushrooms

Pound medallions of veal until ⅛ inch thick. Place in large buttered skillet and sauté briefly. Remove from flame, turn medallions over, and place one slice of prosciutto on top of each. Sprinkle cheese on prosciutto and place mushrooms on side. Place skillet over low flame and simmer, covered, for 5 minutes or until cheese is melted. Remove from skillet and serve. *Serves 1.*

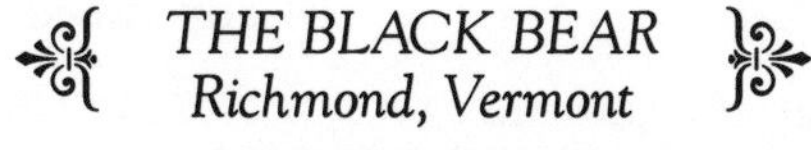

THE BLACK BEAR
Richmond, Vermont

VEAU AVEC CHAMPIGNONS
(Veal with Mushrooms)

Simply elegant! Be sure not to overcook the wine, or it will develop an off flavor.

2 veal cutlets
1 egg with 1 tablespoon water, beaten
1 cup Italian-seasoned bread crumbs
Butter (about ⅓ cup)
1 cup sliced mushrooms
1 cup white wine

Pound veal until thin. Dip in egg-water mixture then in bread crumbs. Coat thoroughly. Sauté veal until lightly brown in butter. Remove to warm platter. Using same pan, sauté mushrooms, adding more butter if necessary. Add wine and cook for a few minutes. Add veal and heat thoroughly before serving. Spoon sauce over veal. *Serves 2.*

VEAL CHASSEUR

This can be prepared earlier in the day and reheated just before serving. However, the tomatoes should not be added until the dish is reheated.

3/4 cup diced onion
1/4 cup diced shallots
2 teaspoons minced garlic
1/2 cup sliced fresh mushrooms
12 medallions veal (2 ounces each)
Flour to dredge veal, plus 1 tablespoon flour to thicken sauce
1 stick butter
3/4 cup beef stock
1/4 cup white wine
1/2 teaspoon tarragon
1/2 teaspoon chervil
1/4 teaspoon chopped fresh basil
1 teaspoon chopped fresh parsley
1/2 teaspoon salt
1/4 teaspoon white pepper
3/4 cup diced tomatoes

Have all ingredients ready to use. Dredge the veal in flour so that it is thoroughly covered. In a very large frying pan melt the butter over low heat. Add the onion, shallots, and garlic, raise the heat to medium, and cook for about 2 minutes. Add the mushrooms and stir. Add the medallions of veal, and cook about 2 minutes on each side. Add the tablespoon of flour reserved for thickening the sauce. Stir to distribute. Add beef stock, white wine, tarragon, chervil, basil, parsley, salt, and pepper. Simmer for a few minutes. Add the tomatoes and continue cooking just long enough to heat the tomatoes. Serve immediately in warmed dishes.

Serves 6.

VEAL LOIN WITH NASTURTIUMS

"The Four Columns Inn uses only organically raised, milk-fed veal. We find this particular recipe complements the meat in an extraordinary way. Nasturtiums can be readily grown in the home garden and are also colorful as well as piquant in a tossed green salad. We love them, especially with the veal."

4 tablespoons unsalted butter
Salt and pepper to taste
8 veal loin scallops, cut 1¼ inches thick, then pounded to ¼ inch thick
4 tablespoons veal glaze
1 tablespoon lemon juice
2 tablespoons rinsed capers
2 nasturtium leaves
16 nasturtium flowers

Melt butter in pan. Salt and pepper veal. Sauté veal on both sides over medium heat until just medium rare. Remove meat from pan and set aside.

Add veal glaze, lemon juice, and capers to pan and boil for one minute; add salt and pepper to taste.

Arrange meat on 4 plates. Quickly add nasturtium leaves to hot sauce — just long enough to wilt. Arrange leaves around the veal. Pour the hot sauce over the meat and leaves. Set the flowers about each plate and serve. *Serves 4.*

VEAL MARENGO

A fine veal casserole to serve with steamed rice and a green vegetable or with spinach egg noodles.

2 pounds cubed leg of veal
4 tablespoons clarified butter
2 cloves garlic, chopped
1 cup dry white wine
2 cups chicken broth
1 teaspoon tomato paste
3 sprigs parsley
2 tablespoons flour dissolved in ½ cup water
1 pound mushrooms
½ cup black olives

Dry veal and brown in butter. Remove from pan and place in a casserole. Add garlic to sauté pan and cook until light brown. Add wine to pan and cook 2 minutes, scraping up brown bits. Add to casserole with chicken broth, tomato paste, and parsley and stir. Bake at 325° for 1 hour. Remove from oven to burner on stove, add flour and water mixture, and cook until slightly thickened. May be prepared ahead to this point. When ready to serve, add mushrooms and reheat. Add olives just before serving.

Serves 4.

VEAL PROVENÇALE

Sauté the veal in small batches so it is not crowded in the pan.

1½ pounds veal, diced
Milk or lemon juice
Flour
2 tablespoons oil
2 tablespoons butter
½ cup peeled, diced tomatoes
½ cup thinly sliced mushrooms
1 clove garlic, minced
½ teaspoon basil
½ teaspoon oregano
Salt and pepper
½ cup dry white wine
4 tablespoons freshly grated Parmesan cheese

Soak veal all day in milk or for just 1 hour in lemon juice. Dry thoroughly. Coat lightly with flour and brown in 2 tablespoons oil and 2 tablespoons butter until lightly cooked and golden. Place tomatoes, mushrooms, and veal in casserole and season with garlic, basil, oregano, and salt and pepper. Top with wine and cheese, cover, and bake at 325° for 45 minutes.

Serves 6.

PORK AND LAMB

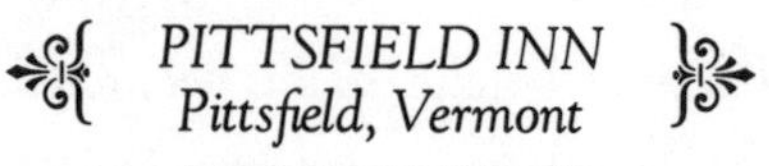

PITTSFIELD INN
Pittsfield, Vermont

COUNTRY STUFFED PORK

If you prefer to make this with a boneless pork loin, buy about a pound of ground pork to use as the stuffing and mix with ingredients as described.

Pork loin (7½ pounds with bone)
½ teaspoon marjoram
½ teaspoon poultry seasoning
¼ teaspoon thyme
⅛ teaspoon cayenne
¼ teaspoon white pepper
¼ teaspoon rubbed sage
¼ teaspoon minced garlic
2 eggs

Remove loin from bone, then cut away all extra meat from bone and trim back loin 1-2 inches on each end. Send all trimmings through grinder or food processor with spices and eggs. Butterfly the loin, stuff with meat preparation, and tie back together. Roast in 350° oven until done, about 2 hours or until internal temperature registers 185°. *Serves 4-6.*

PORK LOIN WITH APRICOT-ROSEMARY SAUCE

Marinated pork loin that is roasted in the marinade and served with a savory sauce.

Center cut pork loin (5 pounds), boned and rolled (reserve the bones)
2 tablespoons vegetable oil
2 tablespoons Italian olive oil
20 white peppercorns
1 bay leaf
1 large clove garlic, chopped
2 tablespoons apricot-flavored brandy
1/4 cup dry vermouth
2 tablespoons fresh lemon juice
1 tablespoon crushed rosemary
4 tablespoons fat from pan drippings
2 cups chicken stock
2 tablespoons arrowroot
2 teaspoons minced rosemary
2 teaspoons minced garlic
3 tablespoons apricot purée (made from strained apricot jam)

Place pork in large stainless steel or glass container. Combine next 9 ingredients and pour over pork. Marinate for up to 24 hours.

Preheat oven to 350°, remove meat from marinade, and place on reserved bones in roasting pan. Pour remaining marinade over meat and roast for approximately 2 hours or until internal temperature reaches 180°. Remove meat to warm platter.

Pour off 4 tablespoons fat from pan drippings and put in saucepan. Add chicken stock and remainder of pan drippings that have been skimmed of fat. Blend in arrowroot, rosemary, and garlic. Add apricot purée and simmer 3 minutes. Strain and serve with meat.

Serves 8-10.

ROAST PORK WITH PIQUANT SAUCE

A moist and juicy pork roast complemented by a thick, dark-red, sweet-yet-tangy sauce. Let the meat sit for about 15 minutes after removing it from the oven to facilitate carving.

Pork roast, center cut (4 to 5 pounds)
1/4 cup light brown sugar
1/4 cup dark corn syrup
1/4 cup cider vinegar
1 can (8 ounces) tomato sauce
1 tablespoon cornstarch
1/2 teaspoon salt
1/8 teaspoon white pepper
1/4 cup water

Cook roast in baking pan at 325° for 2½-3 hours. (Use meat thermometer for accuracy; internal temperature should be 170° when done.) About 1½ hours before roast is done, combine remaining ingredients for sauce in a 1-quart saucepan, mixing well with whisk. Simmer sauce ¾ hour and add pork drippings. Baste roast at least 3 times before it is done. Serve remaining sauce with roast.

Serves 4-6.

INDONESIAN PORK SATAY

This will appeal to creative cooks and sophisticated palates. It's highly seasoned — but not to a painful degree — and highlighted with a heavenly peanut-butter-based sauce.

2 to 3 pounds cubed pork tenderloin (or beef strips or chicken chunks)
1/4 cup walnuts
1 tablespoon coriander seed
3 cloves garlic, peeled
1 onion, coarsely chopped
1 teaspoon red pepper flakes
1 cup orange juice
2 tablespoons brown sugar
2 tablespoons soy sauce
Hot Peanut Butter Sauce (recipe follows)

Blend all ingredients, except pork and Hot Peanut Butter Sauce, thoroughly in blender. Pour over meat and marinate several hours. Skewer and broil or bake in hot (500°) oven until done (about 20 minutes for pork or beef; 10-15 minutes for chicken). Just before serving baste with Hot Peanut Butter Sauce. Serve satays on a bed of rice with sauce on the side. *Serves 6.*

HOT PEANUT BUTTER SAUCE

1 tablespoon butter
1 small onion, coarsely chopped
3 tablespoons chunky peanut butter
1 tablespoon soy sauce
1 teaspoon red pepper flakes
1/2 cup milk

Purée thoroughly in blender.

SEAWARD INN
Rockport, Massachusetts

SEAWARD'S PORK CHOPS

Moist, tender pork chops in a sweet, bright-red sauce full of onion bits. Original, flavorful, and satisfying. Special enough for company.

1/3 cup brown sugar
3/4 teaspoon salt (or to taste)
1/8 teaspoon pepper
1 1/2 tablespoons lemon juice
1/3 cup chili sauce
1/3 cup water
1 medium onion, chopped fine
6 pork chops, about 1 inch thick
Seasoned flour (about 1/3 cup, mixed with salt and pepper to taste)
1/2 cup evaporated milk
Seasoned bread crumbs (about 1 cup)

Combine first 7 ingredients and pour into baking dish. Trim excess fat from pork chops and dip in seasoned flour, then in evaporated milk. Dip one side of chops in seasoned bread crumbs and arrange in baking dish, crumb side up. Cover tightly and bake in preheated oven at 350° for 1 1/2 hours or until tender. Remove cover the last 20 or 30 minutes so that crumbs will brown. Check from time to time to see if more liquid is needed and add tomato juice if so. Serve with lemon-buttered broccoli and mashed potatoes. *Serves 6.*

PUBLICK HOUSE
Sturbridge, Massachusetts

TOURTIÈRE
(French Canadian Meat Pie)

A delightful combination of ground pork and beef, spiced with cinnamon and cloves, sauced with brown beef gravy, and baked in a double crust.

2 pounds lean ground pork
2 pounds lean ground beef
1 medium onion, diced fine
1 teaspoon cinnamon
½ teaspoon ground cloves
2 cups brown beef gravy (recipe follows)
1 cup fine bread crumbs
1 cup diced cooked potatoes
Salt and pepper to taste
Pastry for 2 double-crust 9-inch pies

Sauté pork, beef, and onion until browned. Add cinnamon, cloves, and gravy and simmer for 5 minutes. Add bread crumbs, diced potatoes, and salt and pepper, and stir well. Remove from heat. Divide between pastry-lined pie tins and cover with pastry crust. Brush with egg wash and bake at 375° for 45 minutes or until browned. *Makes 2 nine-inch pies.*

BROWN BEEF GRAVY

½ medium onion, chopped
1 carrot, chopped
1 stalk celery, chopped
2 quarts rich beef stock
4 ounces butter or margarine
4 ounces flour
Salt and pepper

Add chopped vegetables to beef stock and boil for 15 minutes. In small saucepan make roux with butter and flour. Add roux to stock and whip until dissolved. Simmer for 30 minutes. Strain through fine strainer. Add salt and pepper to taste and use as described. *Makes about 2 quarts.*

THE GREY BONNET INN
North Killington, Vermont

SWEETBREADS AND HAM COUNTRY STYLE

Sweetbreads sautéed with mushrooms, scallions, and paprika and spooned on top of cooked sliced ham.

1 pound sweetbreads
2 sprigs parsley
1 onion, sliced
1 stalk celery, halved
½ carrot, sliced
1 slice lemon
2 tablespoons red wine
½ teaspoon wine vinegar
½ teaspoon mixture of pickle spices, salt, and pepper
8 mushrooms, sliced
2 scallions, sliced
½ teaspoon Hungarian paprika
2 tablespoons butter
Salt and pepper
1 pound cooked ham, sliced into 4 equal pieces
Parsley

Soak sweetbreads in cold water to cover for 3-4 hours, changing water 2 or 3 times. Drain the sweetbreads, put them in a saucepan with enough cold water to cover, add parsley, onion, celery, carrot, lemon, wine, vinegar, and spices. Bring the water to a gentle boil and simmer for 10 minutes. Let sweetbreads cool in the cooking liquid, then drain and remove and discard connective tissues and membranes. Flatten sweetbreads between wax paper under a weight for about 2 hours. Cut in ½-inch slices and sauté in a skillet with mushrooms, scallions, and paprika in butter over moderate heat for 10 minutes or until they are golden. Add salt and pepper to taste.

In separate skillet sauté slices of cooked ham in butter for 3 minutes and arrange them on a platter. Spoon the sweetbreads over the slices of ham and sprinkle with minced parsley. *Serves 4.*

ROAST RACK OF LAMB

"This dish is a favorite at the Village Inn. The burnt garlic powder not only generates a lovely aroma, but it imparts a delicious subtle flavor to the lamb."

8-bone domestic lamb rack, trimmed
1/4 cup melted butter
4 tablespoons garlic powder
1/2 teaspoon rosemary
1/2 teaspoon thyme
Pinch of salt and pepper
Fresh mint or watercress for garnish

Have butcher trim and "French" the rack of lamb. Place in shallow baking dish, fat side up. Spread melted butter over lamb with pastry brush. Mix garlic powder, rosemary, thyme, and salt and pepper and sprinkle generously over meat. Preheat broiler to 500°. Place meat under broiler for 5 minutes or until garlic powder mixture "burns" and turns black — it should actually harden and form a crust over the lamb. (Watch carefully in case it catches fire.) Remove meat from broiler and place in preheated 400° oven for 10 minutes for medium rare, longer for well done. Remove and slice through each bone and place on a warm platter. Garnish with fresh mint or watercress. *Serves 2.*

MIDGE'S BUTTERFLIED LEG OF LAMB

"This recipe was given to me by a friend of my mother's long before this way of cooking lamb became well known. It's the only way to cook lamb for a crowd because the carving is so easy!"

1 leg of lamb, 7-9 pounds (native if possible), boned and butterflied
½ cup olive oil
¾ cup red wine
2 tablespoons lemon juice
2 tablespoons parsley
Black pepper (several grinds)
3 bay leaves
1 cup sliced onion
3 cloves garlic, minced
1 teaspoon salt

Mix together all ingredients except lamb and blend well. Marinate lamb in mixture for 6 hours (out of refrigerator), turning occasionally. Broil fat side down first, about 20 minutes each side for medium. For extra flavor cook on outdoor grill.

Serves 10-12.

SIDE DISHES

Center Lovell Inn, Center Lovell, Maine

HOLIDAY INN
Intervale, New Hampshire

VIENNESE GREEN BEANS

"A truly delightful way to 'dress up' an old favorite! The recipe calls for frozen green beans, but if you have them, fresh beans would add a special touch."

1 large package (2 pounds) frozen green beans
½ cup chopped onion
2 tablespoons butter or margarine
2 tablespoons flour
1 teaspoon salt
¼ teaspoon pepper
1 cup chicken broth
2 tablespoons vinegar
4 tablespoons finely chopped parsley
½ teaspoon dill seed
1 cup commercial sour cream

Cook beans until tender. Sauté onion in butter until translucent. Stir in flour, salt, and pepper. Add chicken broth gradually to make light sauce. Add vinegar, parsley, and dill. Cook until bubbly and stir in sour cream. Add drained cooked beans and serve immediately. *Serves 8.*

CENTER LOVELL INN
Center Lovell, Maine

MARINATED CARROTS

A real lip-puckering dish that should be served in small quantities. One pound of small white onions may be used in place of carrots.

1 pound tender young carrots
3/4 cup dry white wine
3/4 cup white wine vinegar
4 cups water
6 tablespoons oil
2 whole cloves garlic
Small bunch parsley, chopped (1/4 cup loosely packed)
1 teaspoon sugar
1 teaspoon salt
1/4 teaspoon crushed black pepper
1 teaspoon prepared mustard (Dijon)
1 teaspoon finely chopped basil

Wash and scrape carrots and cut into medium-sized julienne strips. In a small pot combine white wine, wine vinegar, water, oil, garlic, parsley, sugar, salt, and pepper. Bring to a boil and cook until carrots are done (8-10 minutes — they should still be a little crisp). Let carrots cool in the marinade, then remove and boil down the marinade until it has been reduced to approximately 2 cups. Mix this sauce with the mustard and pour over the carrots. Sprinkle with the fresh basil and chill. *Serves 4-6.*

CENTER LOVELL INN
Center Lovell, Maine

MARINATED MUSHROOMS

Zingy little morsels in a pungent marinade. Those on a low-sodium diet may want to decrease the salt.

1 pound mushrooms
1/4 cup wine vinegar
3/4 cup water
Olive oil
3 cloves garlic, sliced
1 bay leaf
2 whole cloves
4 peppercorns
1 teaspoon salt
1/4 teaspoon freshly ground pepper

Wash mushrooms and then soak in warm, slightly salted water for 10 minutes to clean properly. Drain and put in a saucepan with wine vinegar and 3/4 cup water. Cover and bring to a boil, remove from stove, and let stand until cool. In plastic container, place drained mushrooms with olive oil to cover, sliced garlic, crumbled bay leaf, cloves, peppercorns, salt, and pepper. Stir gently and refrigerate until ready to use. *Serves 6-8.*

RATATOUILLE NIÇOISE

"We serve this as a side dish or as an appetizer with melted mozzarella cheese on top — and either hot or cold. It can be made ahead of time and keeps well."

½ cup olive oil
2 large onions, thinly sliced
2 to 3 crushed cloves garlic
1 eggplant, peeled and cubed
4 large tomatoes, chopped, or 1 large can (1 pound, 12 ounces)
4 zucchini, cubed
2 green peppers, cleaned and diced
½ teaspoon basil
½ teaspoon thyme
Salt and pepper to taste

Heat oil in large saucepan. Add onions and garlic and brown quickly over high heat. Add eggplant and tomatoes and mix, crushing mixture. Add zucchini and green peppers and mix well. Add seasonings and cook 2-3 minutes over high heat, stirring constantly. Cover and simmer about 1 hour. *Serves* 6.

NEW POTATOES BAKED IN CREAM

"Simple but elegant, this side dish is always in demand at our restaurant. Be sure to use the heaviest cream possible."

10 to 15 small, red-skinned new potatoes
2 cups heavy cream
5 medium cloves garlic, finely minced
Salt and white pepper to taste
Chopped parsley or chives for garnish

Scrub potatoes in warm water. Slice them into ⅛-inch-thick slices. Place in an 8-inch-square pan. Add cream, garlic, salt, and pepper, and toss till completely mixed. Cover tightly with aluminum foil and make a hole in the center about the size of a half dollar. Bake in a 350° oven for approximately 25 minutes or until potatoes are tender. Remove foil and bake another 10 minutes or until cream is bubbling and brown color shows on top. Garnish with chopped parsley or chives. *Serves 6-8.*

SCOTTISH LION RUMBLEDETHUMPS

Perfect autumn dish. Serve with sliced turkey or ham, Harvard beets, and corn bread.

6 medium potatoes, peeled and diced
1/2 large cabbage, diced
Salt and pepper to taste
2 tablespoons chopped chives
Up to 1 stick butter
Milk
1 to 1 1/2 cups grated cheddar cheese

Place potatoes and cabbage in separate pans and cover with water. Cover, bring to a boil, and simmer until tender. Remove from heat and drain off water. Mash potatoes with salt, pepper, chives, and butter. Add enough milk to soften the potatoes. Add the cabbage and mix well. Place in a 2-inch-deep baking dish, cover with grated cheddar cheese, and bake at 350° until cheese has melted and potato mixture is hot inside. *Serves* 6.

INDIAN SHUTTERS INN
North Charlestown, New Hampshire

INDIAN SHUTTERS RICE PILAF

"This is an all-time favorite at Indian Shutters and is always included with our hot buffet dinners as well as offered as an everyday alternate to potatoes."

5 to 10 small mushrooms, chopped
1 green pepper, seeded and chopped
1 tablespoon butter
1 pimiento, chopped
6 cups cooked rice

Sauté mushrooms and green pepper in butter until transparent. Add chopped pimiento. Stir into cooked rice. If mixture becomes dry, add a little beef broth or butter to moisten.

Serves 6-8.

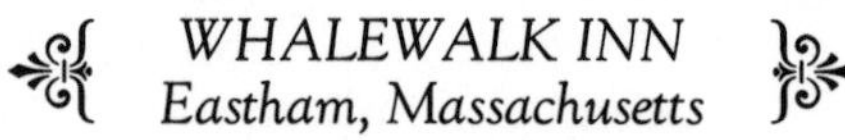

WHALEWALK INN
Eastham, Massachusetts

BAKED PINEAPPLE

Especially good with ham and perhaps a spinach salad — but could also be dessert, topped with whipped cream.

1/4 pound butter
3 cups sugar
1 tablespoon water
1 large can diced pineapple
2 tablespoons cornstarch
Juice of 1 lemon
8 slices toasted white bread, crusts removed

Melt butter and add sugar; stir and cook over low heat for a few minutes. Add about a tablespoon of water, then pineapple with juice. Dissolve cornstarch in a little water and add to the mixture. Stir in lemon juice. Cut toast into small cubes and add. Place in greased 13x9-inch baking dish and bake at 350° for 30-45 minutes.

Serves 4.

THE BERNERHOF INN
Glen, New Hampshire

SPAETZLE
(Austrian Egg Dumplings)

"The tiny egg dumplings that go well with robust stews like beef Burgundy and coq au vin. Gourmet shops sell special spaetzle cutters, but you can improvise with a round cookie cutter (or topless and bottomless tuna fish can) and a flat grater or spatula with holes in it."

2¾ cups flour
1 cup milk
Scant teaspoon each salt, fresh white pepper, and freshly grated nutmeg
3 to 4 eggs, beaten
2 quarts rapidly boiling water, lightly salted
1 tablespoon oil
4 tablespoons butter
4 tablespoons fresh chopped parsley

Combine flour, milk, salt, pepper, and nutmeg in a bowl, and, mixing with a whisk, add enough egg to obtain a thick but fairly loose paste. Let stand for 5 minutes. Using a spaetzle cutter, or an improvisation thereof, cut small bits of dough and drop into boiling water sprinkled with a little oil. Cook for 1 minute or until the spaetzle rise to the surface. If preparing the spaetzle ahead of time, transfer the cooked dumplings with a slotted spoon to a bowl of cold water sprinkled with a little oil (this prevents the dumplings from sticking together). The spaetzle can be prepared up to 48 hours ahead of time to this stage and stored in cold water.

To serve the spaetzle, drain thoroughly, and sauté them in foaming butter in a large frying pan, sprinkling with parsley and salt and pepper. Alternative: freshly cooked spaetzle can be served with melted butter or sour cream. *Serves 6-8.*

NORWEGIAN NOODLE PUDDING

"This is the recipe everyone asks for! Serve it bubbling hot as a breakfast surprise, as an elegant dinner casserole, or as a pleasing dessert with whipped cream. It also doubles as a great midnight snack, served cold . . ."

8 ounces medium-width noodles
1/4 pound butter
1/2 teaspoon cinnamon or to taste
1/2 cup raisins, or more if desired
1/2 cup sugar
3 teaspoons almond extract, or to taste
2 cups milk
3 eggs, beaten
Salt to taste

Do not preheat oven until you have reached that point in the directions. Put noodles on to boil, salting to taste. Melt the butter. Put half the melted butter into a large casserole or baking dish, tilting to spread butter to all sides and over the bottom. Place empty casserole in oven and then preheat to 350°. When noodles are done, strain and rinse with cold water to remove starch. Mix cinnamon, raisins, sugar, and almond extract with the noodles. Beat the milk and eggs together, season with salt and pepper, and add to other ingredients. Add remaining melted butter and stir well. Pour into heated casserole and cook until top is golden brown — at least 1 hour. *Serves 8.*

DESSERTS

Weekapaug Inn, Weekapaug, Rhode Island

PIES

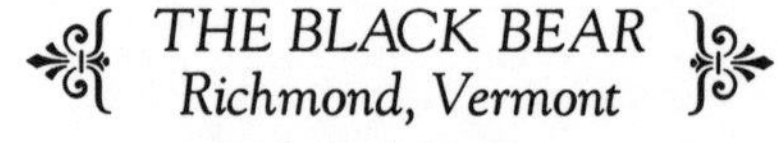

SWEDISH APPLE PIE WITH CINNAMON CREAM SAUCE

Not a pie in the traditional sense but a combination of pie, crisp, and cobbler. Serve à la mode.

3 to 4 medium apples, peeled, cored, and sliced
1 tablespoon sugar
1 teaspoon cinnamon
3/4 cup melted butter
1 cup sugar
1/2 cup nuts
1 cup flour
1 egg
Pinch of salt

Fill buttered 9-inch pie pan two-thirds full of apples. Sprinkle with sugar and cinnamon. Combine remaining ingredients in bowl and spoon over apples. Bake at 350° for 45 minutes or until golden. Serve with Cinnamon Cream Sauce (recipe follows).

Serves 6.

CINNAMON CREAM SAUCE

1 1/2 cups sugar
2/3 cup light corn syrup
1/3 cup water
1 1/2 teaspoons cinnamon
2/3 cup evaporated milk

Bring sugar, corn syrup, water, and cinnamon to a boil over medium heat. Boil 4 minutes. Cool for 10 minutes. Stir in evaporated milk. Serve warm over pie.

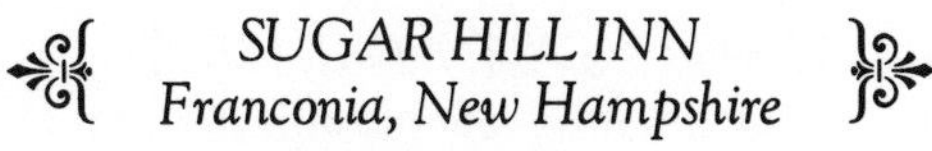

SUGAR HILL INN
Franconia, New Hampshire

APPLE ZAPPLE PIE

Granny Smiths are the apple; applejack brandy, the zapple. Serve with hard sauce, ice cream, heavy cream, or cheddar cheese.

1/2 cup granulated sugar
1/2 cup brown sugar
2 tablespoons all-purpose flour
1/2 to 1 teaspoon cinnamon
Dash of nutmeg
Dash of salt
1/4 cup molasses
1/4 cup applejack brandy or bourbon
6 to 7 Granny Smith apples
Pastry for 2-crust 9-inch pie
2 to 4 tablespoons butter
Sugar

Combine sugars, flour, spices, salt, molasses, and applejack together. Pare and core apples, slice thin, then add sugar mixture, stirring well. Fill bottom crust with apple mixture, dot with butter, and cover with top crust. Vent the top, sprinkle with sugar to sparkle, and bake in 400° oven for 50 minutes or until done.

Serves 8.

WOODBOUND INN
Jaffrey, New Hampshire

FRESH PEACH PIE

Magnificent! You will fantasize about this one in midwinter.

1 cup sugar
3 1/2 tablespoons cornstarch
1/2 cup water
1 tablespoon butter
7 or 8 fresh peaches, peeled
9-inch pie shell, baked
Whipped cream for topping
Slivered almonds for garnish

Combine sugar and cornstarch in a saucepan. Add water and butter and bring to a boil. Mash 3 peaches and add to syrup. Reduce heat, simmer until thickened, and cool. Slice remaining peaches into pie shell, pour syrup mixture over sliced peaches, and chill. Top with whipped cream and garnish with slivered almonds.

Serves 6.

BLUEBERRY BRANDY PIE

Blueberries flavored with cinnamon and blackberry brandy, folded into whipped cream, and chilled in a graham cracker crust.

1 tablespoon gelatin
1/4 cup cold water
4 cups blueberries
1 cup sugar
1/4 cup blackberry brandy
2 tablespoons cornstarch
1 teaspoon cinnamon
2 cups heavy cream
3 tablespoons confectioners sugar
Graham cracker crust (recipe follows)

Soften gelatin in cold water and set aside. Combine berries, sugar, brandy, cornstarch, and cinnamon in a saucepan and cook, stirring constantly, over moderate heat until thickened. Add gelatin and stir until dissolved. Set aside and let cool. Whip heavy cream with confectioners sugar and fold into blueberry mixture. Fill graham cracker crust and chill at least 4 hours. *Serves 6-8.*

GRAHAM CRACKER CRUST

1 1/4 cups graham cracker crumbs
1/4 cup sugar
1 teaspoon allspice
1 teaspoon cinnamon
3/4 stick butter, melted

Mix all together until crumbly. Pat into a 9-inch springform pan and bake at 350° for 8-10 minutes or until lightly browned. Let cool before filling.

LINCOLN HOUSE COUNTRY INN
Dennysville, Maine

BLUEBERRY PIE MARNIER

"The Lincoln House is in the heart of 'the blueberry capital of the world' — Washington County, Maine. We serve this delicious pie throughout the season."

4 cups fresh blueberries
9-inch pie shell, baked
1/4 cup water
3/4 cup sugar
1/2 teaspoon salt
2 tablespoons cornstarch
1 teaspoon butter
1 tablespoon Grand Marnier

Spread 2 cups blueberries in a baked and cooled pie shell. Cook 2 remaining cups with water, sugar, salt, and cornstarch until thickened. Remove from heat and add butter and Grand Marnier. Cool and chill. When cold, pour over berries in the shell. Chill until ready to serve. Serve with freshly made whipped cream or ice cream. *Makes 1 pie.*

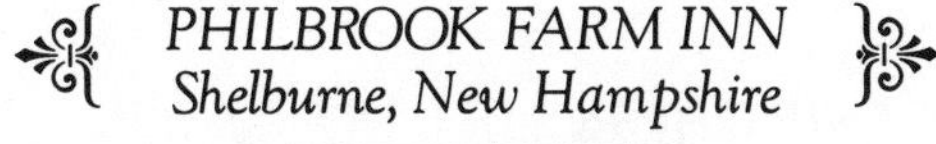

PHILBROOK FARM INN
Shelburne, New Hampshire

FROZEN LEMON PIE

Rewarding on a hot summer day. If all is not served, it can be refrozen.

3 egg yolks
1/2 cup sugar
Juice and rind of 1 lemon
3 egg whites, beaten stiff with 1 teaspoon sugar
1 cup heavy cream, whipped
9-inch graham cracker crust

Beat egg yolks until light colored then gradually add 1/2 cup sugar. Add lemon juice and rind. Lightly add egg whites, fold in whipped cream, and put in pie shell. Freeze 4-5 hours. Garnish with graham cracker crumbs or maraschino cherries and fresh mint. *Serves 6.*

WEEKAPAUG INN
Weekapaug, Rhode Island

KEY LIME PIE

Almost as easy to make as it is to eat. A graham cracker crust works well in hot weather for it doesn't get soggy, but a pastry crust is complementary to the delicate lime flavor.

4 eggs, separated
½ cup lime juice
1 can (13 ounces) sweetened condensed milk
Green food coloring (optional)
9-inch pie shell, baked
½ teaspoon cream of tartar
⅓ cup sugar

Beat egg yolks until light and thick. Blend in lime juice, then milk, stirring until mixture thickens. If desired, add a few drops of green food coloring. Pour mixture into baked pie shell.

Beat egg whites with cream of tartar until stiff. Gradually beat in sugar, beating until glossy peaks form. Spread egg whites over surface of pie to edge of crust. Bake in 350° oven until golden brown, about 20 minutes. Chill before serving. *Serves 8-10.*

THE CHURCHILL HOUSE INN
Brandon, Vermont

MAPLE WALNUT PIE

A Churchill House variation of pecan pie. Use Grade B maple syrup for the best flavor and color.

4 eggs, well beaten
⅔ cup sugar
⅛ teaspoon salt
1 cup strong maple syrup
½ cup butter, melted
9-inch pie shell, unbaked
¾ cup walnuts
1 cup whipping cream

Combine beaten eggs, sugar, salt, and maple syrup. Add melted butter and blend completely. Pour into unbaked pie shell. Cover top with walnuts and bake at 350° for 1 hour or until tester comes out clean. Top with whipped cream. *Serves 8-10.*

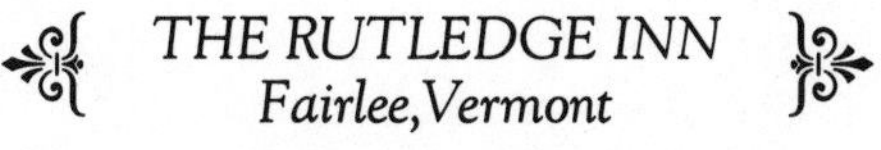

DATE MACAROON PIE

A chewy dessert that stores well in a cool, dry place. Serve any time of the year.

2 cups sugar
1 teaspoon baking powder
24 saltines, crushed
½ cup chopped dates
½ cup chopped walnuts
1 cup egg whites, room temperature (8 large egg whites)
1 teaspoon cream of tartar
1 teaspoon almond extract

Mix sugar, baking powder, saltines, dates, and nuts in large bowl. Beat egg whites until foamy stage, add cream of tartar, and beat till eggs hold soft peaks. Add almond extract, then beat until stiff but *not* dry. Add whites to date mixture. Press into 8-inch buttered pie tins and bake 30 minutes at 350°. Cool and serve with fresh whipped cream. *Makes two 8-inch pies.*

WONDERFUL PIE

The title says it all — wonderful! *Most people can't guess what the ingredients are.*

3 egg whites
1 cup sugar
12 soda crackers
1 teaspoon vanilla
1 teaspoon baking powder
1 cup chopped walnuts
1 cup whipped cream

Beat egg whites until stiff, adding sugar gradually. Crumble crackers and add to egg mixture. Add vanilla, baking powder, and walnuts and mix well. Pour into well-greased 9-inch pie pan and bake 30 minutes at 350°. Cool, top with whipped cream, and refrigerate about 5 hours before serving. *Serves 6-8.*

GREENVILLE INN
Greenville, Maine

ALMOND TORTE

Extremely sweet dessert that should be served warm. The filling is wall-to-wall almonds, beautifully glazed with a sugar-cream syrup. This will keep for several days.

CRUST

1 cup flour
1½ tablespoons sugar
3 ounces butter (¾ stick)
2 egg yolks

Combine flour, sugar, and butter as you would for pie crust. Add egg yolks and mix until combined. Press into pie pan or pan with removable bottom. (If using a springform pan press mixture up sides about an inch.) Bake 10 minutes at 325°. Meanwhile, prepare the filling.

FILLING

1 cup heavy cream
1 cup sugar
¼ teaspoon salt
4 ounces sliced almonds (about 1 cup)
¼ teaspoon almond extract

Combine cream, sugar, and salt. Bring to boil over medium-high heat, stirring frequently. Simmer over medium to medium-low heat 5 minutes, stirring occasionally. Add almonds and almond extract. Pour into crust and bake at 375° for 25-30 minutes or until lightly browned on top. *Serves 8-10.*

THE BIRCHWOOD INN
Temple, New Hampshire

CREAM CHEESE PECAN PIE

If you like both cheesecake and pecan pie, you'll definitely enjoy this.

8 ounces cream cheese
1/3 cup sugar plus 1/4 cup
4 eggs
2 teaspoons vanilla
1/4 teaspoon salt
1 cup light corn syrup
9-inch pie shell, unbaked
1 1/4 cups chopped pecans

Beat cream cheese, 1/3 cup sugar, 1 egg, 1 teaspoon vanilla, and salt. When thick, set aside. Beat remaining 3 eggs. Add 1/4 cup sugar, corn syrup, and 1 teaspoon vanilla and blend well. Spread cream cheese mixture in unbaked pie shell. Sprinkle with pecans. Pour liquid mixture over top. Bake in 375° oven 40 minutes.
Serves 8.

FOLLANSBEE INN
North Sutton, New Hampshire

CHOCOLATE PECAN PIE

The best of both worlds, baked in the same crust. Present while still warm, topped with freshly whipped cream.

1 1/2 cups coarsely chopped pecans (6 ounces)
6 ounces semi-sweet chocolate chips
8-inch pie shell, partially baked
1/2 cup light corn syrup
1/2 cup sugar
2 extra-large eggs
1/4 cup butter (1/2 stick), melted and cooled

Preheat oven to 325°. Sprinkle pecans and chocolate chips evenly into pie shell. Blend corn syrup, sugar, and eggs in medium bowl. Mix in cooled melted butter. Pour mixture slowly and evenly into pie shell. Bake until firm, about 1 hour. *Serves 8-10.*

CHOCOLATE SILK PIE

"This dessert recipe has been The Bernerhof's most frequently requested. It requires no cooking, is easily stored by freezing, can be assembled in 15 minutes, and the beater is a pleasure to lick once you're finished."

CRUST

12 Oreo cookies
2 tablespoons butter, melted

Grind cookies to crumbs, add melted butter, and mix thoroughly. Press crumbs into 9-inch pie tin and place in freezer to firm.

FILLING

6 ounces unsalted butter (room temperature)
2 packages (1 ounce each) Nestle's Choco bake (liquid form)
1 cup sugar
3 whole eggs, beaten

Cream butter and chocolate on medium speed of mixer. Add sugar and thoroughly incorporate. Add half the eggs, increasing mixing speed to allow air to enter. Continue for 3-4 minutes, then add balance of eggs, mixing for 3-4 minutes more or until small peaks hold on surface. Remove crust from freezer and spoon in filling; return to freezer, removing 15 minutes before serving.

Serves 6.

CHOCOLATE FRANGELICO CREAM PIE

A cool, mildly chocolate-flavored pie enlivened by the liqueur. It can be served chilled or frozen.

1½ cups graham cracker crumbs
½ cup butter, melted
2 tablespoons sugar
¼ teaspoon ground cinnamon
12 ounces semi-sweet chocolate morsels
1 quart heavy whipping cream
¼ to ½ cup warm water
4 tablespoons unflavored gelatin
½ cup Frangelico liqueur

Combine graham cracker crumbs, melted butter, sugar, and cinnamon in a bowl and mix well. Pat this mixture on the bottom of a 9- or 10-inch springform pan. Set aside.

Melt the chocolate in a double boiler. Whip the cream in a large mixing bowl until thick. Combine the warm water and gelatin and mix so there are no lumps, adding more water, if necessary, until consistency of maple syrup. Mix the melted chocolate, slightly cooled but still pourable, the liqueur, and gelatin together. Fold in the whipped cream until well blended. Pour this mixture into the springform pan — tap to make sure it settles — then refrigerate for 2 hours before serving. *Serves 10-12.*

OTTAUQUECHEE RIVER MUD PIE

When it is lying on your plate in a heap — with mounds of whipped cream, chunks of crust, and a coating of chocolate sauce — it certainly looks like a mud pie. The taste, however, is divine.

1/4 cup melted butter or margarine
1 cup finely crushed fudge chip cookie crumbs (or crumbs from any chocolate cookie)
1/2 gallon coffee ice cream
Hot fudge sauce and whipped cream

Pour melted butter into cookie crumbs and stir until well blended. Press into a 9-inch pie pan, starting with the sides of the pan, then the bottom. Tamp the crumbs gently in place.

While making the crust, allow the ice cream to soften slightly. With a large spoon, scoop the ice cream into the pie crust. Gently push the ice cream down to eliminate air pockets. Smooth the ice cream with a cake spatula or the side of a knife. The pie should be high in the middle and slope down to the crust. Harden pie in freezer for approximately 1 hour. To serve, cut with a knife dipped in hot water and top with your favorite hot fudge sauce and whipped cream. *Serves 8-10.*

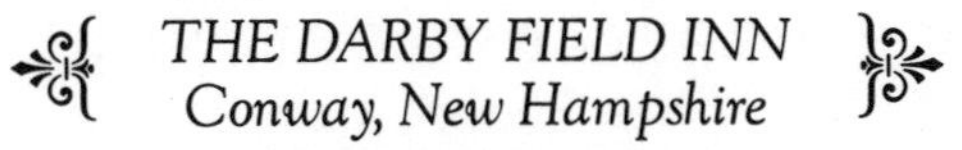

THE DARBY FIELD INN
Conway, New Hampshire

DARBY CREAM PIE

An eggnog-flavored chiffon pie with chocolate-whipped-cream topping. Two layers give it an elegant appearance.

FILLING

1 cup milk
1/2 teaspoon nutmeg
3 eggs, separated
1/3 cup sugar
1 tablespoon gelatin (1 package)
2 tablespoons water
3 tablespoons O'Darby's Irish Cream liqueur
1/2 pint heavy cream
9-inch pie shell, baked

Scald milk and nutmeg together in double boiler. Blend egg yolks with sugar until creamy. Dissolve gelatin in the water and O'Darby's. Remove hot milk from the double boiler and add slowly to the egg and sugar mixture, stirring constantly with wire whisk. Put back into double boiler and cook on low heat, stirring occasionally until thickened. Add the gelatin mixture and blend in thoroughly. Remove from heat and allow to cool (stir occasionally to keep mixture from hardening around the edges). When the filling has cooled, but not set (if filling sets, you'll have to warm it up and cool it again to avoid lumps), whip the egg whites until stiff but not dry and fold into the filling. (If the filling appears lumpy don't despair; use a wire whisk to blend until smooth.) Now whip the heavy cream, fold it into the filling, and put into the baked pie shell. Refrigerate and start work on the topping.

TOPPING

4 ounces milk chocolate
2 tablespoons water
1/2 teaspoon gelatin
2 tablespoons O'Darby's Irish Cream liqueur
1/2 pint heavy cream

Melt chocolate with water in double boiler. Remove from heat, add the gelatin dissolved in O'Darby's, and allow to cool. Whip the heavy cream and thoroughly blend about half the cream into the cooled chocolate mixture, then fold in the remainder. Spread the topping on the pie (make sure the filling is set) and try to hold off for a couple of hours before cutting. *Serves 12.*

MARIE'S OLD-FASHIONED CUSTARD PIE

A real classic. The custard sets after the pie is removed from the oven so do not overbake. Although the dough recipe makes a large quantity, it will keep for 3 to 5 days in the refrigerator or for 3 months in the freezer.

CUSTARD FILLING

4 whole eggs
1/2 cup sugar
1/4 teaspoon salt
1 tablespoon vanilla
2 1/2 cups scalded milk (for creamier custard, use half cream and half milk)
9-inch Never-Fail Pie Crust, unbaked (recipe follows)
1/4 teaspoon nutmeg

Mix eggs, sugar, salt, and vanilla. Slowly stir in hot milk and combine well. Pour into unbaked pie shell, sprinkle with nutmeg, and bake at 475° for 5 minutes. Reduce heat to 425° and bake 10 to 15 minutes more. *Makes 1 pie.*

NEVER-FAIL PIE CRUST

8 ounces lard
8 ounces Crisco
2 teaspoons salt
1 1/2 pounds bread flour
1 whole egg plus enough cold water to equal 1 cup
2 teaspoons white vinegar

With pastry cutter or two knives mix shortenings, salt, and flour until the consistency of coarse meal or the size of small peas. Combine egg, water, and vinegar and pour over flour mixture, stirring with a fork until dough holds together. Form into a ball, cover with plastic wrap, and refrigerate 1 hour. For each 9-inch pie crust, roll out 8 ounces dough. *Makes 7 single crusts.*

THE INN AT WESTON
Weston, Vermont

PEANUT BUTTER ICE CREAM PIE

"We use natural peanut butter in our recipe so you should cut back on sweeteners if using a brand containing sugar." Devastatingly delicious!

2 cups graham cracker crumbs
1 cup chopped peanuts
1 cup coconut
1/2 teaspoon cinnamon
4 tablespoons melted butter
1/2 gallon vanilla ice cream, softened
1 cup ground unsalted peanuts
18 ounces crunchy peanut butter
1/2 cup honey
1/3 cup light corn syrup
1/3 cup milk
Ground peanuts for garnish

Prepare crust by combining graham cracker crumbs, chopped peanuts, coconut, cinnamon, and melted butter. Press into a 10-inch pie plate and set aside.

Mix softened vanilla ice cream with ground unsalted peanuts. Place in freezer while you combine peanut butter, honey, light corn syrup, and milk. Spread half the ice cream mixture into prepared crust using an ice cream scoop. Cover with half of the peanut butter mixture and freeze for 30 minutes — till somewhat set. Repeat ice cream layer and top with remaining peanut butter mix. Pat ground peanuts around the edges and freeze until firm.

Serves 8-10.

PEANUT BUTTER ICE CREAM PIE

This dream of a dessert can be kept in the freezer and used for a spur-of-the-moment party. However, if you use a top-quality ice cream, one that freezes really hard, *you may want to put the pie in the refrigerator for 15 to 30 minutes before serving to make the cutting easier. For a satiny-smooth texture use creamy peanut butter; for added crunch use chunky-style.*

1 cup peanut butter
1 quart vanilla ice cream, softened
Graham cracker or chocolate cookie pie crust

Mix together peanut butter and ice cream and put into the prepared pie crust. Freeze. Serve topped with chocolate syrup or whipped cream. *Serves 8.*

CAKES, COOKIES, BARS, AND CANDIES

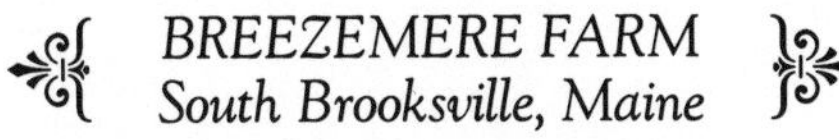

BREEZEMERE FARM
South Brooksville, Maine

MELISSA'S PRIZE-WINNING CHEESECAKE

Melissa is the daughter of Joan and Jim Lippke, innkeepers of Breezemere Farm. She has won several awards for her desserts and has a thriving catering business in Huntington, New York.

1/3 cup graham cracker crumbs
2 pounds cream cheese, softened
1 3/4 cups sugar
1 teaspoon vanilla
4 eggs
3 tablespoons lemon juice
1 cup sour cream
3 tablespoons sugar

Preheat oven to 350°. Grease an 8-inch springform pan all the way up to the rim. Sprinkle crumbs evenly over bottom. With mixer at medium high speed thoroughly cream the cheese till it is perfectly smooth. Add 1 3/4 cups sugar and vanilla. Beat well. Add eggs one at a time, beating only as much as is necessary to mix well. Stir in lemon juice. Pour into prepared pan and place on medium rack in oven. On lower rack, immediately under springform pan, place a larger pan filled with hot water. Bake for 1 1/2 hours. Five minutes before time is up, spread over top sour cream mixed with 3 tablespoons sugar. Allow to cool at least 24 hours for best texture and flavor. *Serves 12.*

THE RAM IN THE THICKET
Wilton, New Hampshire

CAPPUCINO CHEESECAKE

Very rich but not overly sweet. Serve modest portions with whipped cream on top.

CRUST

1 cup flour
1 tablespoon brown sugar
1 tablespoon cinnamon
6 tablespoons melted butter

Blend thoroughly with fork or pastry blender. Pat halfway up sides and over bottom of 10-inch cheesecake pan (with removable sides).

FILLING

2 pounds cream cheese, softened
4 eggs
1/3 cup unsweetened cocoa
2 tablespoons coffee liqueur (optional)
1 teaspoon vanilla
1 cup sugar
3 tablespoons instant coffee powder
2 tablespoons cinnamon
1 teaspoon mace

Thoroughly cream the cheese with electric mixer. Add eggs one at a time, beating well after each. Add remaining ingredients and blend until just mixed well. Pour into prepared pan. Bake at 350° about 45-60 minutes or until center is set. Remove from oven, cover with topping (recipe follows), and bake for 5 minutes. Cool to room temperature and then refrigerate until ready to serve. *Serves 12-16.*

TOPPING

1 cup sour cream
1/2 cup sugar
1 tablespoon cocoa
1 teaspoon cinnamon

Mix together well and proceed as described above.

CHOCOLATE CHEESECAKE

Chocolate lovers will call this intense — and it may be rated as your number one favorite.

CRUST

24 chocolate icebox cookies or graham crackers, crushed
1/4 cup melted butter
1/4 teaspoon cinnamon

Mix together cookie crumbs, melted butter, and cinnamon and press into 8-inch springform pan. Refrigerate until ready to use.

FILLING

12 ounces semi-sweet chocolate
1 1/2 pounds softened cream cheese
1 cup sugar
2 eggs
2 teaspoons unsweetened cocoa
1 teaspoon vanilla
1 1/2 cups sour cream

Preheat oven to 350°. Melt semi-sweet chocolate in double boiler and then let cool. In a bowl beat the cream cheese until smooth. Then beat in sugar, the eggs, 1 at a time, melted chocolate, cocoa, and vanilla. With a rubber spatula fold in the sour cream until thoroughly mixed. Pour into pan and bake 50-60 minutes or more. Cool at room temperature for 1 hour and then refrigerate for 3-4 hours. *Serves 12-16.*

THE LONDONDERRY INN
South Londonderry, Vermont

BLACK VELVET CAKE

"This two-layer sponge cake filled with chocolate mousse and topped with a bittersweet chocolate glaze is a proven favorite of our 'chocoholic' guests! Though at first glance this may appear to be a long and complicated recipe, it is well worth trying and not difficult to prepare as long as the recipe is closely followed."

SPONGE LAYERS

Plain bread crumbs
4 eggs, separated
1/4 cup granulated sugar
3 tablespoons sifted all-purpose flour
Pinch of salt
3 tablespoons confectioners sugar for sprinkling on cake layer

Preheat oven to 350° and adjust rack to 2/3 up from bottom. Butter and dust with bread crumbs two 10-inch springform pans.

In the small bowl of an electric mixer beat egg yolks and granulated sugar on high speed until well blended and a light cream color. Add the flour a little at a time until incorporated.

Add the salt to the egg whites in a separate mixing bowl. Using clean blades on the mixer, beat on high speed until egg whites hold their shape but are not dry.

Fold the whites in thirds into the yolks, being careful to handle no more than necessary. Pour into pans making sure that the batter is smooth and covers each pan equally. Bake for about 18 minutes. Remove from oven and let stand until well cooled.

CHOCOLATE MOUSSE

6 ounces chocolate morsels
1 ounce bitter (baker's) chocolate
1 teaspoon hot coffee
6 eggs, separated
1 teaspoon kirsch or other liqueur

(continued)

In the top of a double boiler heat the chocolates and the coffee until smooth and creamy. Keep hot but do not cook. Beat egg whites as before, but a bit stiffer. Incorporate the 6 yolks into the melted chocolate and add the liqueur. Fold in the whites one third at a time and chill.

BITTERSWEET CHOCOLATE GLAZE

6 ounces semi-sweet chocolate
1 ounce unsweetened chocolate
3 tablespoons prepared coffee
2 tablespoons dark rum
3 tablespoons sweet (or unsalted) butter at room temperature

Melt chocolates with coffee in top of a double boiler, adding rum and whipping until smooth. Allow to set at room temperature for about 15 minutes or until warm, but not cool. Gradually whip in butter until very smooth. Glaze should have a dark, satiny appearance.

To assemble:

To remove sponge cake from springform pan simply run a thin-bladed knife around the edges between cake and pan, release spring, and lift pan from around the cake. Make sure cake is cool when doing this. Slide a long thin knife, such as a roast beef slicing knife, under the sponge cake to free it from the bottom of the pan. Slide the cake onto a serving platter of appropriate design and cover with all of the chocolate mousse. The mousse should be well chilled and very firm at this point. Repeat steps for removing the second sponge cake, which should be sprinkled with confectioners sugar. (This keeps the cake from adhering to one's fingers.) Invert and place on top of mousse-covered layer. Pour chocolate glaze on top of cake, making sure top is well covered with a little running off onto the sides. Chill cake until glaze has set. Remove from refrigerator ½ hour before serving to allow the cake to warm up as this further enhances the flavor.

Serves 12-14.

CHOCOLATE AND RASPBERRY CAKE

A spectacular dessert that is almost *too pretty to eat. But you will succumb . . . happily.*

CAKE

3 egg yolks
1 small whole egg
½ cup sugar
⅔ cup finely ground blanched almonds
½ cup plus 2 tablespoons unsweetened cocoa
¼ cup and 1 tablespoon flour
3 tablespoons melted and cooled butter
4 egg whites
Pinch of salt
3 tablespoons sugar
3 tablespoons raspberry jam to spread on baked layers (if desired, sieve to remove seeds)

In a large bowl beat the egg yolks, whole egg, and ½ cup sugar until mixture is light and fluffy. Add almonds. In a bowl sift together 3 times the cocoa and flour. Fold into the egg mixture alternately with the butter. In another bowl beat egg whites with salt until they hold soft peaks, then beat in 3 tablespoons sugar until they hold stiff peaks. Fold whites into cocoa mixture. Pour into a 9-inch greased cake pan and bake in a preheated 375° oven for 25 minutes. Invert the cake on a rack and let it cool.

FROSTING

1⅓ cups scalded cream
1 pound semi-sweet chocolate chips

Pour scalded cream over chocolate chips and stir till smooth. Chill for 1 hour, then beat until it holds soft peaks.

BRANDY SYRUP

⅓ cup water
3 tablespoons sugar
3 tablespoons eau de vie framboise or kirsch

(continued)

Combine water and sugar and boil, stirring, for 2 minutes. Remove from heat, cool, and add brandy. Heat before spreading on cake.

To assemble:

Slice cake in half. Put the bottom layer, cut side down, on a plate. Brush both layers with warmed syrup. Spread each layer with the raspberry jam. Put one layer on top of the other and frost top and sides with chocolate cream. *Serves 12.*

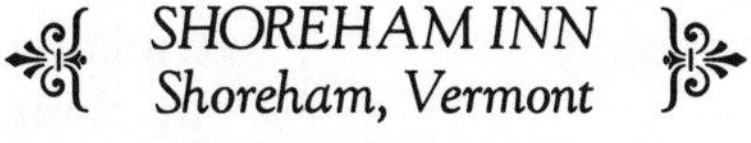
SHOREHAM INN
Shoreham, Vermont

DOUBLE FUDGE INN BAR

Top with ice cream, hot fudge sauce, and whipped cream — then dig in!

2 cups sugar
2 cups flour
1 cup oleo
1 cup water
4 tablespoons unsweetened cocoa
½ cup sour cream
2 eggs
1 teaspoon baking soda

In large bowl, blend sugar and flour. Put oleo, water, and cocoa in saucepan and bring to boil. Add to dry ingredients in bowl. Then stir in sour cream, eggs, and soda. Mixture will be very runny. Bake in greased 15½x10½-inch pan at 375° for 20-30 minutes.

ICING

1 cup chopped walnuts
2½ cups confectioners sugar
1 teaspoon vanilla
½ cup oleo
6 tablespoons milk
4 tablespoons unsweetened cocoa

In bowl combine nuts, confectioners sugar, and vanilla. Put oleo, milk, and cocoa in saucepan and bring to a boil. Add to ingredients in bowl and blend. Spread warm icing on warm cake. *Serves 16.*

WINDFLOWER INN
Great Barrington, Massachusetts

CHOCOLATE LOVER'S CAKE

"This is a dense chocolate cake that our guests rave about! Serve with a dollop of barely sweetened whipped cream."

CAKE

8 ounces semi-sweet chocolate bits
4 ounces unsweetened chocolate
2 tablespoons milk
1/3 cup sugar
10 tablespoons unsalted butter
7 extra-large eggs, separated
1/2 cup flour
2 tablespoons coffee liqueur

Melt chocolates with milk over low heat or in microwave. In a separate pan, melt butter and sugar, stirring until sugar is just dissolved. Blend with the chocolate mixture. Add egg yolks one at a time, beating well after each addition. Mix in flour until just blended. Set aside. Beat egg whites until firm but not dry and gently fold into batter. Pour into greased and floured 10-inch layer cake pan and bake at 400° for about 20 minutes. (Cake should shrink from sides of pan.) Let cool in pan and then turn out onto rack. Brush top with coffee liqueur and let cool.

CHOCOLATE WHIPPED CREAM

4 ounces heavy cream
2 tablespoons sugar
1 tablespoon unsweetened cocoa

Beat all together and spread over top of cooled cake.

CHOCOLATE GLAZE

4 ounces semi-sweet chocolate
2 ounces unsweetened chocolate
4 tablespoons sugar
4 tablespoons water
4 tablespoons unsalted butter, softened

Melt chocolates with sugar and water. Add butter and stir until smooth. Let stand until slightly thickened and pour gently over whipped-cream-covered cake. Smooth over top and sides with spatula.

Serves 12-15.

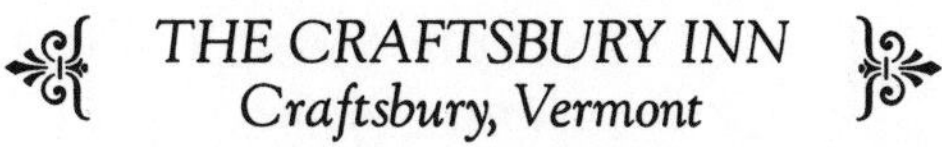

THE CRAFTSBURY INN
Craftsbury, Vermont

CRAFTSBURY INN CHOCOLATE FUDGY CAKE

"Baked fudge" pretty well sums up the richness of this flourless cake.

8 ounces semi-sweet chocolate chips
1/2 cup strong black coffee
1 cup sweet butter
1 cup sugar
4 eggs, lightly beaten

In a double boiler set over hot water, melt chocolate in coffee. Slowly add butter and sugar a little at a time until all has been added and well blended. Remove from heat and slowly add eggs, stirring constantly.

Pour chocolate mixture through a strainer into a buttered and floured 8-inch springform pan that has been wrapped in foil to prevent leakage. Bake at 350° for 50-60 minutes. Cover and refrigerate. May be made 2 days in advance. *Serves 8.*

STAFFORD'S IN THE FIELD
Chocorua, New Hampshire

STAFFORD'S COUNTRY GINGERBREAD

An old family recipe that yields a dark, very moist, and molassesy gingerbread. Top with sliced bananas and lots of whipped cream.

1 cup sugar
1 cup molasses
1 cup oil
3 large eggs
1 teaspoon cinnamon
1 teaspoon ginger
1 teaspoon salt
2 teaspoons baking soda
2 tablespoons boiling water
1 cup boiling water
2 cups flour

Beat together the first 7 ingredients. Mix soda with 2 tablespoons water and add to first mixture. While beating, add 1 cup boiling water and flour alternately — start with flour and end with the water. Pour into lightly oiled 13x9-inch pan and bake 40 minutes at 350°. *Serves 12-15.*

CLEFTSTONE MANOR
Bar Harbor, Maine

WHITE GINGERBREAD

This light, moist spice cake makes a lovely dessert, as well as a breakfast or brunch treat. It packs well, too, so could easily go in a lunch box or on a picnic.

2 cups flour
1 cup sugar
1/2 cup butter
1 teaspoon cinnamon
1/2 teaspoon ginger
1/4 teaspoon mace
1/4 teaspoon salt
1/2 teaspoon baking soda
1/2 teaspoon baking powder
1 egg
1/2 cup buttermilk

Mix flour, sugar, and butter together until mixture resembles cornmeal. Add 1/2 teaspoon cinnamon and toss. Set aside one cup of this crumbly mixture. To the rest add ginger, mace, salt, soda, baking powder, and remaining cinnamon. Toss, then add egg and buttermilk. Beat smooth with electric mixer.

Sprinkle 1/2 cup of reserved crumbly mixture in bottom of an ungreased 8-inch-square pan and spread batter over it. Sprinkle remaining crumbly mixture evenly over top. Bake in a 350° oven for 30-40 minutes.

Serves 6-8.

MARTHA'S BLUEBERRY CAKE

"This recipe comes from an old college friend and is probably the most-asked-for recipe at the inn." Fancy enough for a party.

1/2 cup shortening
2 cups granulated sugar
3 eggs
3 1/2 cups flour
1/2 teaspoon salt
2 teaspoons baking powder
1 cup milk
3 cups blueberries, floured (fresh if possible)
1/2 cup brown sugar
1/3 cup flour
1/2 teaspoon cinnamon
1/4 cup butter

Cream together the shortening and granulated sugar. Add the eggs, beating after each. Combine 3 1/2 cups flour, salt, and baking powder and add alternately with milk to creamed mixture. Stir in blueberries and pour batter into a greased and floured 10-inch tube pan. Mix together brown sugar, 1/3 cup flour, cinnamon, and butter, and sprinkle over batter. Bake 1 hour and 20 minutes at 350°. *Makes one 10-inch tube cake.*

THE BETHEL INN
Bethel, Maine

LEMON ICE BOX CAKE

A deliciously simple dessert that tastes like ice cream.

1¼ cups sugar
4 eggs, separated
Juice and rind of 1½ lemons
3 heaping tablespoons lemon Jello mix
1 cup boiling water
Pinch of salt
½ pint whipped cream
8 vanilla wafers

Mix together ¾ cup sugar, egg yolks, and juice and rind of the lemons. Cook until thick. Dissolve lemon Jello in boiling water and cool until congealed. Mix with sugar and yolk mixture and let stand until firm. Whip egg whites with remaining ½ cup sugar and salt. Fold whipped cream and egg whites into gelled mixture. Roll vanilla wafers into crumbs. Sprinkle half on buttered freezing tray, pour in filling, and sprinkle other half on top. Freeze at least 4 hours. *Serves 6-10.*

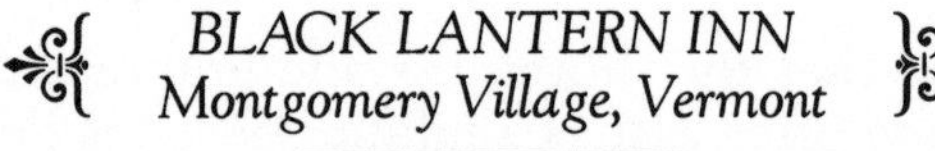

BLACK LANTERN INN
Montgomery Village, Vermont

LAYERED APPLE CAKE

"Very easy. We serve it with whipped cream and grated walnuts." Looks as if it should be front and center in a bakery window.

5 tablespoons sugar
2 teaspoons cinnamon
2 cups sugar
1 cup salad oil
4 eggs
3 cups flour
1 teaspoon salt
3 teaspoons baking powder
¼ cup orange juice
2½ teaspoons vanilla
4 to 6 apples, peeled, cored, and sliced

Grease Bundt pan or tube pan. Preheat oven to 350°. Combine 5 tablespoons sugar with cinnamon. Beat together until smooth and thick the 2 cups sugar, oil, eggs, flour, salt, baking powder, juice, and vanilla. Into prepared pan pour half the batter, then half the apples, and then half the sugar-cinnamon mixture. Repeat layers with remaining halves. Bake for 1¼-1½ hours. Cool in pan until lukewarm. *Serves 8-10.*

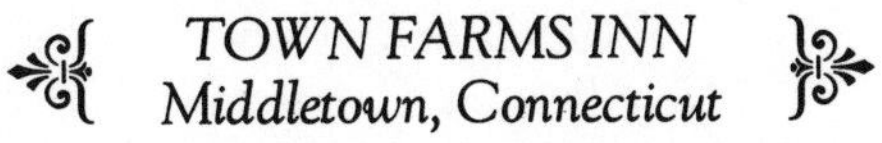

TOWN FARMS INN
Middletown, Connecticut

CARROT CAKE

Possibly the very best carrot cake you will have ever had — chock-full of nuts, raisins, carrots, and pineapple, with an icing that has just the right amount of cream cheese.

1½ cups oil
2 cups sugar
3 eggs
2 teaspoons vanilla
2 cups sifted flour
2 teaspoons cinnamon
2 teaspoons baking soda
1 teaspoon salt
2 cups shredded carrots
1 cup chopped nuts
½ cup crushed pineapple (8-ounce can, thoroughly drained)
1 cup raisins

Beat together oil, sugar, and eggs. Add vanilla. Sift dry ingredients and stir into sugar mixture. Add carrots, nuts, pineapple, and raisins and blend thoroughly. Bake in greased and floured 13x9-inch baking pan at 350° for 1 hour. Cool completely and cover with Cream Cheese Frosting (recipe follows). *Serves 12-14.*

CREAM CHEESE FROSTING

3 ounces cream cheese
1¼ cups sifted confectioners sugar
¼ pound butter or margarine
⅛ cup crushed pineapple (optional)
¼ cup nuts (optional)

Beat all ingredients together until smooth, then spread over cooled cake.

BRANDIED ORANGE NUT CAKE

Still delicious a few days after it is made. Serve with vanilla ice cream.

¾ cup shortening (or margarine or butter)
1½ cups sugar
2 eggs
3 cups flour
¼ teaspoon salt
1 teaspoon baking soda
1 cup sour cream
Juice and grated rind from half an orange
½ cup chopped nuts
½ cup raisins
½ teaspoon vanilla
Topping (recipe follows)

Cream shortening and sugar. Add eggs and mix until smooth. Sift flour and salt. Add soda to sour cream. Add flour and sour cream alternately to creamed mixture. Stir in orange juice and rind, nuts, raisins, and vanilla. Bake at 350° in greased and floured tube pan for about 45 minutes or until cake tests done. Pour on topping and let cake cool completely before cutting.

Serves 12.

TOPPING

½ cup sugar
½ cup orange juice
1 ounce brandy

Combine all ingredients and pour over cake as soon as it is removed from oven.

QUEEN ELIZABETH CAKE

A royal addition to any table. It is said that Queen Elizabeth I herself would go into the kitchen to make this cake. Instead of packaged dates, the inn uses date crystals and additional water. (The crystals are available from Shield's Date Gardens, Indio, CA 92201.)

1 cup boiling water
1½ cups chopped dates (or 1 cup date crystals plus ⅓ cup water)
1 teaspoon baking soda
1 cup sugar
¼ cup butter
1 egg, beaten
1 teaspoon vanilla
1½ cups sifted flour
½ teaspoon baking powder
½ cup chopped nuts
Icing (recipe follows)

Pour boiling water over chopped dates (or date crystals and water), stir in soda, and set aside. Cream together sugar and butter. Beat in egg and vanilla. Sift together flour and baking powder and add to batter, along with nuts. Add date mixture and stir until well blended. Pour into well greased and floured 9-inch-square pan and bake at 350° for 45-50 minutes or until cake tests done. While still hot pour icing over top and sprinkle liberally with coconut. *Serves 10-12.*

ICING

⅓ cup brown sugar
⅓ cup cream
2 tablespoons butter
Shredded coconut

Boil brown sugar, cream, and butter together for 3 minutes and pour over cake. Sprinkle with coconut.

THE VALLEY INN
Waitsfield, Vermont

ROXIE'S CAKE

"This cake smells so good while baking that I must put my dog Roxie outdoors. The first time I made it, when she was just six months old and a very active puppy, I left it on the kitchen counter and later found only the plate, a few crumbs on the floor, and one guilty doggy. Two weeks later I made the cake again but left it in the corner of the counter surrounded by baking supplies. Again the cake disappeared but few baking supplies were moved. Came our daughter's birthday and a request for Roxie's Cake. In a hurry, I left the cake on the counter, closed the door, ran to the store to purchase birthday candles, and came home to find husband had left kitchen door open. I caught not only Roxie but our other dog Spooky eating the cake while it was still on the plate on the counter and quite warm. Lesson to be learned: lock both dogs outdoors, bake cake, place on top of refrigerator, and do not leave the kitchen!" A light, moist pound cake that humans love too.

2½ cups sugar
2 sticks margarine
4 eggs
½ teaspoon baking soda
1 tablespoon boiling water
3 cups sifted flour
1 cup buttermilk
1 teaspoon vanilla
1 teaspoon almond extract

Preheat oven to 350°. Cream sugar and margarine together well. Add eggs, one at a time, beating after each addition. Dissolve baking soda in boiling water and combine with creamed mixture. Slowly add flour and buttermilk, alternately, and continue beating until well mixed. Stir in flavorings. Pour into well greased and lightly floured Bundt pan or tube pan lined with wax paper on the bottom. Bake for about 1 hour. *Serves 12.*

1811 HOUSE
Manchester, Vermont

TRIFLE

Each step is simple to do, but because the gelatin and custard layers have to set up, this is not a spur-of-the-moment dessert.

1 pound cake (Sara Lee or homemade)
Red raspberry jam
¾ cup medium sherry
1 small package raspberry Jello, liquid added according to directions
1 small package strawberry Jello, liquid added according to directions
1 small package "Birds" custard mix (plus 2¼ cups milk)
1 small carton heavy cream, whipped
Strawberries

Slice pound cake and sandwich with raspberry jam. Cut to fit bottom of large glass bowl with a flat bottom. Soak with sherry. Pour liquid raspberry Jello over all, pricking cake with a fork so it will absorb Jello. Refrigerate until set. Pour on cooled strawberry Jello and refrigerate until set. Make custard according to instructions. Cool and pour over. Cover with plastic wrap and refrigerate until ready to serve. Top with whipped cream and decorate with strawberries. *Serves 8-10.*

EDENCROFT MANOR
Littleton, New Hampshire

APRICOT TRIFLE

A fantastic party dessert. Apricot brandy and jam contribute an appealing tartness.

1 classic French sponge cake (9 inches) or your favorite yellow layer cake
Apricot brandy to moisten cake
2 jars (10 ounces each) apricot jam
2 cups pastry cream (recipe follows)
2 cups whipped cream (recipe follows)

Slice cake into 3 layers. Place first layer in trifle or glass bowl and drizzle with brandy until layer is moist. Spread with apricot jam. Spread pastry cream over jam, then whipped cream. Repeat jam/pastry cream/whipped cream sequence twice more, ending with whipped cream. *Serves 15-18.*

PASTRY CREAM

2 cups milk
6 egg yolks
2/3 cup sugar
1 teaspoon vanilla
1/2 cup flour

Bring milk to boil and set aside. Mix egg yolks, sugar, and vanilla in a bowl with a wire whisk, until mixture forms a ribbon. Add flour and mix well (will become rather thick). Add half the boiled milk to the yolk mixture, mixing well. Pour yolk mixture into remaining milk, mixing as you go along. Bring to a boil on medium heat, stirring constantly with the whisk. Sauce will thicken as soon as it reaches the boiling point. Reduce heat and cook 2 to 3 minutes. NOTE: Be very careful at this point; sauce will burn very quickly if heat is too high. Pour into a bowl, cover with plastic wrap, and poke a few holes to allow cream to breathe. Refrigerate for 1-2 hours or until completely cooled.

WHIPPED CREAM

2 cups whipping cream
1/2 cup confectioners sugar
1/2 teaspoon vanilla

Add all ingredients to a bowl. Beat to desired thickness.

THE SCOTTISH LION
North Conway, New Hampshire

SCOTTISH LION TRIFLE

So good it's gotta be sinful!

CUSTARD SAUCE

6 cups milk
3 tablespoons cornstarch
4 tablespoons sugar
4 egg yolks
2 teaspoons vanilla

In heavy saucepan, combine 1 cup milk and all the cornstarch. Stir with wire whisk until cornstarch is dissolved. Add the remaining 5 cups milk and the sugar; cook over moderate heat, stirring constantly until the sauce thickens and comes to a boil. In a smaller bowl, break up the egg yolks with a fork and stir in about a *half cup* of the sauce; then whisk the mixture back into the remaining sauce. Bring to a boil again and boil for 1 minute, stirring constantly. Remove the pan from the heat and add the vanilla extract.

TRIFLE

2 large round sponge cake layers
1/4 cup orange juice
1/4 cup sherry
Raspberry jam
6 medium peaches, sliced
1 pint whipped cream
Chopped walnuts for topping

The trifle may be layered any way you choose; we at the Scottish Lion layer it as follows. Line the bottom of a large trifle dish with one layer of the sponge cake. Mix the orange juice and the sherry together and pour *half* of the mixture over the cake. Cover the layer with raspberry jam. Place another layer of cake over the jam and pour the remaining orange juice and sherry mixture over it; cover with raspberry jam. Next, add a layer of sliced peaches, followed by the custard sauce, more raspberry jam, and another layer of peaches. Top with whipped cream and nuts just before serving.

Serves 6.

SUGAR HILL INN
Franconia, New Hampshire

GINGERSNAPS

"This is a great recipe for teaching small children how to make their first cookies. The cookies come out about silver-dollar-size and little ones can eat a bunch of them."

3/4 cup shortening
1 egg
1 cup sugar
1/4 cup dark molasses
2 cups sifted flour
1/2 teaspoon ground cloves
2 teaspoons ginger
1 1/2 teaspoons baking soda
1 1/2 teaspoons cinnamon
3/4 teaspoon salt
Sugar for rolling

Combine shortening, egg, 1 cup sugar, and molasses in bowl. Sift flour and other dry ingredients into another bowl. Fold dry ingredients into wet mixture and beat. Form dough into small balls like marbles. Roll in sugar and bake on cookie sheet in oven at 350° for about 15 minutes. *Makes 3 dozen.*

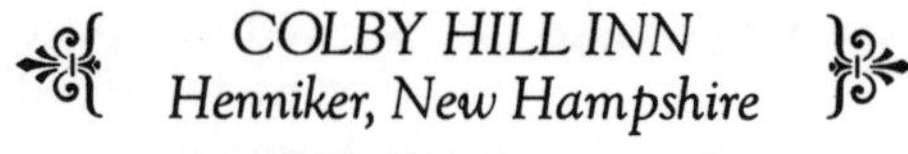

COLBY HILL INN
Henniker, New Hampshire

BROWNIES

Fudge-like and full of nuts.

1 cup butter
8 squares baker's chocolate
3 1/3 cups sugar
4 eggs
2 teaspoons salt
2 cups flour
2 cups chopped walnuts
1 teaspoon vanilla

Melt butter and chocolate in large saucepan. Remove from heat, add sugar, and mix well. Add eggs, one at a time, mixing well after each addition. Stir in salt, flour, nuts, and vanilla, mixing well; pour into greased 15x11-inch cookie sheet with sides. Bake at 350° for 20-25 minutes. Do *not* overcook. *Makes about 3 dozen.*

LEMON SQUARES

The crust has the buttery richness of shortbread, and the tart filling will remind you of lemon meringue pie.

2 cups flour
1/2 pound butter (or half butter, half oleo)
1/2 cup confectioners sugar
4 eggs, beaten
2 cups granulated sugar
1/2 teaspoon salt
6 tablespoons lemon juice (juice from 2 lemons)
Grated rind of 2 lemons
1/4 cup flour
2 teaspoons confectioners sugar

Cream together the 2 cups flour, butter, and ½ cup confectioners sugar. Spread into a 13x9-inch pan. Bake at 350° for 15 minutes. Crust should be a pale gold at edge.

In a bowl, mix eggs, granulated sugar, and salt. Then blend in lemon juice and rind. Sift ¼ cup flour and 2 teaspoons confectioners sugar into egg mixture; fold in. Pour egg mixture over crust and return to oven for 30 minutes. Sift confectioners sugar over top after taking from the oven, if desired.

Makes 10-12 large squares.

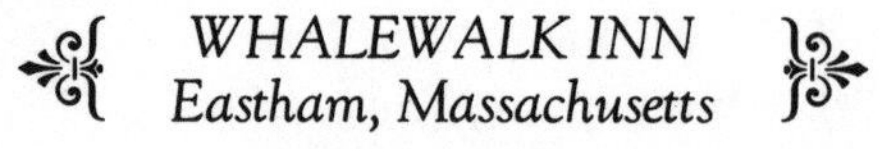

WHALEWALK INN
Eastham, Massachusetts

BUCKEYES

"There are many similar recipes for the following cookie-candy concoction, but the Rice Krispies make these unique."

1 cup confectioners sugar
1/4 cup butter
1/2 cup plus 2 tablespoons creamy peanut butter
3/4 cup Rice Krispies
6 ounces semi-sweet chocolate bits
1/8 cake of paraffin

Mix first 4 ingredients thoroughly, then roll into small balls. Melt chocolate bits and paraffin in the top of a double boiler. Dip balls into chocolate, then place on foil to harden. *Makes 30-35.*

FOLLANSBEE INN
North Sutton, New Hampshire

SWEET TREATS

"Our daughter Nancy found this recipe and she made some for the opening of our inn in June 1978. They were such a hit that we continued serving them. Now daughter Wendy makes the mints. They are time-consuming but something we feel we cannot do without."

6 ounces cream cheese
3 1/2 tablespoons butter
3/4 teaspoon peppermint extract
Food coloring paste
2 pounds confectioners sugar
Superfine sugar

Blend cream cheese, butter, extract, and a very little food coloring paste together with an electric beater. Add more coloring if you desire a darker candy. Mix in the confectioners sugar a little at a time. Make small balls, roll in superfine sugar, and press into candy molds, pop out and place in small fluted papers.

Makes 2 pounds candy.

PUDDINGS, FRUIT AND FROZEN DESSERTS

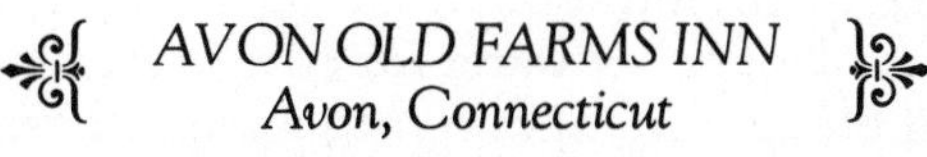

INDIAN PUDDING

"This is a typical New England dessert, which is quite popular with diners at Avon Old Farms Inn. We serve it warm, with a generous dollop of whipped cream."

4½ cups milk
¾ cup yellow cornmeal
¾ cup molasses
1 teaspoon ginger
1 teaspoon salt

In the top of a double boiler combine milk and cornmeal. Cook over low heat, stirring often so that the bottom will not scorch. Cook about 20 minutes. Set aside and add the molasses, ginger, and salt, mixing well with a wire whisk. Pour into a shallow greased baking pan. Place pan into a water bath (a bottom pan with water, for a double boiler effect). Bake at 350° for about 1 hour. Using a wire whisk stir frequently or pudding will get lumpy. Cook until pudding is thick, then turn off heat and leave pan in the oven with door open so pudding may cool. Pudding may be served hot or cold, with whipped cream or ice cream.

Serves 6-8.

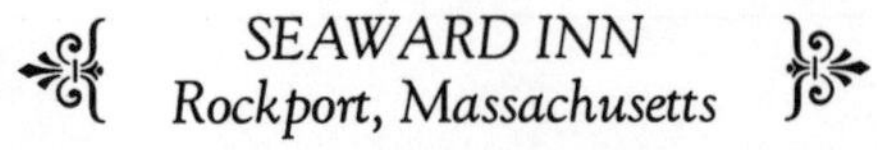

SEAWARD INN
Rockport, Massachusetts

BAKED INDIAN PUDDING

"New England Indian Pudding should be soft. For finest flavor use the best dark molasses."

1 quart milk
5 tablespoons cornmeal
2 tablespoons butter
1 cup "Grandma's" molasses
1 teaspoon salt
1 teaspoon cinnamon
1/4 teaspoon nutmeg
1/4 teaspoon ginger
2 eggs, well beaten
1 cup cold milk

Scald milk in double boiler. Using a whisk, slowly stir in cornmeal and cook over hot water for 20 minutes. Add all but last ingredient and blend well. Spoon into a 2-quart buttered baking dish. Pour over it the cold milk but do not stir. Bake in preheated 300° oven for 1½-2 hours. Serve with heavy cream or ice cream.

Serves 8-10.

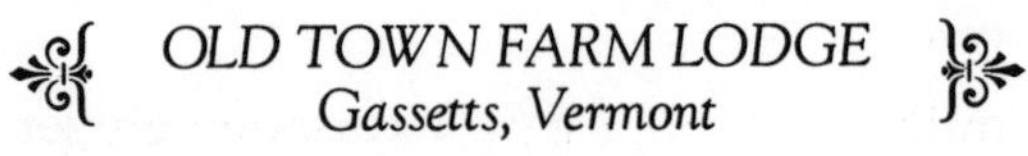

OLD TOWN FARM LODGE
Gassetts, Vermont

GLORIFIED RICE PUDDING

An old-fashioned treat adorned with whipped cream and maple syrup.

3 cups milk
1/3 cup rice, rinsed (do not use quick-cooking rice)
Pinch of salt
1/2 cup sugar
1 teaspoon vanilla
1 envelope unflavored gelatin
Maple syrup
1 cup whipped cream

Put milk in double boiler, add rice and salt, and cook, covered, until soft — about 45 minutes. Remove from heat and add sugar, vanilla, and gelatin, stirring to blend. Pour into a bowl and chill thoroughly. When ready to serve, top with syrup and whipped cream.

Serves 6.

JUDY'S CINNAMON-RAISIN BREAD PUDDING

"This recipe nearly always brings back memories to our male diners of the bread pudding that 'Mother' or 'Grandmother' used to make. It's a standard favorite here at The Birchwood."

4 to 5 slices white and/or whole wheat bread, dried in oven
1/6 cup butter, melted
1/3 cup brown sugar
1 teaspoon cinnamon
1/4 cup raisins
2 jumbo or 3 small eggs, beaten
2 1/2 cups milk, scalded
1 teaspoon vanilla
1/8 teaspoon salt
1/4 cup sugar

Cube bread slices and place in greased 8- or 9-inch-square pan. Pour melted butter over cubes. Sprinkle brown sugar, cinnamon, and raisins on it. Combine remaining ingredients in a separate container and pour over bread. Place bread pudding pan inside larger pan with a little hot water in it and bake in 350° oven for 35-40 minutes. *Serves 6-8.*

INDIAN SHUTTERS INN 
North Charlestown, New Hampshire

GRASSHOPPER PUDDING

A pretty, pale-green dessert to serve in long-stemmed or parfait glasses.

1½ pounds Campfire marshmallows (the brand, in this case, is important)
1 cup milk
½ cup green crème de menthe
¼ cup crème de cacao
1 quart heavy cream, whipped
Fine chocolate cookie crumbs made from Famous Chocolate Cookies (1 package)

Melt the marshmallows with the milk in a 6-quart pan over very low heat, stirring often with a wooden spoon to avoid burning. When completely melted, stir in the crème de menthe and crème de cacao. Set in a pan of cold water to thicken. When thickened, fold in the whipped cream. Sprinkle chocolate cookie crumbs in the bottoms of 12 to 14 dessert glasses. Divide the marshmallow mixture among the glasses and sprinkle more crumbs on top. *Serves 12-14.*

SYCAMORE INN
Arlington, Vermont

OUR BEST APPLE COBBLER

This can also be made with sliced peaches instead of apples, so use whichever fruit is in season.

1 stick butter or margarine
1½ cups quick oats (not instant)
¾ cup brown sugar
½ cup chopped walnuts (optional)
10 apples (approximately), the sourer the better

In medium saucepan, melt butter, then add oats, brown sugar, and nuts. Mix well. Peel, core, and slice apples and place in greased 13x9-inch baking pan. Cover with oat mixture. Pat down gently. Cover with foil and bake at 375° for 25 minutes. Remove foil and bake 20 more minutes or until apples are bubbling vigorously. Serve warm with a little heavy cream poured over. *Serves 12.*

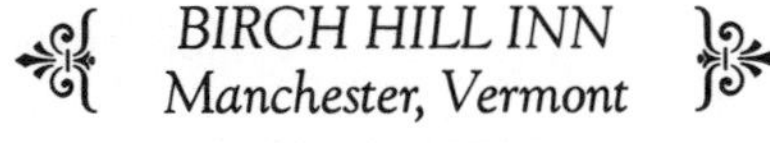

BIRCH HILL INN
Manchester, Vermont

RHUBARB CRUNCH

A great summer dessert — hot or cold. Wonderful crust for rhubarb.

1 cup flour
¾ cup uncooked rolled oats
1 cup brown sugar
½ cup butter or margarine, melted
1 teaspoon cinnamon
4 cups diced rhubarb
1 cup granulated sugar
2 tablespoons cornstarch (or minute tapioca)
1 cup water
1 teaspoon vanilla

Mix together flour, oats, brown sugar, butter, and cinnamon until crumbly. Press half of crumbs into 9-inch-square or 11x7-inch pan. Cover with rhubarb. In a saucepan combine granulated sugar, cornstarch, water, and vanilla and cook, stirring, until thick and clear — about 10 minutes. Pour over rhubarb, top with remaining crumbs, and bake at 350° for 1 hour. Cut in squares and serve with whipped cream or ice cream. *Serves 8.*

RHUBARB CRUNCH

"We have quite a large rhubarb patch and are always trying out different recipes. This one was given to us by Marion Cardwell, who owned and operated the Okemo Lantern Lodge for over 40 years. Marion does not give out too many of her trade secrets so we felt privileged to receive this one."

4 cups chopped rhubarb
1 cup sugar
2 tablespoons flour
2 tablespoons butter
1 cup flour
1 cup sugar
2 teaspoons baking powder
1/4 cup grapenuts or rolled oats
1 egg
1/2 stick butter, melted

Mix together first 4 ingredients and put in a greased 9-inch-square pan. Mix 1 cup flour, 1 cup sugar, baking powder, and grapenuts with the egg. Distribute this mixture over ingredients in pan and top with melted butter. Bake in 350° oven for 40 minutes. Top with vanilla ice cream. *Serves* 8.

AUNT MAGGIE'S GERMAN KUCHEN

"My husband Don's Aunt Maggie from Bavaria, Germany, gave me this recipe, and it has been a family favorite for the 30 years we have been married. Now our inn guests enjoy it as well."

1/3 cup white shortening
1 cup sugar
1 egg, beaten
3 cups all-purpose flour
3 teaspoons baking powder
1 teaspoon salt
1 teaspoon vanilla
1 cup milk
Fruit for filling (blueberries, sliced and peeled apples or peaches, sliced fresh strawberries, plums, etc.)
Streusel (recipe follows)

Cream shortening. Add sugar gradually, then beaten egg. Sift together flour, baking powder, and salt. Add vanilla to milk, then add flour and milk to the egg mixture a little at a time and beat well. Grease and flour a 15x11-inch cookie sheet with sides. Spread batter thin in pan. Add whatever fruit you desire or a combination. Cover with streusel and bake at 350° for 25-30 minutes or until done. *Serves 20.*

STREUSEL

1 cup flour
1 cup sugar
1/2 cup softened margarine

Mix with butter knives until crumbly and put on top of fruit.

FRIED STRAWBERRIES WITH CUSTARD SAUCE

Tantalizing golden morsels in a pool of smooth custard.

2 cups flour
1/4 teaspoon sugar
1/2 teaspoon salt
12 ounces beer
5 egg whites
Strawberries (6 per person)
1/4 cup sugar
2 teaspoons cinnamon

In a medium-sized mixing bowl combine flour, 1/4 teaspoon sugar, 1/4 teaspoon salt, and beer. Mix into a paste.

In another medium-sized mixing bowl, whip egg whites with remaining 1/4 teaspoon salt until stiff peaks form. Fold beer mixture into beaten egg whites.

Wash the strawberries and hull them. (The amount of berries is up to you. We serve 6 per order.) Dip them into the batter and deep fry until golden brown, about 2-3 minutes. Roll the berries in 1/4 cup sugar mixed with 2 teaspoons cinnamon. Serve on custard sauce (recipe follows). *Serves 10.*

CUSTARD SAUCE

2 cups light cream
1/4 cup sugar
2 teaspoons vanilla
3 egg yolks

In a heavy-bottomed saucepan, scald the cream, sugar, and vanilla. Beat the egg yolks in a small bowl until light yellow. Add the scalded cream to the beaten yolks, beating constantly. Transfer to a heavy saucepan and continue cooking over low heat until mixture coats the back side of a spoon. Transfer to a chilled bowl and chill, covered, for 2 hours.

POIRES EN SURPRISE

French vanilla ice cream topped with poached pears, sprinkled with toasted almonds, and draped with rum-chocolate sauce.

1 pound sugar
1 pint cold water
1 teaspoon vanilla
6 medium-sized ripe pears
½ cup slivered almonds
1 egg white, beaten until foamy
2 tablespoons sugar
8 ounces semi-sweet chocolate
1 cup syrup (use syrup in which pears were poached)
2 tablespoons rum
2 egg yolks
¼ cup light cream
1½ quarts French vanilla ice cream

Combine 1 pound sugar, water, and vanilla in pan and cook over medium heat, stirring along bottom of pan to prevent sugar from settling while mixture comes to a boil. As the boiling point is reached, sugar crystals may form along side of pan. Brush them down with pastry brush dipped in hot water. When sugar syrup comes to a boil, remove pan from heat and set aside. Peel pears, cut in half lengthwise, and core. Gently place them in sugar syrup and poach, uncovered, over medium heat for about an hour. Remove from stove and let pears cool in the syrup. (After preparing this dessert, the leftover syrup can be used again for poaching other fruits or in sauces, so don't toss it out.)

Toss almonds in beaten egg white. Remove, drain slightly, and sprinkle with 2 tablespoons sugar. Put on cookie sheet and toast at 325°. Keep an eye on them as they color rapidly. Remove when golden.

Break chocolate into small pieces and melt in top of double boiler over simmering water. Stir until smooth, then add syrup and rum. Keep warm but not hot. Beat egg yolks with cream and stir into chocolate mixture. Keep warm but do not boil. (If made ahead, sauce can be refrigerated and reheated in double boiler when ready to use.)

Place a scoop of ice cream in each of 6 individual glass or china bowls. Place 2 pear halves over ice cream, cavity side down. Sprinkle toasted almonds over top. Serve warmed chocolate sauce in sauce boat and allow guests to help themselves. *Serves 6.*

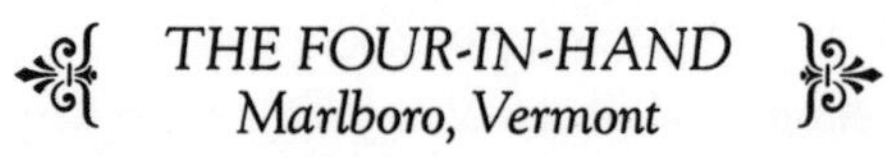

THE FOUR-IN-HAND
Marlboro, Vermont

APRICOTS FOUR-IN-HAND

Exquisite color and flavor combination.

1½ pounds fresh, ripe apricots, peeled, pitted, and cut up
⅓ cup unsalted butter
6 tablespoons brown sugar
⅓ cup good strawberry or raspberry liqueur
½ pint heavy cream
Melba sauce or raspberry purée with seeds removed
Fresh mint leaves or rose petals for garnish

Cook apricots in butter in heavy skillet and add brown sugar and liqueur. Mash mixture as it cooks, then remove from heat. Do not overcook — just long enough to melt the sugar. Chill mixture thoroughly. Spoon into individual serving dishes or stemmed wine glasses. Whip the cream with a shot glass full of Melba sauce or raspberry purée to give a delicate pink color and slightly sweet taste to the whipped cream. Spoon over apricots and garnish with mint or rose petals.

Serves 8.

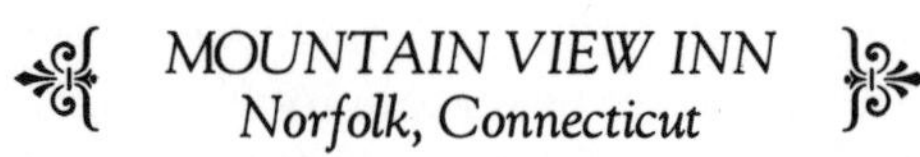

MOUNTAIN VIEW INN
Norfolk, Connecticut

STRAWBERRIES ROMANOFF

Make this for an impressive grand finale.

1 pint fresh strawberries
½ cup Grand Marnier
1 cup sour cream
1 tablespoon brown sugar
1 package strawberry Jello
1 lemon wedge
Whipped cream for topping

Hull and cut strawberries in half or bite-sized pieces. Place in bowl. Pour Grand Marnier over berries and stir. Set aside. Combine sour cream, sugar, and ¼ tablespoon Jello. Wet rims of 8 stemmed glasses with lemon wedge and dip in remaining Jello. Divide strawberries into 8 equal portions in glasses. Pour sour cream mixture over berries, top with whipped cream, and serve.

Serves 8.

BEE AND THISTLE INN
Old Lyme, Connecticut

BLUEBERRY DUMPLINGS

The molasses makes all the difference.

3 cups blueberries (washed and picked over)
1/3 cup sugar
1/4 teaspoon cinnamon
1/4 teaspoon nutmeg
1/4 teaspoon ground cloves
1/4 cup molasses
2 tablespoons lemon juice
1 cup flour
1 1/2 tablespoons baking powder
1/4 teaspoon salt
3 tablespoons butter
1 tablespoon Crisco
1 egg
1 cup milk

Spread berries in a deep 9-inch pie pan. Combine the sugar and spices and sift them over the berries. Dribble the molasses over them and sprinkle with lemon juice. Bake at 375° for 5 minutes (until they start to give juices). Remove pan from the oven and increase heat to 425°. Sift the flour, baking powder, and salt. Blend in the butter and shortening. Stir in the egg and milk. Drop the dough by tablespoons over the berries. Bake 20 minutes or until the crust is slightly browned. Serve hot with heavy cream.

Makes one 9-inch panful.

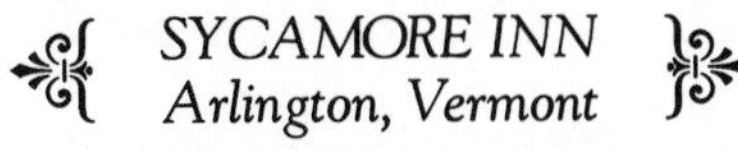
SYCAMORE INN
Arlington, Vermont

EASY CHOCOLATE MOUSSE

Although this must be made well ahead of time, it only takes 5 minutes to prepare!

6 ounces semi-sweet chocolate chips
2 large eggs
3 tablespoons instant coffee (powder or granules)
2 tablespoons boiling water
2 tablespoons rum or brandy (or 2 teaspoons mint or rum flavoring)
3/4 cup scalded milk

Put all ingredients in blender in the order given. Blend at high speed for 2 minutes. Pour into 6 individual dessert dishes and chill at least 3 hours. Serve with whipped cream or ice cream.

Serves 6.

PITTSFIELD INN
Pittsfield, Vermont

CHOCOLATE MOUSSE

There's just a whisper of Amaretto and a light sprinkling of slivered almonds.

4 ounces semi-sweet chocolate
1 pint heavy cream
1/2 teaspoon vanilla
1/4 ounce Amaretto
1/4 cup sugar
3 egg whites
Slivered almonds

Over a double boiler, melt chocolate. Whip heavy cream to medium-hard peaks with the vanilla, Amaretto, and sugar. Beat egg whites to stiff peaks. Slowly add whipped cream to chocolate, being careful not to make lumps (go slowly). Fold in egg whites. Place in dessert cups, top with slivered almonds, and serve well chilled.

Serves 5.

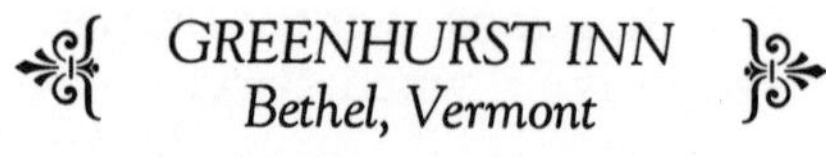

GREENHURST INN
Bethel, Vermont

LISA'S CHOCOLATE MOUSSE

"This recipe was sent to us by our daughter, Lisa, from California. It is so easy and foolproof and causes even our most diet-conscious guests to indulge."

16 ounces whipping cream
8 ounces semi-sweet chocolate
3 tablespoons rum

Whip cream until firm. Place in a cool area but do not refrigerate. (Refrigerating the whipped cream may cause the chocolate to harden into tiny pieces when folded into the cream. If this happens do not despair. The mousse still looks pretty and tastes delicious.)

Melt chocolate in a double boiler or in a bowl in your microwave oven. Allow to cool. Fold cooled chocolate into whipped cream, add rum, pile into pretty glasses and chill.

Serves 6-8.

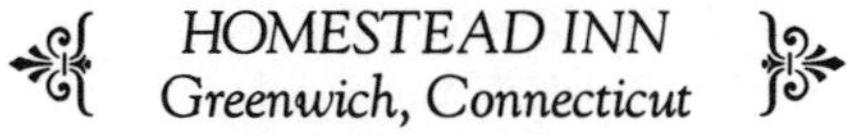

SOUFFLÉ GLACÉ AMARETTO

A luscious, cool, and creamy almond-flavored dessert that takes only minutes to prepare, but does require 4 to 6 hours freezing time.

6 egg yolks
2 whole eggs
3/4 cup sugar
1/4 cup Amaretto
2 cups whipped cream
3 ounces macaroon crumbs

Combine egg yolks, whole eggs, and sugar and beat on high speed until thick and fluffy. Add liqueur. By hand add whipped cream and macaroon crumbs. Pour gently into soufflé dish and freeze at least 4-6 hours.

To serve, top with whipped cream and macaroon crumbs.

Serves 6.

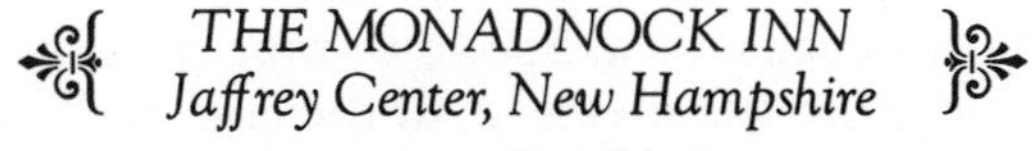

LEMON CREAM PARFAIT

Tangy, sweet, and cold! The perfect treat on a hot summer's eve.

1/4 cup butter
1 1/2 cups sugar
1/4 teaspoon salt
2/3 cup lemon juice
1 tablespoon grated lemon rind
3 egg yolks
3 whole eggs
1 cup heavy cream, whipped

Melt the butter in a double boiler; whisk in the sugar, salt, lemon juice, and lemon rind. Beat egg yolks and whole eggs together and add slowly to mixture in double boiler, stirring constantly. Continue stirring and cook mixture for 12-15 minutes until thick and shiny. Cool to room temperature and fold in whipped cream. Put lemon cream into dessert dishes and freeze.

Serves 6-8.

BEACH PLUM INN
Menemsha (Martha's Vineyard), Massachusetts

BEACH PLUM'S BOMBE WITH RASPBERRY SAUCE

A luscious frozen dessert that can be prepared a day in advance. The raspberry sauce adds tang as well as color.

FILLING

5 egg whites, at room temperature
1½ cups granulated sugar
2 cups heavy cream
2 tablespoons confectioners sugar
2 tablespoons kirsch or rum
½ teaspoon vanilla

Preheat the oven to 250°. Line 2 large cookie sheets with parchment or brown paper. Trace 4 circles 4 inches in diameter on one sheet and 5 circles the same size on the other.

Beat the egg whites until soft peaks form. Gradually beat in the granulated sugar, about 2 tablespoons at a time, and continue beating until stiff peaks form. Spoon or pipe the mixture, using a plain 1-inch tip, onto the sheets to fill the circles. (The meringues are broken into small pieces later, so don't worry if your circles are not perfect.)

Bake the meringues until lightly browned and crisp to the touch, about 1 hour. Transfer them on the paper to a wire rack and let cool completely; peel off the paper. Break the meringues into ¾-inch pieces and place in a large bowl. (If making them ahead, keep the meringues whole and store in an airtight tin.)

Beat the cream until soft peaks form; beat in the confectioners sugar, kirsch, and vanilla. Combine the cream with the broken meringue pieces and gently fold to mix. Spoon into a lightly oiled 8-inch springform pan; smooth the top. Cover with foil and freeze until firm, 6 hours or overnight.

RASPBERRY SAUCE

2 packages (10 ounces each) frozen raspberries, thawed
¼ cup sifted confectioners sugar
1 tablespoon kirsch or rum

(continued)

Drain the raspberries, reserving 1 cup of the syrup. Purée them in a blender or food processor. Pass through a fine strainer to remove the seeds. You should have about ½ cup of purée. Stir in the reserved syrup.

Place the raspberry purée in a small saucepan over low heat and gradually whisk in the sugar. Cook until the mixture thickens slightly, about 1 minute. Remove from the heat; let cool for 5 minutes. Stir in the kirsch, cover, and refrigerate until chilled.

To serve, loosen the edges of the bombe with a sharp knife and release the side of the pan. Cut the bombe into wedges and spoon about 2 tablespoons of sauce over each portion. Pass the remaining sauce in a small bowl. *Serves 10-12.*

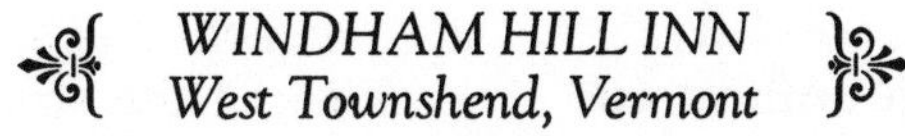

WINDHAM HILL INN
West Townshend, Vermont

STRAWBERRY DELIGHT

Terrific combination of textures — strawberries in whipped cream with buttery pecan crumbs top and bottom. Let sit at room temperature for 10 minutes before slicing.

1 cup all-purpose flour
½ cup chopped pecans
½ cup unsalted butter, melted
¼ cup brown sugar
1 box (10 ounces) frozen strawberries, thawed
1 cup granulated sugar
2 teaspoons fresh lemon juice
2 egg whites
1 cup heavy cream, whipped
Fresh strawberries for garnish

Combine flour, pecans, butter, and brown sugar in 8-inch-square pan. Bake for 20 minutes at 350°, stirring occasionally. Cool. Line a 9-inch springform pan with wax paper, grease lightly, and press ⅔ of crumb mixture in bottom of pan.

Combine thawed strawberries, granulated sugar, lemon juice, and egg whites in large bowl. Beat until stiff. Fold in whipped cream. Spoon into prepared pan and sprinkle remaining crumbs on top. Cover and freeze until firm. Garnish with whole fresh strawberries. *Serves 8.*

PEACH CHARLOTTE WITH STRAWBERRY SAUCE

Prepare 1 to 2 days in advance. If you don't have a charlotte mold, use a 1½-quart soufflé dish. The delicate peach flavor is a nice contrast to the sweetness of the strawberries.

2 dozen ladyfingers
6 egg yolks
⅔ cup granulated sugar
2 cups milk, scalded
1 tablespoon unflavored gelatin softened in 1 tablespoon water
1½ cups already whipped cream
½ cup diced peaches, fresh poached or canned
1 pint fresh strawberries
½ cup confectioners sugar, or to taste

Line a charlotte mold with ladyfingers, making sure each ladyfinger fits securely, leaving no space. Blend egg yolks and granulated sugar till very thick and lemon yellow. Slowly add scalded milk, place back on heat, and cook the custard for about 5 minutes over medium heat, stirring constantly. Do not allow to boil. Add softened gelatin and stir until dissolved. Strain custard through fine strainer into a metal bowl and place in larger bowl of ice cubes and water. Stir until almost set. Remove from ice. Fold in whipped cream and then peaches. Blend until perfectly smooth. Pour into prepared mold. Chill overnight to set.

Purée the strawberries and add confectioners sugar. Chill before serving.

Invert the mold on large plate. Spoon strawberry sauce around charlotte and pass extra sauce separately in a sauceboat.

Serves 6-8.

FROZEN CHOCOLATE CHARLOTTE

Truly a chocolate delight! It keeps very well in the freezer for up to 1 month if properly covered.

2 packages ladyfingers
1/4 cup white crème de menthe or rum
12-ounce package semi-sweet chocolate
3 tablespoons instant coffee
1/2 cup boiling water
6 egg yolks
1/2 cup sugar
1 teaspoon vanilla
6 egg whites
1 1/2 cups heavy cream

Brush flat surfaces of ladyfingers with liqueur and line sides of a 9-inch springform pan. Line bottom with remaining lady fingers, overlapping if necessary. Melt semi-sweet chocolate in the top of a double boiler. In separate container, dissolve instant coffee in boiling water. Set aside. Beat egg yolks at high speed until foamy, then beat the sugar in gradually, beating until thick. Reduce speed and add vanilla, coffee, and melted chocolate. In large bowl, beat egg whites until stiff peaks are formed. Stir 1 cup of egg whites into chocolate mixture, then fold in remaining whites. Whip heavy cream and fold into chocolate mixture. Pour into springform pan. Freeze until firm (4-6 hours). Garnish with chocolate curls before serving. *Serves 12-14.*

THE GOVERNOR'S INN
Ludlow, Vermont

PEACH ICE WITH RASPBERRY MELBA SAUCE

Follow a substantial meal with this light and refreshing dessert, which should be made at least a day in advance.

1 cup sugar
1/2 cup light corn syrup
1 can (29 ounces) peaches (drain and reserve syrup)
1/4 cup peach-flavored brandy
1/4 cup lemon juice
Raspberry Melba Sauce (recipe follows)

Combine sugar, corn syrup, and peach syrup in saucepan. Bring mixture to a boil stirring constantly. When sugar has dissolved, reduce heat and simmer 3 minutes. Cool. Place peaches in food processor or electric blender, add the brandy, and process until smooth.

Combine syrup, peach purée, and lemon juice. Pour into 8-inch-square pan and freeze.

When ready to serve, place a scoop of peach ice in each champagne glass and top with Raspberry Melba Sauce.

Serves 8-10.

RASPBERRY MELBA SAUCE

1 package (10 ounces) frozen raspberries, thawed
Water (or brandy or raspberry liqueur)
1/3 cup red currant jelly
2 tablespoons cornstarch

Drain berries and reserve juice. Add water to juice to equal 2/3 cup. Combine juice, jelly, and cornstarch in saucepan. Cook until clear and thickened. Stir in raspberries. Chill and serve over Peach Ice. Ample for Peach Ice recipe, with a little left over to try on ice cream.

MISCELLANEOUS

(Stuffings, Sauces, Herb Butter, Vinegar, Relish, Conserves, and Beverages)

Greenville Inn, Greenville, Maine

SPINACH STUFFING AND WHITE SAUCE

Place a mound of the stuffing on a dinner plate, cover with cooked white fish or chicken breasts, and spoon on the sauce. Or fill crêpes with stuffing and top with sauce.

STUFFING

2 packages (10 ounces each) good fresh spinach
2 medium shallots, finely diced
3 to 4 ounces butter
5 ounces good cheddar cheese, grated
2 fresh tomatoes, diced, seeded, and cooked (optional)
2 ounces cottage cheese (optional)
Salt and pepper to taste

Wash and remove stems and bruises from spinach. Cook until tender in a small amount of water. Drain, cool, squeeze out moisture, and finely chop. Simmer shallots until just translucent in butter in a saucepan large enough to accommodate all the ingredients. Add remaining ingredients and toss lightly until the cheddar melts and everything is thoroughly mixed.

Makes about 2½ cups.

WHITE SAUCE

Slivered almonds (about ¼ cup)
2 tablespoons butter
Finely diced green pepper (about ¼ cup)
Flour
1 pint light cream, heated
Grated cheddar (optional)
Salt to taste

Blanch almonds in butter. Strain and save butter in pan. Gently cook pepper in butter until translucent. Do not overcook or it will be bitter. Bind up pepper and butter with flour. Add hot cream and salt to taste. Toss in cheese and stir until melted.

Makes about 2 cups.

PUBLICK HOUSE
Sturbridge, Massachusetts

CORN BREAD STUFFING WITH SAUSAGE MEAT

This makes a full-flavored and substantial stuffing for chicken or turkey. Allow about ¾ cup per pound of bird.

1 pound sausage meat
2 tablespoons water
1 medium onion, chopped
1 cup finely diced celery
Salt
1 teaspoon poultry seasoning
8 cups corn bread crumbs

Cook sausage meat in a frying pan with water over low heat. When sausage is cooked remove from heat. Cook the onion and celery in the sausage fat; add salt and poultry seasoning, and combine this with the sausage meat and corn bread crumbs. Add chicken stock or milk if a more compact stuffing is desired.

Makes about 10 cups.

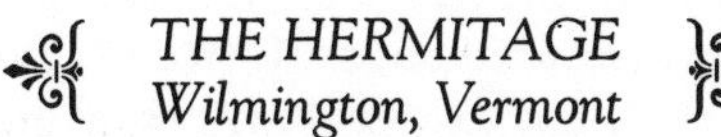
THE HERMITAGE
Wilmington, Vermont

BRANDIED PEACH SAUCE JENSONI

A luscious sauce to serve with roast pheasant or duck.

½ cup raisins
½ cup brandy, warmed
2 cups rich game stock
2 tablespoons chopped fresh parsley
2 ounces sautéed blanched almond slices
Cornstarch slurry (about 1 tablespoon cornstarch or arrowroot powder dissolved in 2 tablespoons water)
2 ripe peaches, peeled and sliced

Plump raisins in warmed brandy for 20 minutes. Heat stock in saucepan; add parsley, almonds, and raisins with brandy. Thicken with cornstarch slurry. Add peaches and keep warm until ready to serve.

Makes about 3 cups.

ORANGE SAUCE À LA LARCHWOOD

Chicken base tones down the sweetness. Enjoy this with roast duckling or chicken.

1 cup brown sugar
1 cup water
6 ounces orange juice concentrate
1 tablespoon chicken stock base (like Spice Islands)
1/8 teaspoon allspice
1/2 cup granulated sugar
2 tablespoons cornstarch
1/4 cup water
Thinly sliced orange

Combine brown sugar and water in saucepan and dissolve over medium heat. Add orange juice concentrate, chicken stock base, allspice, and granulated sugar. Once all the ingredients are dissolved, increase the heat to a boil and thicken with cornstarch and water. Add orange slices to the finished sauce as a garnish.

Makes about 2 cups.

SCHNITZEL ROSINE SOSSEN
(Raisin and Pineapple Sauce for Pork Cutlets)

"When we had a German restaurant we wanted something different in the pork line so we experimented with various makings and came up with this sauce. It is very good with pork cutlets, and our guests return often requesting that dish along with carrot bread, potato pancakes, red cabbage, and of course apple strudel."

8 slices bacon, cut into pieces
1 large onion, chopped
1/2 cup flour
1 handful raisins
1 small can pineapple pieces with juice
Water and white wine in amounts equal to the pineapple juice

Sauté bacon pieces, drain off some fat, add onion, and cook until soft. Add flour and stir. Blend in remaining ingredients and simmer until smooth but not thick. Pour over cooked breaded pork schnitzels. *Makes about 1 cup.*

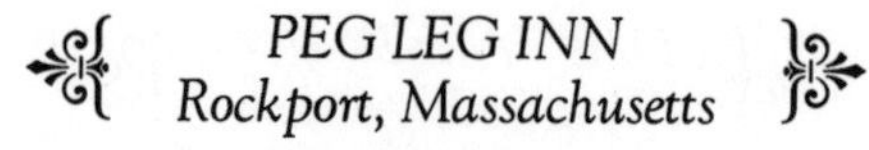

MONTMORENCY SAUCE

The sweetness makes it suitable for sautéed chicken breasts or roast duckling, as well as more robustly flavored meats such as pork chops.

1 can (28 ounces) pitted Bing cherries
1/4 cup lemon juice
1/4 cup molasses
6 drops Tabasco sauce
1 tablespoon Dijon mustard
2 tablespoons cornstarch
1/4 cup water

Drain the liquid from the cherries into a medium saucepan, reserving the cherries. Add lemon juice, molasses, Tabasco sauce, and mustard to the liquid and bring to a boil. Mix cornstarch in water to make a paste, then add to cherry liquid, whisking constantly until thick enough to coat the back of a spoon. Remove from heat and add cherries. Serve over sautéed chicken breasts or roast duckling.

Makes about 4 cups.

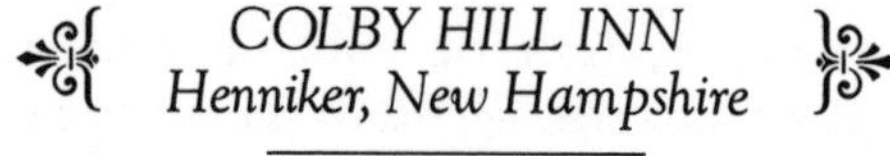

BUTTER-VINEGAR SAUCE

"My mother always used this recipe. It is especially nice served on asparagus, spinach, or Swiss chard."

4 tablespoons butter
1/4 cup flour
1/2 cup vinegar
1/4 cup sugar
1/4 cup water

Melt butter and slowly add flour, stirring constantly. Add vinegar, sugar, and water, bring to a boil, and simmer 10 minutes. More vinegar or water may be added if too thick.

Makes about 1 cup.

THE WOODBOX INN
Nantucket, Massachusetts

HERB BUTTER

This zesty herb butter adds flavor to just about anything. It freezes and stores well, too. Place a slice on top of a cooked filet mignon right before serving for a special touch.

1 pound butter, slightly softened
1/2 tube anchovy paste
1/2 bunch parsley, chopped
2 tablespoons each fresh chopped basil and thyme
1 ounce Lea and Perrin's Worcestershire sauce
1 clove garlic, chopped
1 shallot, chopped
1/2 teaspoon each pepper and paprika

Whip butter in mixer till fluffy and add rest of ingredients. Place in a line on aluminum foil, roll foil, and twist ends to form log. Freeze, slice, and use as desired. *Makes 1 pound butter.*

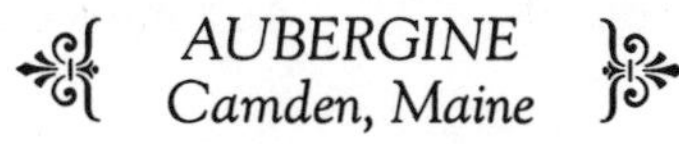

AUBERGINE
Camden, Maine

HERB VINEGAR AUBERGINE

Herbs picked at the greatest heat of a sunny day should go into this vinegar. The predominant quantity should be of lemon balm, then basil, and tarragon the least. Use for salad dressings, deglazing in fish sauces, and for finishing chicken, fish, and vegetable dishes when a piquant flavor is desired.

1 gallon white distilled vinegar (in a glass jug)
Fresh lemon balm, basil, and tarragon

Pour off 3/4 cup from a 1 gallon jug of white distilled vinegar. Stuff jug with the freshly picked herbs and set it in full sun for 2 sunny days or until color and scent are well developed. Store in cool, dark place for 2 months before using. *Makes 1 gallon.*

ZUCCHINI RELISH

"This relish is a good way to use up some of that over-abundant zucchini you have in your garden. It can be used with meat loaf, stew, sliced meats, and even hot dogs. We serve it at dinner and cookouts. It is a favorite with our guests."

1/3 cup pickling salt
12 cups coarsely ground zucchini
2 green peppers, coarsely ground
2 sweet red peppers, chopped
4 cups coarsely ground onions
1 teaspoon turmeric powder
1 teaspoon curry powder
1 teaspoon celery seed
1 tablespoon cornstarch
1/2 teaspoon pepper
3 cups vinegar
4 1/2 cups sugar

In large enamel pan, mix pickling salt into vegetables. Let stand overnight. Drain, rinse with cold water, and return to enamel pan. Mix together rest of ingredients and add to vegetables. Boil 20 minutes. Pour into sterilized jars and seal.

Makes about 12 pints.

ENGLISH MEADOWS INN
Kennebunkport, Maine

BEACH PLUM CONSERVE

"Beach plums grow in straggling bushes among sand dunes on the Maine Coast — we are fortunate to have many here in our meadow. We dry the fragrant blossoms for our potpourri. The beach plums have a peculiarly delicious flavor when stewed with sugar or made into jelly or conserve. The latter confection is like the Mirabelle conserve so popular in France. Serve with hot breads or muffins."

Pick beach plums when they are red, cover with water, and bring to a boil. Drain, add fresh water, and cook until the plums are soft. Remove the pits, then add as much sugar as there is liquid. Place marbles in the bottom of the kettle to prevent the conserve from sticking to the bottom and burning. When the conserve jells when poured from a spoon, remove from the stove, pour into glasses, seal, and label.

ENGLISH MEADOWS INN
Kennebunkport, Maine

RHUBARB CONSERVE

For best flavor, let this meld a few days — preferably a few weeks — before serving.

4 pounds rhubarb
3 pounds granulated sugar
2 pounds brown sugar
1/2 cup preserved ginger
1/3 cup preserved orange
Grated rind and juice of 2 lemons
1 pound seedless raisins

Wash, peel, and cut rhubarb in 1-inch pieces. Mix all the ingredients together and let stand 30 minutes. Simmer for 2 hours, pour into jars, seal, and label. *Makes about 8 pints.*

OLD-FASHIONED LEMONADE STAND LEMONADE

"Here is a treasured old-fashioned memory — fresh, crisp, cold, and delicious lemonade. On a hot afternoon our guests especially enjoy it while sitting under a shady tree. An ounce of gin or vodka may be added."

1½ cups sugar
½ cup boiling water
1 tablespoon grated lemon rind
1½ cups freshly squeezed lemon juice
5 cups cold water
Lemon and lime slices for garnish
Fresh mint sprigs

Combine sugar and boiling water, stirring until sugar dissolves. Add lemon rind, lemon juice, and cold water; mix well. Chill. Serve over crushed ice garnished with lemon and lime slices and fresh mint sprigs. *Makes 7 cups.*

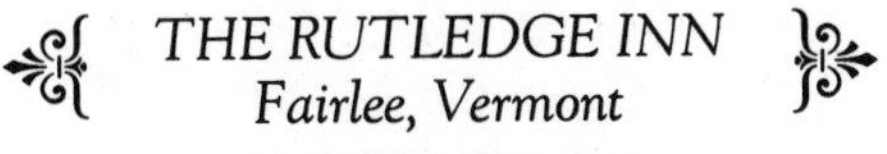

THE RUTLEDGE INN
Fairlee, Vermont

GINGER FRESH FRUIT DRINK

A refreshing appetizer for lunch or dinner, or increase the amounts and serve as a party punch.

1 teaspoon cut up crystalized ginger
1⁄4 cup crushed pineapple
1⁄3 cup orange sections
1⁄3 cup canned peaches
1⁄3 cup sugar
1⁄4 cup lemon juice
Ginger ale

Mix ginger, pineapple, orange sections, and peaches in blender until smooth. Combine sugar and lemon juice and add to ginger mixture, stirring until well mixed. At serving time put 2 tablespoons in a 10-ounce glass, fill with chilled ginger ale, and present with straws. *Serves 12.*

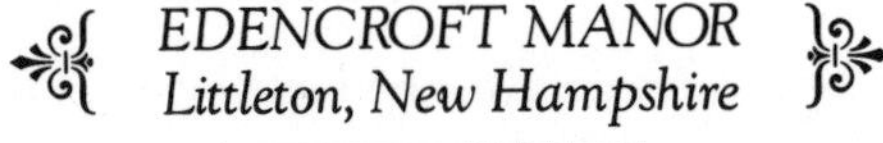

EDENCROFT MANOR
Littleton, New Hampshire

CHAMPAGNE MIMOSA

Perfect with brunch or lunch on a sultry summer's day.

3 ounces champagne
2 ounces orange juice
2 dashes bitters

Fill an 8-ounce tulip glass with ice. Pour champagne, orange juice, and bitters onto ice, stir gently, and serve with a straw. Garnish with orange slice. *Serves 1.*

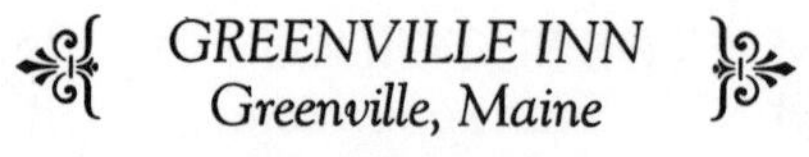

STRAWBERRY SHORTCUT

This drink was named and devised by the inn.

1½ ounces dark rum
1½ ounces dry vermouth
Squeeze of lime
Grenadine for color
4 soft strawberries
Crushed ice

Place ingredients in blender for 5 seconds and serve in 4-ounce champagne glass or brandy snifter. *Serves 1.*

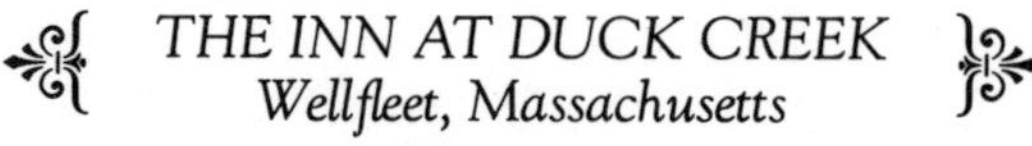

ICED MOCHA ESPRESSO

Great for a coffee lover who doesn't have room for dessert, or as part of a brunch.

2 ounces strong, chilled espresso
2 ounces heavy cream
1 ounce Kahlua
1 ounce crème de cacao
Whipped cream
Twist of lemon peel
Whole coffee bean or cinnamon

Fill a large (16-ounce) goblet or tall iced-tea glass with small ice cubes. Add chilled espresso, heavy cream, Kahlua, and crème de cacao and stir to mix. Top with whipped cream and add a twist of lemon and whole coffee bean or dash of cinnamon. *Serves 1.*

DIRECTORY OF NEW ENGLAND INNS

(The numbers in parentheses after the inns' names refer to the pages on which their recipes may be found.)

CONNECTICUT

Avon Old Farms Inn
(190, 212, 273)
Routes 44 and 10
P. O. Box 535
Avon, CT 06001
(203) 677-2818

Bee and Thistle Inn
(88, 117, 153, 283)
100 Lyme Street
Old Lyme, CT 06371
(203) 434-1667

The Blackberry River Inn
(25, 97, 179)
Route 44
Norfolk, CT 06058
(203) 542-5100

Boulders Inn (264)
New Preston, CT 06777
(203) 868-7918

The Homestead Inn
(88, 171, 285)
420 Field Point Road
Greenwich, CT 06830
(203) 869-7500

The Inn on Lake Waramaug
(182, 208)
New Preston, CT 06777
(203) 868-0563/(212) 724-8775

Mountain View Inn
(46, 173, 282)
Norfolk, CT 06058
(203) 542-5595

Old Lyme Inn (83, 131, 168)
Lyme Street
Old Lyme, CT 06371
(203) 434-2600

Town Farms Inn (144, 263)
River Road
Middletown, CT 06457
(203) 347-7438

MAINE

Aubergine (105, 187, 201, 297)
6 Belmont Avenue
Camden, ME 04843
(207) 236-8053

The Bethel Inn (47, 262, 292)
Bethel, ME 04217
(207) 824-2175

Breezemere Farm
(10, 89, 101, 251)
Box 290
South Brooksville, ME 04617
(207) 326-8628

MAINE *continued*

The Captain Jefferds Inn (16, 74)
Pearl Street
Box 691
Kennebunkport, ME 04046
(207) 967-2311

Center Lovell Inn
(141, 178, 227, 228)
Center Lovell, ME 04016
(207) 925-1575

Cleftstone Manor
(11, 54, 260, 279)
Eden Street, Route 3
Bar Harbor, ME 04609
(207) 288-4951

Le Domaine Restaurant & Inn Français (100)
Box 496
Hancock, ME 04640
(207) 422-3395

English Meadows Inn
(26, 29, 299)
R.F.D. 1, Route 35
Kennebunkport, ME 04046
(207) 967-5766

The Gosnold Arms
(40, 98, 193, 248)
North Side Road
New Harbor, ME 04554
(207) 677-3727

Granes FairHaven Inn (22, 37)
North Bath Road
Bath, ME 04530
(207) 443-4391

Greenville Inn
(18, 42, 214, 242, 302)
Greenville, ME 04441
(207) 695-2206

The Kennebunk Inn
(50, 53, 79, 124, 186)
45 Main Street (Route 1)
Kennebunk, ME 04043
(207) 985-3351

Lincoln House Country Inn
(41, 123, 202, 239)
Dennysville, ME 04628
(207) 726-3953

Oakland House (21, 25)
Herricks
Sargentville P.O., ME 04673
(207) 359-8521

The Pentagöet Inn (65)
Castine, ME 04421
(207) 326-8616

The Pilgrim's Inn (116)
Deer Isle, ME 04627
(207) 348-6615

Spruce Point Inn (139, 145, 179)
Boothbay Harbor, ME 04538
(207) 633-4152

Weld Inn (65, 74, 186)
Weld, ME 04285
(207) 585-2429

MASSACHUSETTS

Beach Plum Inn (174, 281, 286)
Menemsha
Martha's Vineyard, MA 02552
(617) 645-9454

The Benjamin Choate Inn
(39, 92)
25 Tyng Street
Newburyport, MA 01950
(617) 462-4786

The Bramble Inn (125, 203)
Route 6A, Box 159
Brewster, MA 02631
(617) 896-7644

Chez Pierre at the Charlotte Inn
(180, 183, 192)
South Summer Street
P. O. Box 1185
Edgartown, MA 02539
(617) 627-8947

Coonamessett Inn (162, 184)
Jones Road and Gifford Street
Falmouth, MA 02541
(617) 548-2300

Country Inn at Princeton
(132, 204)
30 Mountain Road
Princeton, MA 01541
(617) 464-2030

The Four Chimneys Inn
(10, 55, 73)
38 Orange Street
Nantucket, MA 02554
(617) 228-1912

The Harvest at the Village Inn
(81, 126)
16 Church Street
Lenox, MA 01240
(413) 637-0020

Hawthorne Inn (14, 62, 67)
462 Lexington Road
Concord, MA 01742
(617) 369-5610

The Inn at Duck Creek
(132, 176, 194, 302)
East Main Street
Box 364
Wellfleet, MA 02667
(617) 349-6535/(617) 349-9333

Jared Coffin House (90, 142)
Nantucket, MA 02554
(617) 228-2400

Longfellow's Wayside Inn
(63, 206)
Sudbury, MA 01776
(617) 443-8846

Peg Leg Inn (28, 198, 280, 296)
Two King Street
Rockport, MA 01966
(617) 546-2352

Publick House
(66, 97, 169, 185, 221, 293)
On the Common
Sturbridge, MA 01566
(617) 347-3313

The Queen Anne Inn (84, 288)
70 Queen Anne Road
P. O. Box 747
Chatham, MA 02633
(617) 945-0394

The Red Lion Inn
(60, 107, 133, 141, 210)
Stockbridge, MA 01262
(413) 298-5545

Seaward Inn
(36, 60, 64, 220, 274)
Rockport, MA 01966
(617) 546-6792

The Victorian (17, 19)
South Water Street
Edgartown, MA 02539
(617) 627-4784

The Victorian (15, 138, 159, 230)
583 Linwood Avenue
Whitinsville, MA 01588
(617) 234-2500

Whalewalk Inn (232, 261, 272)
Bridge Road, Box 169,
Eastham, MA 02642
(617) 255-0617

The Wildwood Inn (53, 63, 234)
121 Church Street
Ware, MA 01082
(413) 967-7798

Windflower Inn
(76, 90, 103, 156, 172, 258)
South Egremont Road, Route 23
Great Barrington, MA 01230
(413) 528-2720

The Woodbox Inn (72, 181, 297)
29 Fair Street
Nantucket, MA 02554
(617) 228-0587

NEW HAMPSHIRE

The Bernerhof Inn
(80, 233, 244)
Route 302
P. O. Box 381
Glen, NH 03838
(603) 383-4414

The Birchwood Inn
(28, 196, 243, 275)
Route 45
Temple, NH 03084
(603) 878-3285

Colby Hill Inn
(49, 202, 270, 296)
Henniker, NH 03242
(603) 428-3281

The Darby Field Inn
(57, 151, 247)
Bald Hill
Conway, NH 03818
(603) 447-2181

Edencroft Manor
(20, 77, 268, 301)
R.F.D. 1, Route 135
Littleton, NH 03561
(603) 444-6776

Follansbee Inn
(13, 157, 243, 272)
North Sutton, NH 03260
(603) 927-4221

Hanover Inn (106, 161, 205)
Main Street
Hanover, NH 03755
(603) 643-4300

Holiday Inn (51, 200, 226)
Intervale, NH 03845
(603) 356-9772

Indian Shutters Inn
(199, 232, 276)
Old Claremont Road (Route 12)
North Charlestown, NH 03603
(603) 826-4445

The John Hancock Inn (61, 144)
Hancock, NH 03449
(603) 525-3318

Lovett's by Lafayette Brook (30, 128)
Profile Road
Franconia, NH 03580
(603) 823-7761

The Monadnock Inn (77, 208, 285)
Box B
Jaffrey Center, NH 03454
(603) 532-7001

The Pasquaney Inn
(62, 107, 197)
Newfound Lake
Star Route 1, Box 1066
Bridgewater, NH 03222
(603) 744-2712

Philbrook Farm Inn
(24, 33, 61, 239)
North Road
Shelburne, NH 03581
(603) 466-3831

The Ram in the Thicket
(59, 72, 119, 140, 219, 252)
Wilton, NH 03086
(603) 654-6440

The Scottish Lion (67, 231, 269)
Route 16
North Conway, NH 03860
(603) 356-6381

Snowvillage Inn
(48, 114, 122, 158, 163, 241)
Snowville, NH 03849
(603) 447-2818

Stafford's In The Field
(56, 170, 238, 259)
Chocorua, NH 03817
(603) 323-7766

Sugar Hill Inn
(113, 143, 191, 218, 237, 270)
Route 117
Franconia, NH 03580
(603) 823-5621

Woodbound Inn (12, 237)
Jaffrey, NH 03452
(603) 532-8341

RHODE ISLAND

Larchwood Inn (111, 189, 289, 294)
176 Main Street (Route 1A)
Wakefield, RI 02879
(401) 783-5454

Weekapaug Inn (114, 240, 271)
Weekapaug, RI 02891
(401) 322-0301

VERMONT

Birch Hill Inn (19, 224, 277)
West Road
P. O. Box 346
Manchester, VT 05254
(802) 362-2761

The Black Bear (211, 236)
Bolton Valley
Richmond, VT 05477
(802) 434-2126

Black Lantern Inn (51, 75, 229, 262)
Montgomery Village, VT 05470
(802) 326-4507

The Churchill House Inn (18, 109, 207, 240)
R.F.D. 3, Route 73 East
Brandon, VT 05733
(802) 247-3300

The Combes Family Inn (110, 160, 250, 278)
R.F.D. 1
Ludlow, VT 05149
(802) 228-8799

The Craftsbury Inn (154, 177, 259)
Craftsbury, VT 05826
(802) 586-2848

1811 House (21, 267)
Manchester, VT 05254
(802) 362-1811

The Four Columns Inn (82, 102, 213)
Newfane, VT 05345
(802) 365-7713

The Four-In-Hand (147, 164, 282)
Marlboro, VT 05344
(802) 254-2894

The Governor's Inn (16, 58, 93, 94, 135, 182, 290, 300)
86 Main Street
Ludlow, VT 05149
(802) 228-8830

Greenhurst Inn (23, 127, 152, 284)
Bethel, VT 05032
(802) 234-9474

The Grey Bonnet Inn (222)
Route 100
North Killington, VT 05751
(802) 775-2537

The Hermitage (96, 175, 293)
Coldbrook Road
Wilmington, VT 05363
(802) 464-3511

The Highland House (253)
Route 100
Londonderry, VT 05148
(802) 824-3019

Hill Farm Inn (38, 167)
R.R. 2, Box 2015
Arlington, VT 05250
(802) 375-2269

The Inn at Manchester (112, 256)
Route 7
Manchester, VT 05254
(802) 362-1793

The Inn at Norwich (188)
Norwich, VT 05055
(802) 649-1143

The Inn at Weston (195, 215, 249)
Route 100
P. O. Box 56
Weston, VT 05161
(802) 824-5804

VERMONT *continued*

Knoll Farm Country Inn
(99, 165, 298)
Bragg Hill Road
R.F.D. 1, Box 180
Waitsfield, VT 05673
(802) 496-3939

The Londonderry Inn (104, 146, 254)
Route 100
South Londonderry, VT 05155
(802) 824-5226

Longwood Inn (91, 108, 147)
Route 9
P. O. Box 86
Marlboro, VT 05344
(802) 257-1545

The Middlebury Inn (43)
14 Courthouse Square
Middlebury, VT 05753
(802) 388-4961

Mountain Top Inn (52, 78, 146, 245)
Chittenden, VT 05737
(802) 483-2311

Mountain View Inn
(66, 118, 265)
R.F.D. Box 69
Waitsfield, VT 05673
(802) 496-2426

The October Country Inn
(31, 32, 44)
Bridgewater Corners, VT 05035
(802) 672-3412

The Old Tavern (68, 129, 134, 145)
Grafton, VT 05146
(802) 843-2231

Old Town Farm Lodge
(115, 161, 274)
Route 10
Gassetts, VT 05144
(802) 875-2346

Pittsfield Inn (216, 284)
Pittsfield, VT 05762
(802) 746-8943

The Rutledge Inn (142, 241, 301)
Lake Morey
Fairlee, VT 05045
(802) 333-9722

Shoreham Inn (121, 166, 257)
Shoreham, VT 05770
(802) 897-5081

Stone House Inn (45, 69)
North Thetford, VT 05054
(802) 333-9124

Sycamore Inn (120, 166, 277, 283)
Route 7
Arlington, VT 05250
(802) 362-2284

The Valley Inn (266, 295)
Route 100, Box 15
Waitsfield, VT 05673
(802) 496-3450

The Vermont Inn
(121, 177, 209)
Route 4
Killington, VT 05751
(802) 773-9847

The Village Inn of Woodstock
(34, 223, 246)
41 Pleasant Street (Route 4)
Woodstock, VT 05091
(802) 457-1255

West Dover Inn (76, 87, 155)
West Dover, VT 05356
(802) 464-5207

The White House (27, 143, 211)
Route 9
Wilmington, VT 05363
(802) 464-2135

Windham Hill Inn (127, 217, 287)
West Townshend, VT 05359
(802) 874-4080

Woodstock Inn (86, 130, 150)
Woodstock, VT 05091
(802) 457-1100

INDEX TO RECIPES